Round-Trip to America

Round-Trip to America

THE IMMIGRANTS RETURN TO EUROPE, 1880–1930

Mark Wyman

Cornell University Press

ITHACA AND LONDON

First published 1993 by Cornell University Press.
First printing, Cornell Paperbacks, 1996.

Lines from "When I Journeyed from America" quoted from Harriet M.
Pawlowska, ed., *Merrily We Sing: 105 Polish Folksongs* (Detroit: Wayne
State University Press, 1961); reprinted with permission of the publisher.

Library of Congress Cataloging-in-Publication Data

Wyman, Mark.
    Round-trip to America: the immigrants return to Europe, 1880–1930 /
Mark Wyman.
        p.   cm.
    Includes bibliographical references and index.
    ISBN: 978-0-8014-2875-3 (cloth : alk.paper)

    1. Europeans—United States—History. 2. Immigrants—United
States—History. 3. United States—Emigration and immigration—
History. 4. Return migration—Europe—History. 5. Europe—
Emigration and immigration—History. I. Title.
E184.E95W96   1993
973—dc20   93-18180

Library of Congress Catalog Card Number 93-18180

Paperback printing   10 9 8 7 6 5

for the memory of

VERNON CARSTENSEN

friend, mentor, gadfly
to a generation of unfeathered bipeds

Contents

Part Four   A Round-Trip Journey Concluded

Acknowledgments

Just as a returned immigrant usually had a host of friends who gave assistance going and coming, so I have relied on many persons and institutions as I progressed from initial probing to research, writing, revision, and publication of this book. At the top of the list are two good friends, Adam Walaszek of the Jagiellonian University in Kraków, Poland, and George Gilkey of the University of Wisconsin–La Crosse. Both have a high degree of expertise with different areas of the issue— Walaszek with the Polish question of return, Gilkey with the Italian— and both devoted much time to this project. Two other scholars who gave important help were Keijo Virtanen of the University of Turku, Finland, and Gerard Moran of Dublin, Ireland.

Many others opened doors to sources that I would not otherwise have obtained. David DeChenne of Nokomis, Illinois, helped me find my way through the intricate pathways of Bulgarian labor migration while stimulating my thinking on the subject in many ways. Abroad, Dorothy Skårdal of the University of Oslo helped locate Norwegian materials, Reidar Grunde Simonsen provided a copy of his Oslo master's thesis, and Marjolein C. 't Hart sent her Groningen master's thesis. Marcin Kula permitted the use of Polish illustrations, and Birgitta Ekström of Hangö Museum in Finland provided the photograph of the Hangö memorial. Salvador Fajardo of the State University of New York at Binghamton made me aware of the importance of return migration in the early Spanish colonial empire and its place in literature.

Illinois State University provided a sabbatical leave that permitted European research.

Other individuals who gave assistance include Joseph W. Wieczerzak of the Polish National Catholic Church Commission on History and Archives, Odd Lovoll of St. Olaf College, Robert Vitas of the Lithuanian Research and Studies Center, Kerby Miller of the University of Missouri, and Norma Ashbrook of Bloomington, Illinois.

Special thanks are due to three scholars who read early versions of the manuscript: George Gilkey, John Bodnar of Indiana University, and Milton Cantor of the University of Massachusetts–Amherst. Translation help came from Adam Walaszek, Annikka Peterson, Taimi Ranta, Sigmund Gronmø, Enrica Brunelli, Kermit Westerberg, and Edith Goldschmidt.

The following research institutions, archives, and libraries were important in locating and providing sources: Milner Library of Illinois State University (especially the Inter-Library Loan Department); Archive of the Metropolitan Curia of Kraków, Poland (Wychodźstwo Collection on Emigration); Instytut Badán Polonijnych of Jagiellonian University, Kraków, Poland (director Władysław Miodunka and Mirosław Frančič); the Archive of Modern Records, Warsaw, Poland (Polish post-1918 governmental records); the Irish Folklore Commission (chairman Bo Almqvist, Barbare óFloinn, and Máire Dillon); Dublin Diocesan Archives (archivist David Sheehy); libraries of University College, Dublin, and Trinity College, both in Dublin, Ireland; the Polish Museum of America Library, Chicago; Swenson Swedish Immigration Research Center, Augustana College (archivist Kermit Westerberg); the University of Turku Emigration History Research Center, Turku, Finland; Main Library, University of Illinois at Urbana-Champaign; Archives, University of Illinois–Chicago (archivist Mary Ann Bamberger); Chicago Historical Society (curators Archie Motley and Ralph Pugh); Regenstein Library, University of Chicago; U.S. National Archives, Washington, D.C.

Material from the Irish Folklore Commission Questionnaires is used with the permission of the head of the Department of Irish Folklore, University College, Dublin.

MARK WYMAN

Normal, Illinois

PART ONE

Migrants
and Immigrants

CHAPTER I

A Two-Way Migration

The Polish priest was surprised as he went over the parish census for 1894. He had known for some time that people were emigrating from the village of Miejsce, and so there was nothing startling in the total of 121 persons going to America in the ten years since the first traveler set out across the Atlantic.

What surprised him was the return flow: fifty-eight persons had come home to stay, just under half the overseas migration. Admittedly the totals masked several twists and turns in the emigrant stream: two eager travelers had crossed the ocean three times, and five others had each made two trips to America. Five more had died in the United States, one of them in a coal mine accident, another in a strike. A girl simply disappeared. In addition, there were others who left Miejsce on seasonal trips for employment elsewhere in Europe, two of them for lengthy stays in Romania. The Polish community was on the move, but the movement was not all in the same direction.

All this was a bit more complex than the usual "America fever" stories that circulated around central Europe. It made the Miejsce priest cast a more sympathetic eye on the outflow, for in it he saw encouraging signs. "Whenever there is a chance to buy a piece of land," he wrote for the *Gazeta Koscielna*, "a man leaves his wife at home and goes to America." Earnings from overseas labors came back to Miejsce. What's more, the travelers had brought or sent back $280 to remodel the parish church. The exodus was not a disaster, then, as some critics were charging. Polish emigration to America "is not a loss but a gain for this

3

province," the priest insisted. He urged that emigration from other localities also be investigated.[1]

What surprised the Polish priest in 1894 continues to offer unexpected findings to those who look beneath the surface of American immigration. For the incoming tidal wave of peoples has always had an outflow, a reverse movement of immigrants turning their backs on the United States. Ignored by Fourth of July orators, overlooked by historians who concentrate on the newcomers' assimilation, return migration looms so large in world history, with critical implications for the homelands and the United States, that it cries out for attention. A leading British historian once lamented the lack of study on the subject and termed it "almost the further face of the moon." An economist recently admitted his surprise that motivation for return "has been totally ignored by the majority of econometric studies on pre–World War One migration." And a folklorist seemingly threw up her hands when she discovered that American research, "be it based in history, sociology, or folklore, has ignored, for the most part, the phenomenon of return in favor of the immigrant experience within the United States." Returned immigrants rejected America and, it seems, American scholars have rejected them.[2]

There is no lack of material to examine, however, no scarcity of tales to unravel. Immigrants have been heading back to Europe from the earliest days of the rush to the New World. It was a common activity in the Spanish empire, and as early as 1613 Cervantes described the estrangement and romantic difficulties of an Estramaduran, returning wealthy after twenty years in the New World only to discover that all his friends in Spain had passed away. Colonial New England experienced an ebb tide also, during the early years whose glories are sung each Thanksgiving: from 1640 to 1660, in fact, those returning to England outnumbered those going to America. A century later, in 1751, Benjamin Franklin worried that the reverse flow to England might counterbalance the numbers coming from there.[3]

And when the tourist Charles Dickens boarded a vessel in New York Harbor in 1842 to head back to his native England, he encountered nearly a hundred returning immigrants: "As we came to know individuals among them by sight, from looking down upon the deck where they took the air in the daytime, and cooked their food, and very often ate it too, we became curious to know their histories, and with what expectations they had gone out to America, and on what errands they were going home, and what their circumstances were." From the ship's carpenter Dickens learned that some had been in America three months,

At Hangö, Finland, the America Fever is recalled in this statue of birds flying off to America, erected in 1967 by the Suomi Society with the assistance of communities in southern Finland. Hangö itself was a major jumping-off point for Finnish emigration and is sometimes called Finland's "Plymouth." The sculptor is Mauno Oittinen. Photograph by Hangö Museum.

others only three days, "and some had gone out in the last voyage of that very ship in which they were now returning home." In this supposed Land of Plenty, it was perhaps disconcerting to see these former residents living on food donated by others on board; one man survived on the "bones and scraps of fat he took from the plates used in the after-cabin dinner, when they were put out to be washed." Dickens had seen returning immigrants and the view was shocking.[4]

The perils of ocean travel in these early periods, during the age of sail, helped keep return totals low. But by the middle of the nineteenth century a different picture emerged as railroads crisscrossed the continents and steamships began to ply the Atlantic. Not only were the European masses on the move for America, Canada, and elsewhere, but for large numbers it had become a round-trip. During this era of mass immigration, from approximately 1880 until 1930 when restriction laws and the Great Depression choked it off, from one-quarter to one-third of all European immigrants to the United States permanently returned home. The total may have reached four million persons.[5]

European peasant villages that once seemed impenetrable in their backwardness, their isolation, now boasted residents who could describe the wonders of the New World—skyscrapers, elevated trains, deep tunnels. (Had not they themselves worked on these wonders?) Men and women who formerly quailed at the thought of a visit from the landlord now proudly described how they had seen the president of the United States in person, and one returned Slovenian even claimed to have shaken the hand of "Tedi." European politicians suddenly had to contend with subjects who knew different governmental systems, and clergymen confronted parishioners who had come into contact with other religious ideas. Life was not the same in Miejsce, nor in the Mezzogiorno, nor in thousands of peasant communities across the Continent.[6]

The U.S. Immigration Commission team that toured Europe after 1907 encountered some of the results of this increasing homeward flow:

> The investigators . . . were impressed by the number of men in Italy and in various Slavic communities who speak English and who exhibit a distinct affection for the United States. The unwillingness of such men to work in the fields at 25 to 30 cents a day; their tendency to acquire property; their general initiative; and most concretely, the money they can show, make a vivid impression. They are dispensers of information and inspiration, and are often willing to follow up the inspiration by loans to prospective emigrants.

Others told of a Sicilian saloon flying a U.S. flag (in Killarney it was later claimed that every pub was run by a "Yank," someone back from America), and a visitor to a southern Italian village reported that the only barbershop that "looked like the real thing" was run by a re-migrant, modeled on his former establishment in New York City. For many the stay abroad led them to attempt entirely new approaches, such as the "Amerikansky Schtore" in Hungary's Nyitra district; it offered a wide variety of goods under one roof and also broke tradition in allowing no bargaining: each item had a posted price. A new home built along U.S. styles—the "American house"—was the proud result of remigration for many others.[7]

Politics drew other returners who threw themselves into efforts to change governmental and economic systems at home. They had learned labor organizing through struggles in the American northwoods and in Pittsburgh steel mills; they experienced politics firsthand in the ballyhoo of American election campaigns. Now they came home to challenge the old order. Many could no longer "be sufficiently submissive to the pettiest official of the town." Three who returned eventually became prime ministers of their homelands, in Norway, Finland, and Latvia. Thousands of others took the lead in forming or helping shape village organizations, labor unions, even political parties.[8]

They had plenty of fellow remigrants—both men and women, but mainly men—to turn to for support. Ships heading eastward filled their steerages with Europeans who had had enough of the Americas or who had saved the amount they planned to save. As the return totals began to mount, American phrases became common in the speech of isolated hamlets and American clothes added variety to village gatherings. Nearly one Italian in twenty had resided for some time in the United States by the beginning of World War I, if no allowance is made for repeat crossings, and by 1920 in Norway's heavy-emigration county of Vest-Agder a quarter of all males over age fifteen had lived at least two years in America.[9]

Stories of these returning men and women worked their way rapidly into the very fabric of Continental life. Songs, folktales, jokes—these and other aspects of popular culture began to reflect experiences across the ocean. A woman who returned from America and led the fight against society's hypocrisy was featured in *The Pillars of Society* (1877), the first social drama by Norwegian playwright Henrik Ibsen. Irish, German, Finnish, Italian, and Jewish authors all dealt with the theme that Cervantes had addressed more than two centuries earlier: the emigrant who came back from the New World a changed (perhaps wealthy) person, confronting the old ways of home.[10]

STATISTICS OF RETURN

Determining the size of the return flow to Europe with any precision is impossible because of both inconsistent counting by governments and shipping lines and inaccuracies and incongruities in their efforts. Some

THE WORLD OF THE RETURNED EMIGRANTS
EUROPE 1914

NORWAY

SWEDEN

FINLAND

Gulf of Bothnia

Ostrobothnia

Bergen

Christiana (Oslo)

Helsingfors (Helsinki)

Stavanger

Stockholm

Hango

St. Petersburg

SCOTLAND

RUSSIA

IRELAND

GREAT BRITAIN

North Sea

DENMARK

Smaland

Baltic Sea

Vilna

Minsk

Dublin

Hull

ENGLAND

Liverpool

Malmö

Hamburg

Bremen

London

NETHER-LANDS

Berlin

Posen

Warsaw

Congress Poland

English Channel

BELGIUM

GERMANY

Leipzig

Łódź

Kiev

Le Havre

Düsseldorf

Prague

Kraków

Lvov

Paris

Bohemia

Moravia

Galicia

Bay of Biscay

FRANCE

Munich

Vienna

Slovakia

Odessa

Lyons

SWITZERLAND

AUSTRIA

Budapest

HUNGARY

PORTUGAL

Genoa

Croatia

ROMANIA

Black Sea

Marseille

ITALY

Bosnia

Belgrade

Madrid

Herzegovina

Monte negro

SERBIA

BULGARIA

SPAIN

Rome

Mezzogiorno

Adriatic Sea

ALBANIA

TURKEY

Constant (Istanb

Naples

Tyrrhenian Sea

GREECE

km

0 125 250 375 500

mi

0 125 250 375 500

Border of Austria-Hungary

Mediterranean Sea

Sicily

Ionian Sea

Athens

Aegean Sea

European countries made attempts at certain ports, then neglected those entering national territory by land after having debarked elsewhere. Tourists and business travelers were lumped together with returning emigrants; those paying a visit were not separated statistically from those coming home to stay. One researcher discovered that the Finnish Central Office of Statistics sometimes did not bother to include return figures. Further, he found that some Finns traveled without a passport and some with a false passport, or several would journey on the same passport, providing endless complications to the search for satisfactory totals. Finland's official statistics "are incontrovertibly extremely deficient," another Finnish scholar concluded. Similar stories are told of other countries.[11]

And the question must be raised, what do return migration percentages measure? If 1,000 persons were immigrants in 1902 from Country A, and 500 persons returned there that year from America, the 1902 rate was 50 percent; but most of the 500 returnees had arrived in earlier emigrations, perhaps from twenty years or more previous.

Because of these problems, historians must either speak in broad generalities when discussing return migration or admit the uncertainties of their statistics. Frank Thistlethwaite of Cambridge, in his catalytic address on immigration to the Eleventh Congrès International des Sciences Historiques in 1960, used numerous qualifiers and hedging: repatriation from the United States "may have been over 30%," he said; it varied sharply between groups and over time; the totals are muddled with numerous "repeaters" such as the "birds of passage" who came briefly for seasonal work; many persons traveled from one country to another before eventually returning to their native sod.[12]

Twelve years later, Sweden's Lars-Göran Tedebrand surveyed the field and concluded, "On account of the unsatisfactory position as regards sources, there exists no international demographic and statistical investigation of the emigrants who returned from North America." Studies of recent migrations offer little hope for breakthroughs. As late as 1981, when papers were published from a European conference on International Return Migration which focused on the years since World War II, the editor could conclude only that "returns are quite difficult to assess with any statistical accuracy."[13]

Rough estimates may be made, however. A major source is the U.S. government's attempt from 1908 to 1923 to count both immigration and emigration. The grand totals were 9,949,740 immigrants from all countries entering the United States in those years, and 3,498,185 leaving; 88 percent (3,078,403) of those returning were Europeans. Many of these were undoubtedly repeaters; further, Europeans' crossings to Canada and Mexico complicate the totals. The return rate among all groups was 35 percent for the period. The country-by-country breakdown for Europe in the U.S. government's compilations for 1908–23 is presented in the accompanying table.

A survey of estimates by European and American scholars, beginning in the 1920s and continuing through the present, suggests the following return percentages among European national and ethnic groups. These are for emigration from the United States to Europe in the 1880–1930 period unless otherwise noted:

Austro-Hungarians: 17–27 percent for the pre-1909 era of mass migration from the multiethnic dual monarchy.[14]

Croatians: Between 33 and 40 percent for 1900–14; a more recent estimate for Croatians and Slovenians together is 36.3 percent.[15]

Danes: The 8.6 percent in U.S. records from 1908–14 is regarded as less than the true level for earlier years. One scholar estimates the return at 20 percent.[16]

English and Welsh: Probably higher than the U.S. figures of 16 percent for the English and 7 percent for the Welsh from 1908 to 1918, but certainly lower than the British government's combined 55 percent return for both groups from 1895 to 1918. A more recent estimate of 19.3 percent includes Canadians.[17]

Finns: 20 percent overall, according to a recent study for the 1860s to 1930.[18]

French: Compared to other large European nations, France sent small numbers to the United States. A recent study puts the remigration rate for the opening decades of the century at 48.2 percent.[19]

Germans: From 1884 through 1892, ranging from 13 to 23 percent.[20]

Greeks: The 46 percent rate for 1908–23 in U.S. statistics is probably close to the figure for the entire period 1880–1930, although the Balkan wars and World War I brought sharp changes.[21]

Hungarians: One recent estimate is 46.5 percent, although the percentage for 1899–1913 has been estimated at 24.3 percent.[22]

Irish: 10 percent of the post-famine emigrants returned, according to the most recent studies.[23]

Italians: Rising from 34 percent for 1901–6, according to several different official Italian statistics, to 38 percent for 1907–14, with extremely high percentages in certain years. A 1926 Italian government investigation claimed a 63 percent return rate for 1902–23. A recent examination, however, places the overall percentage at 50 percent from the 1880s to the early 1920s.[24]

Migration between the United States and Europe, 1908–23

Race or nationality	Immigration into U.S.	Emigration from U.S.	Net gain	% Emigrating
Bohemian, Moravian (Czech)	77,737	14,951	62,786	19%
Bulgarian, Serbian, Montenegrin	104,808	92,886	11,922	89%
Croat, Slovene	225,914	114,766	111,148	51%
Dalmatian, Bosnian, Herzegovinian	30,690	8,904	21,786	29%
Dutch, Flemish	141,064	24,903	116,161	18%
English	706,681	146,301	560,380	21%
Finnish	105,342	30,890	74,452	29%
French	304,240	62,538	241,702	21%
German	669,564	119,554	550,010	18%
Greek	366,454	168,847	197,607	46%
Hebrew	958,642	52,034	906,608	5%
Irish	432,668	46,211	386,457	11%
Italian (north)	401,921	147,334	254,587	37%
Italian (south)	1,624,353	969,754	654,599	60%
Lithuanian	137,716	34,605	103,111	25%
Magyar	226,818	149,319	77,499	66%
Polish	788,957	318,210	470,747	40%
Portuguese	128,527	39,527	89,000	31%
Romanian	95,689	63,126	32,563	66%
Russian	210,321	110,282	100,039	52%
Ruthenian (Russniak)	171,823	28,996	142,827	17%
Scandinavians (Norwegian, Danish, Swedish)	448,846	97,920	350,926	22%
Scottish	301,075	38,600	262,475	13%
Slovak	225,033	127,593	97,440	57%
Spanish	153,218	61,086	92,132	40%
Welsh	26,152	3,376	22,776	13%

Source: U.S. Secretary of Labor, *Eleventh Annual Report, 1923* (Washington, D.C. 1923), 133.

Jews: Complicated because of the different countries involved, and a recent estimate of 4.3 percent is obviously based on post-1900 remigration. One scholar estimates that, before the era of czarist pogroms and revolutionary upheaval, the Jewish (then called "Hebrew") return rate was likely in the 15–20 percentage range.[25]

Lithuanians: 20 percent from 1898 to 1914, according to the most recent study.[26]

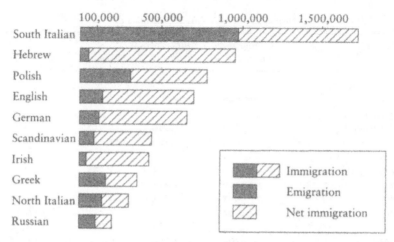

From 1907 to 1923, the U.S. government kept track of return migration as well as immigration. This bar graph by economist Harry Jerome shows the sharp differences between ethnic groups in both inflow and outflow. From Harry Jerome, *Migration and Business Cycles* (New York, 1926), 43.

Norwegians: 25 percent from 1880 on, according to both Norwegian government statistics and recent examinations.[27]

Poles: 30 percent in both the pre-1918 independence and post-independence periods, but marked by sharp yearly swings, according to the most recent study.[28]

Scots: 46 percent from 1895 to 1918 according to British figures, considered too high because no differentiation was made between tourists, visitors, and returning emigrants. One recent scholar considers U.S. official percentages for the Scots (14 percent) too low.[29]

Slovaks: Estimates range from 20 to 36.5 percent.[30]

Swedes: 19 percent from 1881 to 1930, according to official Swedish statistics, supported by recent scholars.[31]

THE ISSUES

Thus do statistics attempt to summarize the millions of individual experiences, stories, tragedies, and triumphs of those remigrants who would forever after be identified by their connection with the republic across the Atlantic. This was the "Yank" (Irish), the *Americano* (Italian), the *Amerikanci* (Slovene), the *Amerikan-kävijöitä* (Finnish), the *Amerykanty* (Polish). Nicknames based on their use of American phrases were also part of the identification: in Greece they were the "all-right boys," the "okay-boys," the "hello-boys." An Irish wag called them the "I-guessers."[32]

Whatever their names or nicknames, these American immigrants who permanently returned to their European homelands in the 1880–1930 years are the focus of this book. (I use the term *immigration* to mean entering the country in question for residence rather than a visit. *Emigration* refers to leaving the country in question with the intention of residing elsewhere, even temporarily.) Large numbers of Europeans also emigrated to Canada, Argentina, and Brazil, where many had similar experiences; they are outside of the scope of this study, however. Rather than making an extensive, and predictably unsuccessful, attempt to determine the exact totals returning home, I have accepted the fact that large numbers returned and address four main questions:

- How were immigrants who planned to return home different from those who expected to put down roots in America—especially in motivations for leaving Europe and expectations for life in the United States?
- How were these temporary immigrants different while living and working in America, and how did this experience change them?
- What were the temporary immigrants' influences on America?
- What did remigrants carry back (in their hands as well as in their heads), and how was the homeland affected by their return?

I define the temporary immigrant as one who left Europe intending residence in the United States and who remained at least one year before returning home. Often the length of residence is unclear in the historical records, however. Related issues include the relation of American economic changes to return migration, differences between national and ethnic groups, rural and urban contrasts as well as differences in levels of economic development between both Europe and America, and the impact on national policies of both the United States and the European nations.

In asking such questions this book is an attempt to respond to calls for a broader approach to the study of immigration. Frank Thistlethwaite called for coverage of Continental issues and a probe of the emigrant's thoughts and motivations as well as acculturation; he urged a framework for studying return that would include premigration activities as well as life in the United States and back again in Europe. Conditions merited such urgings at the time of Thistlethwaite's plea in 1960, for European scholars had largely ignored emigration while in the

United States the traditional emphasis was on those who came, stayed, and succeeded. This earlier approach denied Americans "the chastening values of disapproval" inherent in return migration, argues Wilbur Shepperson. A happy ending was not always the conclusion of the immigration story; instead, "an exhausted immigrant silently sails for home; he debarks, and we are left in doubt about the temper of his mind or the lure of the dream that provoked the tilt with America." To the leading student of Greek return migration, "we would be derelict both as scholars and citizens if we continued to ignore the reasons why people leave the United States and go elsewhere to live." Even the question of the Italians' estrangement from American life has been linked to Italy's experience with remigration.[33]

The danger, of course, is that in telling this epic involving millions we will overlook individual stories. Long ago Robert Foerster, a historian of the Italian emigration, attacked this "specious simplification of what is inevitably complex." Foerster noted that, when migrating birds fly high, "the view is of large outlines, assuring them of direction, yet they must be able to alight on a branch."[34]

This book will seek to "alight on a branch" as it tells the story of the millions of "hello-boys" and "I-guessers" who took the eastward lap of their round-trip to America carrying tomato seeds as well as Methodism, tuberculosis as well as double-bitted axes. Man and woman they had tried America, had labored in its factories and hotels and along railroad tracks in isolated mountain passes; they had acquired expertise in sweatshops and tunneling. And now they turned their backs on the promised land. Surveying the scene from his small parish in central Europe, the Polish priest in Miejsce decided that, because of their return, emigration to America was not a loss but a gain for his province. The issue would remain an open one, however, as returns from America began to mount and villagers as well as officials discovered that their emigrating neighbors were back home again. It had become a two-way migration.

CHAPTER 2

Seasonal Migrations
and the America Fever

Once the Atlantic spray dashed against the lofty sails and prows of packets and clipper ships with their clusters of immigrant families huddled below deck. These travelers were drawn from the English Midlands and Stavanger, from Friesland and Limerick. But winds of a different sort began to sweep the Continent as the nineteenth century drew toward its close, and packets and clipper ships gave way to steam-powered vessels that did not stop for calm seas. The vast changes during these years decreed that the human migration story would be transformed again, fueled by new technology and the often cruel interplay of economics, politics, and myth.

Two stories about Italians tell much about the transformation. One came from a U.S. State Department observer in Germany: "A laboring population heretofore unknown in Württemberg is becoming now quite numerous," he reported in 1878. These were Italians, pushing north for work in German railroads, mines, and other enterprises. They impressed onlookers with their industrious activity but also because they were "so easily satisfied," he reported. The Italian workers lived on polenta with occasional cheese; they made "no clamor for more 'luncheon' and 'more drink.'"[1]

Italian prime minister Giuseppe Zanardelli's visit to the Mezzogiorno provided the occasion for another story. After officials in one southern community escorted him from the train station to the square, the mayor turned to Zanardelli with the official greeting: "I welcome you in the name of the five thousand inhabitants of this town, three thousand of whom are in America and the other two thousand preparing to go."[2]

Thus did a continent feel the changing currents that directed many to trek into neighboring countries for work, then increasingly turned thoughts westward as the "America fever" became an epidemic. In this chapter I examine these issues involving temporary migrations that became intercontinental, spurred by the rise of the transatlantic carrying trade as a massive business enterprise. The role of ticket agents, and the land pressures that transformed news of American wages into the stuff of peasant dreams, is also addressed.

EMIGRATION "IN ORDER TO"

The immensity of the movement westward drew together thousands upon thousands of emigration tales, as 23 million Europeans emigrated to the United States in the fifty years from 1880 to 1930. Country totals could be especially dramatic as the so-called New Immigration from south and east Europe joined and increased the flood: 13.5 million Italians headed to North and South America from 1880 until the outbreak of World War I, and 1.9 million Poles crossed to the United States in less than twenty years. Europe's highest per capita losses, however, were suffered by Ireland, part of the so-called Old Immigration, which saw the emigration of 1.7 million of its citizens from 1881 to 1930. Norway, also part of the Old Immigration, ranked second in per capita losses until the 1890s, by which time one-fifth of all Norwegians lived outside its boundaries; Italy then replaced it in second. Sweden, meanwhile, lost a million emigrants during a period not much longer than the lifetime of an individual, starting from a mid-century population base of only 3.5 million.[3]

This mass movement came from overcrowding, land pauperization, and other worsening home conditions; it turned on wars and threats of wars, political upheaval, ethnic persecution, and natural disasters such as volcanic eruptions and the vineyards' phylloxera. The rise of steamship companies and their ubiquitous ticket agents suddenly made the New World reachable for millions, while American industrial expansion promised work even for "greenhorns." Within the unpredictable fluctuations of this exodus were unmeasureable pinings and yearnings that somehow came together to create what was everywhere called America fever. And somewhere during this era large numbers of Europeans began to look on emigration to America as they had traditionally regarded seasonal job-seeking nearby: not as a permanent relocation but only a temporary one.[4]

One scholar has argued that in east-central Europe two motives for emigration dominated, emigration "because" and emigration "in order to." The latter classification grew in importance, stimulated by a changing American economy and the increasing ease—psychological as well as physical—of the transatlantic journey. And as emigration "in order to" became more popular, short-term emigration to the United States entered its boom years.[5]

MIGRATION WITHIN EUROPE

The new migration was all built on the centuries-old European tradition of seasonal migration for work in nearby areas. This practice was so old, so extensive, that recent scholars have referred to it as "a way of life" among Russian and Galician Poles; as "the thing to do . . . an accepted and socially supported form of behavior" in many areas of east-central Europe; as "a way of life for hundreds of thousands of Slovaks" and "as almost an ordinary routine of village life" in the Italian Apennines. It was known everywhere in Europe.[6]

Sweden's probes into its emigration problem would eventually discover that, from 1850 to 1930, about 300,000 Swedes traveled to work in European countries, 40,000 of them to Germany. But it was from Italy that the migration was especially large. A study of four Italian villages found that from 16 to 37 percent of the twenty-year-old men were "away from home" at any time in the years from 1820 to 1900. Italy's Commissariato dell'Emigrazione reported in 1912 that 900,562 Italians were then in the rest of Europe, led by the 400,000 in France, the 180,000 in Germany, and the 135,000 in Switzerland. France examined the makeup of its resident population in 1911 and found 1,160,000 foreigners within its borders—including some 287,000 Belgians, 117,000 Germans and Austro-Hungarians, and 110,000 Spanish and Portuguese, in addition to the 400,000 Italians.[7]

Migration was a tradition among Poles also. When a compilation was made of the outflow from the Galician village of Zaborów, the dominance of seasonal migration was apparent: during the 56 years that followed 1882, the village of only 160 farms said goodby to 2,168 seasonal migrants, who returned; 721 nonseasonal migrants, who also returned; and only 782 persons who permanently emigrated.[8]

This upsurge in migration became manifest to the hierarchy of the Roman Catholic diocese of Kraków in 1907. Diocesan leaders authorized a survey of migration from Galician parishes that year and found the following numbers leaving for various destinations:

Jordanów: to Saxony-Prussia, 400; to Budapest, 10; to America, 400.

Łetownia: to Saxony, Silesia, Denmark, 1,500; to Budapest, 50; to America, 20.

Maków: to Saxony, 220; to Prussia, 483; to Budapest, 140: to America, 290.

Osielec: to Prussia, 300; to America, 70.

Raba Wyźnia: to Prussia, 50; to Budapest, 25; to America, 50.

Rabka: to Prussia, 60; to Saxony, 20; to America, 110.

Sidzina: to Prussia, 60; to America, 130.

Spytkowice: to Prussia, 30; to Saxony, 20; to America, 450.

Zawoja: to Prussia, Silesia, Wrocław, 500; to Saxony, 1,500; to America, 200.[9]

This movement within Europe was not new to the late nineteenth century, despite claims to the contrary by some writers. The modern world has struggled hard to maintain the comforting, nostalgic thought of a static peasant culture rooted to the soil, unchanging. Oscar Handlin wrote of "the enormous stability in peasant society. . . . From the westernmost reaches of Europe, in Ireland, to Russia in the east, the peasant masses had maintained an imperturable sameness." He described a world where the village's self-sufficiency only rarely yielded to products or influences from outside, while cities were "regions of total strangeness into which the peasant never ventured, where not the people alone, but the very aspect of the earth, was unfamiliar."[10]

But recent examinations into the past of European communities contradict the view of peasant life as stable and unchanging; this picture is inaccurate not only for the nineteenth century but for many centuries before. The Nordic countries' population "has been very mobile for centuries," one scholar found, and another showed that conditions in central Sweden's Dalarna province were driving people to seek work elsewhere perhaps as far back as the Middle Ages. Internal migration within Norway was "common at least from the 1750s," and death records for one Bergen church in 1809–10, covering those over fourteen years old, showed that only 27 percent of the deceased had been born in the city. Similarly, Hungary had long known travel into rich agrarian areas for seasonal employment, "a tradition with a past of several centuries." Abel Chatelain's painstaking examination of internal French migration shows evidence of extensive travels for employment dating at least from the Middle Ages. It was the same in Italy, where two scholars who examined the exodus from a northern community for 1865–1921 noted that this emigration really demonstrated "continuity in an apparently long-standing pattern of intense but short-distance migration." The inhabitants traditionally traveled for work away from home, but not overseas. Balkan men similarly trekked across much of southern Europe looking for jobs. An Irishman was therefore speaking for generations and an entire continent, not just for his 1881 peers, when he told the royal commissioners investigating the vast farm labor migration into England, "We are like wild geese, your honor."[11]

These job seekers often met angry responses from the natives as they entered an area. England's trade union for agricultural laborers began to oppose the use of Irish farm workers vigorously in the 1870s, especially after outsiders helped break a South Warwickshire strike. Urban workers also fought the outsiders, and by 1905 it was reported that Italians had been excluded from almost all British shops and factories. Germany's Chancellor Bismarck was so upset by the hordes of Poles spilling into East Prussia, threatening to "polonize" the district, that he ordered foreign workers expelled from Prussia in 1885. This ban was dropped five years later and attempts were made to rotate Polish farmer workers in Prussian jobs, or to hire Ruthenians and Czechs instead; some urged importation of Chinese. On the eve of World War I some 500,000 seasonal farmhands—the *Sachsengänger*—were working in Germany, four-fifths of them from Congress (Russian) Poland. There were so many Poles employed in nearby Denmark that a migrant protective law was labeled "the law of the Poles"; Danish workers later won a temporary ban on the use of foreign workers.[12]

Church leaders were also concerned, but for different reasons. Italian Catholic organizations followed their countrymen into France and worked to prevent their exploitation; on one occasion they forced the return of 300 Italian boys from textile mills in southern France. Priests in the Kraków diocese surveyed their parishes in 1891, 1907, and 1913 and filled their reports with condemnations of the short-term migration, especially that going to Prussia. Singled out as especially dangerous destinations in the reports were Silesia, Saxony, Brandenburg, Westfalia, Poznań, and Budapest. The priest at Suski lamented in 1907 that each year from six to ten illegitimate children were born to girls from the parish who had gone away for seasonal work in Prussia; the young men came back with heavy drinking habits. A later survey noted minor improvements but still pointed to moral decline, winter drinking bouts, sexual delinquency, laziness, and religious straying by the returning "Prussian hooligans." "Whoever comes back from Budapest is indifferent toward the faith," asserted the priest from Stroza.[13]

And so priests from the diocese were called to a convention in Kraków on 28 November 1907, to address problems of the "emigration fever," especially that directed toward Prussia. Seasonal migration, the convention heard, represented a desire for freedom, as youths tried to "escape from the priest's eye and from the parents' eye," with the result that at railway stations "one might see very sad pictures and scenes of dirty and loud youngsters looking for freedom" as they awaited the train for Germany. Speakers complained that the returning young men spread this immorality in the parishes, and because they had lived and worked among Protestants they often lost their Catholic faith.

The Kraków representatives proposed several possible solutions: (1) Stop the emigration by improving local job opportunities, creating employment offices, and dividing up the landlords' extensive holdings. (2) Encourage people to go to America rather than Prussia. (3) Protect the short-term migrants by urging those from the same parish to stay together, with the elders watching over the younger travelers; and before leaving for their seasonal labor the villagers should go to confession and attend mass. (4) While in Prussia, migrants should be visited by Polish priests, and "good Catholic newspapers" should be mailed to them.[14]

To the seasonal migrant, these short-term wanderings brought results that ranged from economic success, even survival, to demoralization. A search for employment could usually satisfy immediate financial problems at home, whether in Norway, Galicia, or Italy. And that need could be great: for example, up to three-fourths of the population of Swinford, in western Ireland, was heavily dependent in the early 1880s on money sent or brought back by its sons and daughters who had gone to England for work. Some French geographers have argued that during the turn of the century many communities would have become uninhabited without temporary job-seeking migration to maintain families in their homes. The ability of seasonal migration to meet such needs depended, of course, on the wages paid, the worker's ability to scrimp and save, and the amount of travel required. One study of a Galician village in 1899 reported that income brought by migrant workers returning from Germany was 20 percent more than the net income derived from the village's entire farm production.[15]

For many seasonal workers the journeys resulted in more than wages. The major impact for some was an ethnic consciousness as, for the first time, they encountered people of other groups and nationalities. In 1893 one young Pole accompanied his parents from their Galician mountain village to Budapest, where he saw his first Italians, Slovaks, Czechs, Croats, Germans, and Hungarians. He later recalled that until then he had not realized he was a Pole; the lesson remained with him as he moved on to other lands overseas. Many migrants experienced this ironic rise in ethnic consciousness as they left their own people: as they wandered among others they learned who they were.[16]

And seasonal migration had yet another major result for Europe's peoples: as it grew ever more common, with traditional travel at harvesttime spurred by the spread of a cash economy and industrial recruitment, it produced what scholars have variously called a "migrant mentality" or "a propensity to migrate." Movement was everywhere; it had become the accepted thing. Łódź grew to become the "Manchester of Russia," shooting from a population of 31,000 in 1860, to 314,780 in 1897, as its factories relied heavily on seasonal peasant-migrants. One study showed that, in the 1880s, 60–70 percent of the labor force in Łódź, Warsaw, and the Daborwa mining region was drawn from this source; to the south, one-fourth of Budapest's factory workers were foreigners. Italians poured into southern France; Poles were so numerous in parts of the German mining-industrial zone that one Ruhr community was dubbed "Poznań on the Rhine." America's tales were not the only myths drawing Europe's surplus labor, German historian Dirk Hoerder has argued: industrial capitals such as Vienna and Paris had similar reputations.[17]

This internal migration was stimulated and enlarged as subsistence farming weakened and a new capitalism took hold, encouraged by steamboats on the rivers and seas and railroads crisscrossing the Continent. There was a psychological change too. Peasants who had formerly accepted their lot, expecting only to work up to match the level of their parents, could now dream of going further, of advancing into higher levels of economic achievement and even social status. They were becoming future-oriented, and migration would no longer be undertaken only to avoid starvation.

From this transformation came a change in the destinations of many temporary migrants. Until the age of steam, seasonal job seekers usually avoided lengthy journeys. But just as a hike for employment in a nearby hamlet often became precursor for a journey to a distant factory, so this internal migration now began to lead overseas. The propensity to migrate was pushing in new directions, but it would still be round-trip. Those interested in improving their lives at home therefore began to travel in tandem with the older, existing stream of those who emigrated with the aim of permanent settlement abroad.[18]

That these streams mingled should not obscure the fact that overseas migration in the era remained secondary to the massive and continuing trek for employment about the Continent. The United States was still, and would remain, second choice. Among Poles, temporary short-term migration within Europe was twice as high as emigration to America, and similar reports came from most other areas. From 1906 to 1911, almost 3 million people left Austrian territories to work elsewhere in Europe, nearly a half-million annually. These numbers far exceeded those heading abroad. For European peasants struggling to survive, temporary migration to adjacent territory was the easier, logical choice; if conditions were right nearer home—or in Łódź, in Manchester—they would not brave the Atlantic. A Norwegian folk saying reflected this preference: "Cod were an America for the people." If cod were abundant, they would provide the extra cash needed. Travel beyond coastal waters was unnecessary.[19]

THE STEAMSHIP'S IMPACT

It was the steamship, however, that caused the America fever to grow from isolated outbreaks into an epidemic. Now faster vessels brought North and South America securely within an Atlantic economy where both goods and workers could be transferred easily and cheaply. Crossing by sail was irregular, slow, and the ships lacked large capacities. But steam soon met its early promise, adding screw propellers and stabilizers, presenting a waiting Continent with enormous vessels built specifically for ferrying large numbers of immigrants at low cost in steerage.

The steamship soon outgrew its early tests on rivers and along coastlines. Egged on by their governments, British and American firms entered into a development race, joined by the Germans whose first transatlantic steamship was operating by 1856. Before long the Atlantic was crossed by ships run by large firms of many nations—Cunard, White Star, C.G.T., Inman, Holland-America, as well as the two major German companies, Hamburg Amerikanische Packetfahrt Actien Gesellschaft (HAPAG) and Norddeutscher Lloyd. Despite initial reluctance by the sailing public to give them its business, the less-dashing steamships began to advance in emigrant popularity. As late as 1856 more than 95 percent of all emigrants came to America by sail, but by 1865 the portion was down to 25 percent. By 1873 it dropped to 3.2 percent. Steam had won. The victory was achieved with shorter crossing times, vastly improved shipboard conditions, and lower costs.[20]

With the passage from Europe shortened from the sailboats' erratic

35–42 days down to two weeks or even less by steam, the impact was dramatic. "The great ocean liners that were coming into being in those days made travel safe and comfortable," recalled one Irishman, "and brought America so near to this country, that it was just round the corner, as compared with twenty years before that time." Similar reductions were reported for other parts of Europe, with crossings under two weeks increasingly common as the century neared its close.[21]

Conditions on board improved drastically as ships no longer transported westbound emigrants in the same crude quarters filled earlier with cows, flax seed, corn, and other agricultural products. The first mass sailings, back in the late eighteenth century, had carried up to 5,000 persons to America in one season, but under such difficult conditions below deck that the image of wretchedness remained. In those early days of sail, emigrants traveling in steerage received drinking water, a place to cook, and a place to sleep, but they were expected to bring their own food and bedding. The dungeonlike conditions were a hell for travelers, especially during foul weather when they were unable to go on deck; when the hatchways were finally lifted after a long stormy stretch, a stench-curdled steam arose. Travelers from the first- and second-class cabins wondered how anyone in steerage could survive.[22]

Many did not. After reports of up to 10 percent of steerage passengers dying at sea, the U.S. Congress in 1819 passed the first of many laws attempting to reduce overcrowding and improve conditions. Britain was undertaking similar actions. One U.S. official complained that "if crosses and tombs could be erected on water, the whole route of the emigrant vessels from England to America would long since have assumed the appearance of a crowded cemetery." This reputation kept many leery of oceanic travel until steamship lines were firmly established.[23]

Low fares eventually became a crucial part of the steamship's appeal, although fares on sailboats in the 1860s were generally within the same range: ticket costs from two to five British pounds ($9.72–24.30)—often without food, however—were reported as the age of sail drew to a close. But the sailboat's time of crossing, uncertainties about scheduling, poor conditions, and shipboard dangers all worked against it as steamship competition increased. And the new shipping lines vigorously battled in fare wars that saw the ticket price dip to as low as $10 to cross on HAPAG in steerage during the mid-1880s, and in 1894 Irishmen could cross for $8.75.[24]

Sharp variations in fares became the rule. The sixteen- or seventeen-

Steamship ticket from 1891 for a Norddeutscher Lloyd journey from Bremen to Detroit, by way of Baltimore. The agent responsible was Missler of Bremen, one of the most active in areas of Prussian and Austrian Poland. Provided by Marcin Kula.

day trip from Naples to New York cost $15 for steerage in 1880, $25 in 1881, $24 in 1888, $28 in 1899, and $25 in 1907; in 1912 the Italian government reported a range of fares from $33 with HAPAG to $40 with Italia, Duca di Aosta, and Norddeutscher Lloyd. British firms' tickets to New York fell from $34 to $12.50 during the 1894 fare wars, then hit $25 to $27.50 in 1899. That was the year Norddeutscher Lloyd reported a steerage rate to New York of $36.50–38.50 from the port of Bremen, where many Poles embarked. There were other expenses, too; in 1912, however, the total cost for an Italian, Slav, or Hungarian was only $40. Probably $30 was the average fare for most of the period.[25]

Peasants did not have such money. But, with the economic transformation going on about them, they were increasingly able to collect it, borrow it, obtain it by selling land or cattle, or to receive a ticket from someone who had gone ahead. In Finland a farmhand or lumberjack earned two or three marks a day in the early twentieth century; the ticket to America cost 200 Finnish marks—more than $40. But only one-third of the emigrants from Finland paid their own way; another third took out a loan, and one-third got the ticket from a relative or friend in America. Even at $30 or $40, the price was within reach for many.[26]

Thus, although the age of the indentured servant was long past, the lower classes in Europe were again presented a chance to emigrate to America. The U.S. consul in Düsseldorf pointed to the $25 fare from his district in 1888 and agreed that it put emigration "within the means of the poorest classes to emigrate." As the prefect of Cosenza wrote in his 1894 report to the Italian government, "going to America has become so popular recently that young men feel ashamed if they have not been overseas at least once. As late as ten years ago America evoked images of danger and distance. Now people feel more confident about going to New York than to Rome."[27]

The growing competition between shipping lines and nations eventually fueled this movement so that emigration developed its own momentum. Its dynamism was great enough to overwhelm countervailing economic factors and governmental policies, and to beat down critics. And, on the local scene, where individuals made their final decisions, the major instrument of this steam-driven transformation of emigration was the steamship company agent.

TICKET SELLERS SCOUR A CONTINENT

They were ubiquitous. The representatives of "one of the best organized, most energetically conducted branches of commerce in the world"—according to the U.S. commissioner-general of immigration—the steamship lines' agents covered the Continent's parishes, villages, and cities, visiting the marketplace, seeking out the curious, and winning converts in numbers that would have made an evangelist drool. Agents came into the village of Orsomarso in the Italian south one festival day in 1891, the state prefect reported: "Early in the morning they set up a podium in the town square. From there they addressed the people, offering explanations and especially dispelling doubts, whenever peasants approached them and showed interest in departing."[28]

The agent became important in the emigration picture only after steam power had cheapened and eased the ocean crossing, resulting in a new level of business competition—a "period of steam-ship rivalry, agents' commissions, and misrepresentations," according to the man-

Agent Missler of Bremen scoured Polish areas for emigrant customers, using personal contacts and posters such as this. The journey from Bremen to America was advertised as "only 9 days." Provided by Marcin Kula.

ager of the Italian Society of Emigration. The agent did much more than sell tickets: he often served as a source of credit, loaning the traveler funds for passport and passage; he helped auction off the emigrant's property, even providing clothing for the journey.[29]

But, above all, he located customers. Asked how three agents could round up 1,600 passengers to travel on a single steamer bound for America, an Italian answered simply, "Three villages were scoured." To "scour" a village, the agent needed ready answers to questions about the crossing, the costs, the dangers, as well as the opportunities in America. He had to be especially quick in countering the peasant's fear of failure overseas: Angelo Antonio di Dierro, a recently arrived Italian, told congressional investigators (through an interpreter), "All I know is the men when he met them he used to talk to them about coming to America; he said, 'You will find good wages there, and if you can't find anything there you can always come back.'"[30]

You could always come back—this must be added to the list of new encouragements to emigrate in the latter decades of the century. It was born with the entry of the steamship into the carrying trade and became an extra, convincing argument used by agents as they accosted reluctant peasants who still saw their long-term futures in their villages among their own people, not overseas in some American factory town. With these new arguments on their lips the agents swarmed over Europe: 6,254 employed by Norway's thirteen ship ticket agencies by 1881, eight of them working full time in the district of Sogn alone; "several thousand" operating in Ireland by the 1890s, employed by the five largest Irish firms, in addition to others working there for U.S. and Canadian governmental bodies, railroads, and land companies; and 5,000–6,000 agents from only two companies participating in the "great hunt for emigrants" across Galicia, the Dillingham Commission was told. That commission, carrying out its investigations mainly between 1907 and 1910, concluded that Austria, Hungary, Greece, and Russia were scenes of the most extensive promotional work by steamship ticket agents. But it was the same in virtually all regions of Europe. An Irish immigrant's comment spoke for legions: "One agent is fighting with the other who will sell the ticket."[31]

The agent's commission was the motor behind this activity. It was also the bait that lured public officials, local businessmen, school teachers, and even religious leaders to become ticket sellers. The commission ranged from $1.90 to $5 per ticket, occasionally as high as $8. It was a large sum in a peasant village. And if a would-be emigrant

Posters were used to attract emigrant customers all over Europe. W. Wolff of White Star's Anchor Line distributed this poster in the early steamship era when some vessels combined sails and steam power. Provided by Marcin Kula.

could find others to purchase tickets—at least ten, according to one report—then he or she might travel free.[32]

Giuseppe Granozio from Salerno recalled agents reading out loud the posters on walls in his village, advertisements proclaiming that in America "$2 would be paid a day certainly; . . . The particulars of sailings were written on the bill, together with a sketch of the steamer." Ireland was also covered with these: "You would see them everywhere," John Heghney from Fantni, county Tyrone, told congressional investigators. Another Irishman, Patrick Cavanaugh, elaborated:

> They are posted up through the town and through the country. . . . Sometimes they have little hand books, I could not read them, but they will tell you what they are doing here in the winter time—cutting wheat and one thing and another, and big wages. . . . [The posters] are about half the size of this table . . . red and white and blue and white. . . . They are printed so that people could hardly pass them without seeing them. . . . the whole town and country is placarded with those.[33]

But posting handbills, helping raise travel expenses, and trumpeting America's wealth were only part of the work of the steamship agent. He also accompanied emigrants on portions of their journey, passing them on to confederates in an intricate series of links that ultimately formed a chain reaching all the way to the steel mill door in Chicago or the mine pit in Pennsylvania. In some cases the chain was connected to the padrone system, providing jobs for a fee. A Macedonian thirteen-year-old who was leaving home presumed that Selo, a former emigrant accompanying him, would serve "like a guide on a mountain." He discovered, however, that they were met at the first stop by agents who pinned red buttons with white stars on their coat lapels, so that agents at the next station would find them more easily. By the time they arrived at dockside in Cherbourg, "we were not five but more than a hundred. . . . It seemed to me that the whole world had discovered America at the same time that Selo had and was in a hurry to get there."[34]

The buttons were unusual enough, and blossomed among crowds in European railway stations in such profusion, that they aroused the curiosity of the touring U.S. commissioner-general of emigration (and former head of the Knights of Labor), Terence V. Powderly. The U.S. consul in Trieste told Powderly that the buttons were given out by the Austro-American Line so that its ticketed travelers could be recognized along the route. "For instance," the consul wrote, "the local agents of the Austro-American Line at Lemberg, Prague and Brussel forward emigrants to Trieste via Vienna. These three agents inform the agent of the said line at Vienna that they have shipped emigrants who will arrive at Vienna on a certain day. The Vienna agent appears at the appointed time at the railway depot. He soon recognizes his people on their arrival by their buttons" and starts them on the next leg of their journey.[35]

One major concern of the agents was to assure that the pipeline to America remained clear, unclogged, and moving. Agents knew that if the trip was a disaster the next letter home would scare off future customers. As one Greek crossing in steerage explained to an interviewer, agents would not allow an emigrant who had been refused admittance to America ever to return to his village, "for the reason that one emigrant who has failed to enter the United States can keep 300 more from trying it." And so they worked diligently, desperately, to avoid this, providing helpers at difficult points along the route, making certain that meals were available, arguing with officials and resorting to bribery if needed—and even steering unhappy returners away from their home villages so their reports would not deter others.[36]

The agent was needed; quite often he was crucial. When Josef Cybulski wrote in 1891 to advise his brother back in Congress Poland about the trip, the reliance on the agent was spelled out:

Show the red card in Prussia. Pin it to the side or in the center of your cap, and show the white card only in New York when you arrive in America, then they will direct you to me. With the red one, they will direct you in Prussia to Bremen and to the agent from whom you will get a steamship ticket. . . .

Do not exchange the money as soon as you cross the border, but only as much as you will need for the train trip through Prussia. Change ten rubles only, and the rest you can exchange at Missler's when you pay for the steamship ticket, because at the border they cheat. [37]

Cheaters were occasionally caught. Eighty "runners" of HAPAG and Nordsdeutscher Lloyd were arrested in Galicia in the summer of 1888, leading to a string of sensational lawsuits in the controversial "Wadowice Trials" that threw open to public view the machinations of agents, public officials, and others in defrauding emigrants while reaping fabulous profits.[38]

The Wadowice Trials of 1889–90 centered on the activities of the HAPAG agency at Oswiecim, which had transported 12,406 emigrants through the city during the previous year. It was revealed that the firm had in its employ policemen, customs agents, railway conductors, and porters, all receiving monthly stipends. Emigrants who had not purchased their tickets from HAPAG were threatened with arrest, for conductors informed the unwary peasants that only HAPAG had the right to carry travelers to America. The resulting arrests of emigrants who refused to cooperate gave rise to the court cases, which eventually exposed the operation. It was revealed that the agency's office had been remade to appear as a government establishment—complete with large portrait of the emperor and employees who acted like Austrian officials. Emigrants were forced to show all their travel documents and money, fetching them from hiding places in shoes, hats, and coats; stubborn victims were searched. Often leaflets or other advertising materials were sold as tickets.

Another agony concerned the peasant's required medical exam, which invariably found that he or she was not healthy enough to be accepted into America. When the doctor left the room, however, clerks advised the victim to offer a bribe to be allowed to continue on the journey. After that, it was announced that the peasant's clothes—long, ornamented coats and traditional dresses—were not permitted in America; the only way to continue on was to cross the street and purchase acceptable American garb right there in Lowenberg's store.

The climax of the emigrant's troubles in Oswiecim came when the head of the agency pretended to telephone to Hamburg, asking whether there was room there for the traveler. Then another imaginary call was put through to America: "Is there still any free land left in America? Will this emigrant be accepted?"—and the peasant had to pay, of course, for these "calls." Even that did not ènd the fraud. In Hamburg, high charges were made for the emigrant's food and lodging until the ship sailed.

Despite such subterfuge, wrote Polish scholar Leopold Caro wonderingly in 1909, the agent was widely considered to be the emigrant's benefactor! Caro's disbelief was echoed across the Atlantic as American officials and others involved in immigration issues began to question how voluntary the influx could be under such goading by agents. When 100 unemployed Bulgarians were interviewed in Chicago by Grace Abbott for an article in the influential *Charities* magazine in 1909, 77 said they had been induced to emigrate by steamship agents, and 63 of the 66 who had been promised jobs in America reported that they had received that promise from steamship agents. Something more than economic conditions started these Bulgarians to America, Abbott concluded: "The cause is found in the activity of the steamship companies." The U.S. immigration commissioner argued that the shipping companies were to blame for this "artificially induced" immigration into the United States, and the Dillingham Commission investigators agreed: "To say that the steamship lines are responsible, directly or indirectly, for this unnatural immigration is not the statement of a theory but of a fact."[39]

In the opinion of a Polish immigrant in 1888, probably three-fourths of the Polish immigration would have stayed home without the activities of the shipping company agents. Sixteen years later, in 1904, immigration inspector Braun conceded that exceptional conditions drove people from some areas, but he still argued that "the volume of immigration into the United States would not exceed one-half of the present figure but for the activity of the transportation companies in their hunt for business." And Caro raised the obvious point: if the agents were not necessary to stir up business, why did the shipping lines employ them in such enormous numbers?[40]

Some contemporaries, however, saw other factors behind the increasing exodus from Europe and more recent scholars usually emphasize a variety of causes. A writer in *Charities* in 1904 attributed the "radical change" in immigration to U.S. prosperity and economic opportunity, to racial and religious oppression overseas, to cheaper and easier transport, and only last to the activity of steamship agents. Terence Powderly, although quite critical of the agents, came to similar conclusions after his 1907 tour for the immigration service.[41]

The argument that massive immigration was all caused by steamship company agents was attacked by a contemporary prominent sociologist, himself an immigrant, who instead saw the remigrant's role as crucial. Isaac Hourwich, in his critique of the Dillingham Commission report, asserted that an annual emigration of one million could barely support twenty thousand agents: "This scarcely equals one per cent of the volunteer force of immigration promoters who have returned from America within the past ten years"—that is, returned emigrants and visitors. Hourwich considered it "clearly against all sense of proportion to magnify the 'propaganda' of a few thousand ticket agents into a contributing cause of this modern *Völkwanderung.*"[42]

NEWS FROM OVERSEAS

Frequently it was specific information from America that drew the emigrant. As an Italian politician put it, "the strongest emigration agent is the postage-stamp." Branko M. Colakovic's interviews with 500 Yugoslavs who had crossed the ocean before 1925 led him to conclude that the pull from America was more important than the push from even the harshest Yugoslav conditions. Higher wages were crucial, and pamphlets from American railroads and state immigration bureaus bombarded the would-be immigrant with statistics to support the agents' claims. "It was almost heaven," a Finn said in recalling tales of the wealth that allegedly awaited workers in the United States. "You could almost just grab the money!" And Swedish children in Småland called the distant land where their relatives were heading not America but *mer rika*—"more rich."[43]

Reports by those coming back and others who had gone ahead quickly expanded the peasants' knowledge of the lands across the ocean. Some of this knowledge was spread on an organized basis, as with the Jewish groups that passed information on the best routes to cross the Russian border, dangers along the way, and preferred trachoma treatments (to pass the scrutiny of U.S. Customs agents). America lost its reputation as a land of mystery through detailed letters:

When you board the train at the Castle Garden station, you should sit in the upper part of the train. You will pay 5 cents to reach the ferry at 34th St. You will pay 3 cents for the ferry. When you arrive at

Underspeitu, ask at the depot for College Point. They will tell you and show you how you are to travel. You will pay 25 cents to College Point, L.I., and there you will ask for P. Kugler. . . . I wish you all a happy trip. [44]

Such letters soon brought a change in the distant land's reputation. America was no longer the unfamiliar, the unreachable. In earlier times, an Italian writer observed, peasants considered the United States "a mysterious land where misery is unknown [and] where in a few years a person can become a Croesus, a Rothschild." But by 1909 it was seen simply as a country of labor, where work was hard but rewarding. Similarly, Polish scholars found that peasants began to regard emigration to the United States as they would a trip to the next city or to a neighboring fair. Swedes, it was reported, found that because of improved travel facilities and the increasing numbers of relatives abroad it was easier to move to America than to Stockholm or Gothenburg. And the Sicilian, a 1914 reporter concluded, "goes and comes from America with the same indifference with which he undertook a trip to Catania 50 years ago."[45]

One reason for this new ease of travel was that prospective travelers knew the conditions that awaited them, knew them in dollars and cents with an exactness that would have surprised some of their future employers. The peasant was able to calculate with some precision, at least for the city that drew him on. Emily Balch found Slavs in southern Bohemia "amazingly well informed as to conditions in America" in 1905, and recent studies of the information reaching perspective Irish emigrants, and of the American reports carried in a Swedish workers' newspaper, conclude that the information was accurate. Josef Wroblewski could be specific when he wrote to his brothers in America concerning his plans to emigrate: "But first I ask you for advice, whether it is worth going, for if I don't earn $1.50 a day, it would not be worth thinking about America."[46]

The American possibilities contrasted sharply with wages across Europe, especially with what was paid in peasant Europe. By the turn of the century in Hungary, field hands worked only 88 days a year on the average, earning 111 kronen (just over $22) for the year. Farm laborers in Austria were reported to be receiving 10–20 cents daily plus board in the winter, and 20–30 cents in the summer. Similarly, in Ireland it was "the pay" that "coaxed the people to America," a resident of Glenagivney recalled. "There was a big difference between eight shillings ($2) a week and $8 a week." The Dillingham Commission investigated the wage question and found that, though recent labor scarcities in Calabria had raised farm workers' wages, they were still only about two and one-half lire (50 cents) a day. And this was for labor that was usually only sporadic. For example, yearly income totals of male farm workers across Italy ranged from a high of $103.20 in the northern Piedmont to a low of $50.37 in the Marches of east-central Italy, with $74–84 paid in the Mezzogiorno.[47]

These earnings of European peasants must be contrasted with actual American wages, of course, for stories claiming gold in the streets could not have lured many for long. But the true wages in the United States stood far above what most would-be immigrants were receiving at home—far enough above them to constitute "gold" in their eyes. This was especially true when contrasted with wages in Europe's peripheries, in peasant Europe. The U.S. Labor Department determined that laborers in New York were averaging 61 hours a week in 1880, receiving $1.30 as an average daily wage; it was 60 hours and $1.57 in 1890, and 44 hours and $1.51 in 1900. California was slightly higher in average wage, the rest of the country generally slightly lower. Paul Douglas estimated average *weekly* earnings for unskilled labor in the United States at $8.82 in 1890, $8.94 in 1900, and $10.68 in 1910. In coal mining— a frequent occupation for immigrants—Douglas found wages averaging $10.80 weekly in 1890, falling to $10.74 in 1900, rising to $15.42 in 1910 and to $37.80 by 1920 with the impact of wartime-induced demand.[48]

This wage differential was crucial for Europeans wishing to return and take up their lives again at home. Those leaving permanently could expect to recoup travel and other expenses over many years, but temporary migrants had to plan differently, comparing different possibilities; a southern Italian saying of the period placed the yield from America at 1,000 lire a year, at least double what one could earn in Germany. The short-term migrant needed high wages in America to justify a short stay. This helped assure that return migration would draw its greatest numbers of participants from peasant societies such as in southern Italy, where wages were miniscule. It also meant that these industrial migrants would seek employment in America that promised immediate rewards. "With comparatively few exceptions," the Dillingham Commission concluded, "the emigrant of to-day is essentially a seller of labor seeking a more favorable market."[49]

U.S. employers soon took advantage as they realized that they could obtain a steady supply of workers simply by urging their employees to send back requests to friends and relatives in Europe. The 1885 Foran

Act with its ban on labor recruitment proved no obstacle. Steel mill foremen in Pittsburgh relied almost totally on white ethnic networks to fill their labor needs by 1910, according to one study. This meant that immigrant workers were reaching industrial jobs soon after their arrival, whether directed by subagents, padroni, relatives, or others. And they knew where they were going. A typical finding by the Dillingham Commission was that a large number of incoming Bulgarians listed the steel mill town of Granite- City, Illinois. Many of them gave specific addresses within Granite City, such as a large Macedonian mercantile house, an immigrant saloon, a Macedonian saloon-lodging-mercantile house, and similar immigrant businesses. Those putting down simply "Granite City" were presumably headed for the city's steel mills.[50]

An agent of the Seaboard Railway, a southern line, told immigration commissioner Powderly in 1906 that 90 percent of the immigrants he checked at Ellis Island had arrived with a fixed destination, "and no amount of persuasion could influence these people to be diverted." They all claimed that letters from friends and relatives guided them. Taking this into account, Powderly agreed that shifting the destinations of the immigrants to the South "cannot be done at Ellis Island." These new industrial immigrants knew where they were going before they left Europe. By the time they reached Ellis Island, they were not open to other possibilities. This mass migration went "according to well-defined individual plans rather than in a haphazard way," the Dillingham Commission found, and later investigations have revealed the alertness of European emigrants to changing American conditions. They were a "calculating people," John Bodnar concluded.[51]

They had much to calculate. Falling wheat prices in Europe, one result of the increased world competition brought by the steamship and railroad, combined sporadically with booming American industrial conditions to create lures that were difficult to resist. A reporter sat in Oderberg Station on Austria's Northern Railroad Line and watched the emigrants surging through on the first leg of their journey abroad, drawn from all parts of the empire. By their volume, he observed, "one can judge the prosperity of the United States" or the condition of its labor market. This idea has occurred over the years to many economists, also, who have sought specific factors behind the immigration-economy relations. In 1926 Harry Jerome linked new waves of immigration to U.S. production of pig iron. Although in 1954 Brinley Thomas found no simple correlation between short-term business upturns and immigration, he demonstrated ties between long-term American economic investment and growth, when matched with European agricultural devastations and overpopulation. Jeffrey Williamson, however, concluded in 1974 that the structure of the European sending economy was the key: emigration from Sweden, for example, was more responsive to upturns and downturns in the local economy than was emigration from England.[52]

LAND PRESSURES

The increase in landless farm workers, day laborers, and contract farm workers in many areas was also crucial for emigration. By the turn of the century, Italy reported that half its labor force consisted of contract laborers and *giornalieri* (day workers); another 39 percent was made up of renters, partnership tenants, and sharecroppers. Only 11 percent owned their own land. The situation was especially acute in southern Italy.[53]

Those without land were "superfluous" people, and their numbers were rising across much of the Continent. By 1900 landless agrarian workers constituted perhaps 25 percent of the total population of central and east-central Europe. The landless in Congress Poland were increasing twice as fast as the rest of the population during the closing decades of the nineteenth century; by 1910 more than two million peasants in Congress Poland had no land. Half of those emigrating from there in 1912 were reported to be landless.[54]

Finland also had a growing landless population, especially in socalled Emigration Finland, the district of Southern Ostrobothnia. By law, only one child could inherit a family's farm, which theoretically provided adequate farms for many while sharply increasing the numbers without land. Kuopio province at the end of the century reported the highest proportion of landless in Finland, and it also showed the highest rural population decline; without nearby alternatives, the landless had to leave. A similar restriction on land division among heirs in Norway produced the same results. Sixty-eight percent of the 165,206 emigrants from Norway were from rural areas in the 1896–1906 period, and later government investigations found that almost four-fifths gave "lack of access to profitable occupations" as their main reason for emigrating.[55]

Ireland's problem was a backward agriculture combined with overpopulation, "congested districts," in the British parliamentary phrase. By 1910 a quarter of the island was classified as congested, and the seven most congested counties provided more than a third of all Irish emigrants from 1881 to 1910. Without land, without jobs, they too chose to leave.[56]

Disastrous rural conditions were behind much of the emigration to America, but these were not identical or even similar in all regions. There were significant differences between suffering agrarian populations, and these had an impact on emigration. One major contrast was between dispersed landholding and the dominance of large estates.

Various studies have documented the differing impact on emigration and return migration of landholding variations. Hungary, for example, stood out in east-central Europe in its predominance of large estates—with a resulting landless agrarian proletariat—but other areas had the problem of too many landholders, owning farms too small to support a family. The latter condition, pauperization, often resulted from the custom of partible inheritance, under which farmers divided land among all their children, and it increased the attractions of temporary migration. Examining eastern Slovakia, the Banat, and Transylvania, Josef Barton found a broad distribution of landholdings in the middle sector of the peasantry—and heavy emigration. Partible inheritance "tied men to their village," he found. This led to another set of local land relations, "the sharing in the land's produce through participation contracts, which both gave the landless cultivator some stake in the land and provided a means to acquire property."[57]

Similarly, Galicia saw an increase from 1850 to 1890 of peasant-owned tilled land by 750,000 acres, but along with this a proliferation of "dwarf" holdings. The disastrous results were seen by Balch in 1910, as the Galician peasant continued to cut up land among his descendants, holdings that were already sufficient to support only one household. But soon he was driven to seek outside work or borrow money:

> Thus the peasant, with mortgage payments which he could not meet or with children for whom he could not provide an adequate patrimony, saw himself face to face with an intolerable decline of social status for himself or for his children; namely, reduction to the position of a propertyless day laborer. This is the sting which induces many a man among the Slovaks, the Poles, the Ruthenians, to fare over seas or to send out his son to the new land from which men come back with savings.[58]

Some areas of southern Italy presented similar conditions, despite legends to the contrary. True, Sicily had *latifondi*—large estates—in abundance, and tenants were present in enormous numbers in such provinces as Apulia and Umbria, but in Basilicata and Calabria and even along the Sicilian coastlands there were many small and medium-sized holdings. These farmers, surviving only with difficulty, cast their eyes on neighboring holdings, watched their opportunities, and used temporary emigration as a means to raise funds to purchase more land. Barton ranked Italian districts according to their degree of rural property concentration and found a "striking pattern" when he compared these with emigration data: migration rates were highest in regions where property was least concentrated. These were very poor, backward areas, but property was still widely distributed among peasants. And although fairly evenly divided, it was generally cut up into tiny plots, difficult to survive on. Similar patterns were seen in many other areas, providing an impetus to the idea of emigrating temporarily.[59]

In some areas primogeniture, or impartible inheritance, was still unable to hold back pauperization, as children without land sought by any means to acquire some property, any property. They often succeeded but could acquire only bits and pieces. As a result, pauperization developed even amid impartible inheritance. This was true of Congress Poland, where the number of landless peasants grew by 386 percent from 1870 to 1891; although the number of individual peasant landholdings was increasing 121 percent during the same period, the average size of holdings was declining. More than 30 percent of Finnish farms were under five acres by 1901. The agony of much of the European peasantry was summed up by a central European folk saying: if a dog lay on one man's property, its tail would be on his neighbor's. Some strips of land, in fact, were only 1.5 meters wide. Many farmers owned fifty or sixty of these narrow plots.[60]

Such persons had a specific interest in this new, reachable America. Those high-paying industrial jobs abroad could become the means to expand the farm at home, especially now that ocean travel had become regular and predictable and the price of the ticket might be borrowed or, better still, provided by a relative who had gone ahead. A round-trip ticket to America could be a long-term investment at home. One study of emigration from a Galician village around the turn of the century found that, the more property a person had, the greater the chance that he would emigrate. Those with some land wanted more, and now America would be the means to obtain it. One-third of the villagers owning 5–10 hectares emigrated, planning to purchase additional land when they returned. This was emigration "in order to."[61]

"DROVES OF MALES"

But more than land size, more than economics propelled the movement westward. The America fever was a changing contagion that defied exact analysis, and the rising phenomenon of temporary migration directed overseas was becoming part of it. Not all of this exodus was predictable, neither in 1890 nor in retrospect today. Sometimes communities with poor conditions sent fewer emigrants than communities that were thriving. As a Dutch authority observed, "evidently, where judging the need for emigration, the demographers and economists apply standards whose validity the agrarian population has not yet recognized." Often the wrong people left. Slovaks in Hungary did not emigrate from the Magura region during hard times but waited until the rising sugar beet industry brought good times. Others waited out economic downturns until friends and relatives had settled in America first.[62]

Ethnic feuding, wars, revolts, and government restrictions stirred others to leave despite favorable economic conditions at home. The empires—Russian, Austro-Hungarian—with difficulty kept lids on their boiling nationality disputes. The czar's 1899 orders for conscription of Finnish young men set off an immediate rush for the borders, and sporadically other groups within the Russian empire also fled to escape the government. From 1899 to 1910, 43.8 percent of Russia's emigrants were not Russians but Jews, and Poles made up 27 percent. Only 4.4 percent of those leaving Russia were Russians.[63]

As this emigration to America mushroomed, its makeup began to shift. It remained a heavily rural, peasant movement, but no longer did family groups dominate. Single women arrived, but their numbers were overwhelmed by those of men, especially young men. "They came in droves of males," a U.S. congressman remarked, and the change was dramatic enough to draw attention: the U.S. Census report for 1910 observed that with the increased immigration from southern and eastern Europe the foreign-born showed "a very marked excess of males"—154.6 males to 100 females from Austria, 160.8 to 100 from Hungary, 190.6 to 100 from Italy, 137.3 to 100 from Russia. Foerster found that, among outward-bound Italians, the percentage of males rose rapidly with every pronounced spurt in immigration; in fact, from 1870 to 1910, 78 percent of the emigrants from Italy to the United States were male. Those leaving the Austro-Hungarian empire showed male percentages from 1899 to 1910 ranging from a low of 57 percent for Bohemians and Moravians to highs of 91 percent for Romanians, 92.3 percent for Dalmatians, Bosnians, and Herzegovinians, and 95.7 percent for Bulgarians, Serbians, and Montenegrins.[64]

But the phenomenon affected the Old Immigration as well. Scandinavian emigrants from 1881 to 1890 included forty-six dependents for every fifty-four breadwinners; by 1901–10 this had fallen to nineteen dependents for eighty-one breadwinners. This makeup was similar to that of earlier job-seeking migrations into neighboring regions, and an analysis of overseas emigration from Dalarna province in central Sweden concluded that "in many ways the turn-of-the-century emigrants were much more like the traditional short-distance or internal migrant" than were earlier groups heading to America.[65]

The transformation in the makeup of this emigration was apparently not driven by racial or regional factors but by economic ones. In the decade ending in 1910, in fact, almost 70 percent of *all* immigrants into the United States were males, mainly young males. Women continued to arrive, but many found work not in the factories but as servants, or they remained within family groups. And for both men and women it was a migration of youth. Some of the Austro-Hungarian groups had more than 80 percent in the 14–44 age category after 1900; for U.S. immigration as a whole, persons in that age group accounted for 83.4 percent of the total in the exploding influx of 1906–10. This changing flow had a large impact on the emigration districts of Europe, too: the exodus of men from Slovak regions of Hungary was so heavy that by 1910 there were only 532 men in Slovakia for every 1,000 women.[66]

Part of the change in the exodus was that immigrants increasingly planned only a short stay in America—nothing to put down roots for, just enough to pile up some savings that could be used for better living or a specific project at home. Permanent residence was no longer the aim: the goal in every case of emigration from one Hungarian community "was to work for the good of the family," one investigator found. As a Polish immigrant in Pennsylvania explained in a letter sent back to his brother in 1890, "Now dear brother, you wrote that your harvest has not been too good and that it is difficult for you, so if you want to come to America, then come. You could remain for two years in America, earn some money so that you could pull yourself out from under that misery and be a man."[67]

Behind the abundant reminiscences of immigrants who stated that their original plan was to return to Europe lie some impressive statistical data. When Italy after 1901 began requiring passport applicants to state whether they were going abroad permanently or only temporarily—and canceling their names from community registers if permanent—the results showed that more than three-fourths planned to return. In 1909, for example, only 22 percent of the departing emigrants' names were canceled as permanently lost; in 1912–13, 19 percent. Historian Dino Cinel cautions that "a declaration of intent is not a guarantee of what will happen; but it is a strong indication."[68]

When the Austro-Hungarian governor of Carniola ordered an investigation into the devastating exodus of Slovenians, he found that two-thirds of those departing were unmarried and that, among the property holders leaving, 5,999 had *not* sold their properties at home while only 135 had done so. He concluded that this Slovenian emigration was "of the transient type." Bulgarians traveling to America were interviewed in Chicago by Grace Abbott in 1908, who found that 78 percent of those questioned said they had mortgaged their land to undertake the trip, hoping to earn "enough money so that they could return home and buy more land."[69]

Similar accounts came from other districts. A Polish priest reported the departure for America of twenty married men from Tarnawa Dolna in 1902, but he assured that they would stay no more than four years: "No one left forever." Similar Polish reports provide additional backing for this trend, including the pleading letter from a younger brother at home urging his kin overseas to let him join them: "Let me also try America! I would not spend there longer than two years." Other districts across the Continent produced similar tales. That a majority of immigrants eventually remained in America should not obscure the probability that this had not been their original intention. As a Finn recalled from his earlier emigration journeys, "very few, it can be said, intended to leave their country for ever."[70]

THE FEVER SPREADS

Encouraged by the abundance of steamship lines, drawing hope from both accurate and fanciful reports on American wages, and driven by pauperized landholdings as well as threats of czars and brigands and local landlords, the swirling interest in America soon constituted a potent mix that could sometimes be explosive. "There is an emigration fever," the Kraków priests announced in their 1907 statement. They warned that young people without jobs, without enough land, were searching for opportunities elsewhere, and once such a person learned of conditions overseas "there is practically no one—even his parents—who can stop him" from leaving. Westward-journeying vessels soon filled with these travelers: Italy's emigration to the United States rose from 307,309 for the decade of the 1880s, to 651,893 for the 1890s, and topped two million for the years 1901–10. Even though Sweden's record for the 1880s of 391,776 was not matched in succeeding decades, later decade totals still exceeded 200,000. "Once a person from this area, man or woman, has been seized by this epidemic American fever, there is nothing one can do about it," a doctor informed the Swedish Royal Commission. And the movement was so extensive in parts of Norway, a writer observed in 1910, "that in many places one begins to wonder about the occasional strong youth who decides to remain instead of traveling to America."[71]

The direction was the same—to the west, to the new worlds of North and South America, principally to the United States but also to Canada, Brazil, Argentina, and other Hispanic countries. If the direction was the same, it was nevertheless true that in the backgrounds of these travelers lay fundamental differences: they came from static, unchanging villages as well as regions torn by industrial upheaval; they knew wars and phylloxera and pogroms as well as the familiar rites and *festas* of the peasant year. These varied experiences would propel some away from their pasts forever. Others would seek to return, always planning their return, for their expectations of life in the New World had now become the stuff of dreams for a new and golden future in Europe.[72]

And so this heavily male, mostly young emigration said its farewells in "American wakes" and other village gatherings, loaded trunks and bags, and began the journey. Now the United States would have to deal with newcomers whose heads danced with stories of fabulous wages abroad but held no expectations of becoming citizens, only of becoming workers in America.

PART TWO

American Realities

CHAPTER 3

Immigrants in an Industrializing Economy

The "picker" machine in the Massachusetts textile mill beat the cotton to clean it as it came out of bales—beat it with knives circling in 1,500 unending revolutions a minute inside the "beater box." Like all machines it was ultimately tended by a human, in this case a recently arrived Pole named Frank Chmiel, age thirty-five. He did not speak English and had no previous mechanical experience.[1]

Much of the success of American industry in the years following the Civil War was based on the fact that men like Frank Chmiel could be taught to operate such a complex, fast-moving device. For this was a major part of the "revolution" that made possible the industrial revolution, under which minute subdivisions were created in each work process, usually through extensive use of machinery. Laborers soon began replacing skilled workers, becoming tenders of machines rather than merely shovelers or loaders. This transformation also meant that the unskilled—immigrants and Americans, farmboys and children—could be brought to the factory and taught specific tasks without a lengthy apprenticeship. A "melter" had always been a highly skilled job in a steel mill, but by 1901 Charles Schwab of Carnegie Steel was arguing that he could take a green hand and make a melter of him in six or eight weeks. Henry Ford's foundry had 95 percent unskilled laborers by 1914, trained to do just one operation, which Ford said "the most stupid man can learn in two days." That was what the machine age amounted to for many workers in American industry.[2]

In mining, the changes were equally spectacular and led to large-scale

45

displacement of skilled Americans as well as veteran English, Welsh, and Scots coal miners who had come into the coalfields after the Civil War. With new undercutting machines, the pick miner was largely done away with, the Dillingham Commission reported, thereby increasing the proportion of unskilled workmen who loaded coal after machines had cut it down. Only a few days' apprenticeship was needed to teach this to inexperienced workers. Noting similar changes in metal mining, a Finnish historian summed up: "Thus the Finn, who had never been a miner, became one in the United States."[3]

It was this transformation that brought immigrant Frank Chmiel to the Throndike Company's picker machine in Massachusetts in 1902. Chmiel's entry into American industry was fairly typical; unfortunately, his problems with the cotton picker were not at all unusual either. He had been instructed for two weeks before working on his own, but the day after Chmiel was put on the picker the rolls feeding cotton began to clog. Failing to free them by pulling cotton away from the emerging rolls, he removed the protective cover on the beater box—as he had seen his instructor do—and reached in to pull the cotton through the feed rolls, even as the knives jabbed into them at 1,500 revolutions a minute. His arm was cut off.

Chmiel may have occupied a crucial spot in America's industrial transformation, but that held little importance for the U.S. judicial system. Though the common law of liability was changing by 1902, it still effectively decreed that few employers were forced to pay compensation to employees injured on the job, especially when the worker had removed a machine guard and thereby contributed to his own injury. The weight of legal precedent did not take account of greenhorns: rather, court traditions envisioned a perfect, English-speaking employee who never grew tired after long hours amid smoke and din, was never distracted, was not made nervous or desperate by fears of being fired, and always understood perfectly his instructions as well as each rattle and hum of the machine.[4]

But reality was different. This case dealt with an immigrant Pole, not speaking English, having no previous mechanical experience; probably he was a peasant farmhand before coming to America. His instructor at the machine observed before the court, "As to whether Mr. Chmiel learned slowly or rapidly, I say he didn't have a good head to learn; . . . . Frank showed that he wasn't good to learn, and didn't learn well, because I showed him how to oil, and then told him how to oil there, and the third time asking him to do it he didn't do it."

Despite such testimony and the employee's peasant background, the court stated that the Thorndike Company could not be expected to have had "any reason to suppose that [Chmiel] was so dull as to require a caution not to put his arm where it would come in contact with the beater knives making 1,500 revolutions a minute." He received no compensation.[5]

It was part of the new order of things that the industrial system booming across Europe and North America would rely for much of its thrust on inexperienced, vulnerable greenhorns like Frank Chmiel. As British labor historian E. J. Hobsbawm has observed, "the bulk of industrial workers in all countries began, like America's, as first-generation immigrants from pre-industrial societies. . . . And like all first-generation immigrants, they looked backwards as much as forwards."[6]

In this chapter I take up issues arising from the massive influx of unskilled European peasants into American industry, the role of the padroni, job mobility, and efforts to reduce living costs while increasing savings. Throughout, attention is paid to the work environment and its impact, whether resulting from employer actions, the mix of machinery and men, or the shifting economy.

IMMIGRANT LABORERS

New and untried as the immigrants from European villages were, industry nevertheless depended on them, and the America fever brought an unending flow of workers willing to labor long hours for low wages. Even these conditions were often improvements over their earlier peasant drudgery outside the money economy or at the subsistence-level wages of day labor. One study of such new laborers around the world found several common features, regardless of country or period of history: originating in backward areas and lacking prior contact with industrial processes, these usually unskilled and illiterate laborers were attracted to industrial centers to take specific jobs—jobs often held in disdain by native workers. But they saw themselves initially as only short-term workers for their new employer, and only temporary residents of their new homes.[7]

These characteristics were present in abundance in the United States among the workers brought by the millions into the industrial boom developing by the 1880s. A government study found that, by 1900, 73.2 percent of the Italian, Slavic, and Hungarian immigrants resided in the seven major industrial states that produced 61 percent of the nation's manufactured and mining products. To Americans these were seekers after a new life, the "wretched refuse" of distant shores. But as one authority has defined the issue, "from the point of view of the Atlantic Economy, all those Jews, Italians, Poles or Armenians who traveled to America were essentially migrant-laborers searching for work, people displaced by a changing, industrializing society." The contrasting views of who the newcomers were became important, she notes, because these "often accounted for divergencies in action and behavior."[8]

They came into an America caught up in an economic explosion. Railways grew from only 35,000 miles of track at the end of the Civil War to 242,000 miles by 1900, including five transcontinental railroads. Only 1.6 thousand tons of steel had been produced by American mills in 1867, but output rose to 7.2 million tons in 1897. By 1900 steel was being sold to England, heretofore considered the world's industrial leader; American pig iron production had doubled Britain's by then. In fact, the United States had more than 30 percent of world manufacturing output as the century ended. Chicago's stockyards handled 1.5 million head of livestock during their first year of operation in 1866, but this rose to 14.6 million by 1900 and hit 18.6 million by 1924; employment reached 60,000 during World War I.[9]

Considerable credit for this growth must go to the immigrant laborers. One economist has estimated that Europe lost one-quarter of its labor force to the New World from 1850 to 1914, and within the United States one-third of the increase in the labor force from 1870 to 1910 was accounted for by immigration. The immigrants' presence was crucial.[10]

They flocked to industry, which meant they largely flocked into cities. Although by 1900 only 38.8 percent of America's foreign-born lived in cities of more than 100,000, these same cities were home to 73.4 percent of the Russians, 61.2 percent of the Italians, 60 percent of the Poles.[11]

Immigrants predominated in many occupations, such as the ready-made clothing industry, in which they outnumbered native-born workers two to one by 1910; they were dominant by 1.5 to one in blast furnaces, rolling mills, public works construction, and maintenance-of-way labor. But specific areas and firms frequently showed much higher proportions of the foreign-born: the Carnegie Steel works of Allegheny County, Pennsylvania, employed 14,359 common laborers in 1907, and 11,694 were East Europeans. One of Henry Ford's plants counted 12,880 employees in 1914, and 9,109 of these were foreign-born, a majority of them Poles, Russians, Romanians, Italians, Sicilians, and

Austro-Hungarians. John Fitch's 1910 study of the steelworkers observed that in blast furnaces, "aside from the Irish foreman, there are seldom any but Slavs or Hungarians employed," called "Hunkies" or "Ginnies." A survey of Michigan copper miners and smelter workers found that 80 percent were foreign-born, the largest group Finns, who constituted more than one-fourth of the total.[12]

According to the Dillingham Commission, whose investigation ran through the 1907–11 period, 57.7 percent of all iron and steel manufacturing employees east of the Mississippi were foreign-born, and 64.4 percent of them had been farmers or farm laborers abroad. The same study reported that, in Pennsylvania's bituminous coal mines, 76 percent of the miners were foreign-born and less than 8 percent of these came from the British Isles or Germany. "The term 'American miner', so far as the western Pennsylvania field is concerned, is largely a misnomer," the principal investigator concluded.[13]

The Italian became the road builder in America, the track layer, the shovel man; lacking mechanical skills, "he could contribute nothing more, and *nothing more was asked of him*, than the strength of his arms," Francesco Cerase has written. By 1890 some 90 percent of Italian wage earners in New York were engaged in public works construction; soon they constituted a monopoly of the sanitation department crews in San Francisco and did 99 percent of Chicago's roadwork. The great majority of railroad builders in the mid-seaboard, New England, and the central states were Italians during the period.[14]

These immigrants did not often turn to agriculture, despite their backgrounds. Taking up the digging of sewer lines in America proved easier than becoming an American farmer. Another reason farming did not attract these Italians, or many others drawn from the New Immigration, was that it did not suit their goals. These workers sought money, now.[15]

Many were attracted to the United States precisely because they could plan a short-term visit: help from the shipping company agent, speedy ships, low fares, the knowledge of routes and jobs and wages—all these made it easier to plan a reduced stay abroad. "The absence was to be temporary," Julianna Puskás has written of Hungary's emigrants; "they would soon return with the money made overseas to make a better life for themselves in the environment they were attached to, the place where they *wanted* to live." Poles entering Pittsburgh's industries were said to consider their sojourn there a temporary necessity that would enable them to achieve their larger goal of increasing land holdings at home. A Ukrainian woman recalled that when she came in 1912 she planned to stay "just two or three years. Everybody had the same idea—make a little money and go back home."[16]

Several basic points followed the decision for a temporary stay. A wife's presence was unneeded in America and could even be a detriment if she did not add to the savings but depleted them. Women continued to arrive, but in smaller numbers than males and usually as unwed single females; as such, they found ready work as household servants as well as in the sweatshops of the rising ready-made clothing industry. From 1870 to 1920 the yearly percentage of males entering the United States fell below 60 percent only fourteen times and was never under half; it exceeded 70 percent five times in the 1900–10 decade. The peak immigration year of 1907 also produced the highest male percentage: 72.4 percent.[17]

Even when already married, vast numbers of male immigrants pouring into American industry arrived singly, without spouses. A Pole's letter home in 1891 brought out some of the implications:

> I am not thinking of bringing you here her, dear wife, because I plan to return in the fall. . . . Yes, dear wife, save your *groszy*; do not spend it on unnecessary things because I would like to earn a few *groszy*. So I beg you, dear Wife, manage your affairs with as little expense as you can so that I too might have some kind of rest for my bones in my later years. . . . The 100 *rubles* which I sent to you, dear wife, to Dobrzyn, do not lend them. But if you think it wise, then lend them to some reliable person, but if not, then it is better to hold on to them. And dear wife, what I am earning I will bring with me when I return.[18]

The Dillingham Commission's later examination of various major industries found that, among the New Immigrant workers, most men were either unmarried or left their wives abroad. Percentages of married men in the meatpacking industry who had wives overseas included Bulgarians, 90.2 percent; Serbians, 79 percent; Romanians, 72.7 percent; Russians, 53.2 percent, and southern Italians, 42.4 percent. This compared to the Germans, 3.7 percent; Swedes, 1.9 percent; and Irish, 0.9 percent. A similar pattern appeared in the plate glass industry, copper mining and smelters, and coal mining. If a short stay to obtain money was planned, such surveys showed, a wife could be in the way. Better leave her at home.[19]

In the contest between assimilating the immigrant to America and keeping him tied to his homeland, the absence of wives added one more factor in favor of the village connection. In historian George Gilkey's succinct phrase, "at home their dream was of America; in America their dream was of home." And so the immigrants longed for the sights and sounds of their kin. "I cannot cease thinking, not an hour passes without my thinking about home," Aleksander Wolski wrote back to his mother in Poland, an idea repeated frequently in immigrant letters. For many of the immigrant workmen like Wolski, emotions were directed across the Atlantic unceasingly—rather than into their new lives in America. "I have been thinking a great deal this week and now have this letter from you," a Finn in Michigan wrote; "I could not read it without crying. It was supper time and they asked why I was crying and what the problem was."[20]

The postal system mothered a busy two-way traffic. From America a flow of orders and requests headed back across the Atlantic on use of funds mailed home, with warnings and advice about the farm. It was said of Zaborów, Poland, that although many left to try their luck in other lands, "the village remained the main area of aspirations and dreams." But letters came from the village also, and with them came attempts to control its members abroad. If the son in Chicago drank heavily, did not save his earnings, or broke other family rules, the village was able to criticize him and exert pressure from afar. And it did. This influence was often aided by village priests who traveled and by the establishment of clubs in America named for the European hometown. Members raised money for a new church bell at home, a new community center, or similar projects. In all, a temporary migrant often remained inextricably part of the village to which he would return. It was his future that awaited him there; although working abroad, he was still a functioning member of his community. He looked backward as well as forward, but in both directions he saw the village. From the emigrant came money, an increasing cascade of wealth tumbling down on the village; from the village came concern about his behavior. Each had influence on the other.[21]

Some European observers of this process questioned why large numbers planned only a temporary stay, "with a mentality that was not favorable to the exhausting process of adapting to the new society" (in the words of Italian scholar Livi Bacci). They could not but wonder at the living conditions adopted by their compatriots overseas. A Croatian writer in 1910 worried that, "if our people would emigrate permanently, without the intention of returning, they could cultivate the soil in America and their life abroad would not be so difficult."[22]

But generally it was Americans, not Europeans, who wondered at the temporary nature of their residence. The matter began to draw attention as early as 1888, when the head of Pittsburgh's Department of Charities was asked whether the New Immigrants planned to become U.S. citizens: "Well, I will give you an instance of what I have heard them say when I questioned them in regard to whether or not they came to remain here. They come here in order to get a certain sum of money, but not to remain here. I have interrogated them. They have come in my place for relief." This idea became attached to the New Immigration. The Dillingham Commission found that in the packinghouse industry almost half of those workers surveyed had been in the country for less than five years, and the commission contrasted this record with the fact that Old Immigrants in the textile mills "were usually home seekers . . . [and] mingled with the native element and imbibed many of its admirable qualities." Popular writer Kenneth Roberts informed *Saturday Evening Post* readers in 1920 that the New Immigrants came, "to a great extent, with the intention of making as much money as they could, and of going back home to settle down when they had saved a sufficient quantity of money."[23]

A NEW WORLD FOR WORKERS

With dreams of dollars in their heads, and their womenfolk safely back in the Old Country, the immigrants moved into American industry. More than 60 percent of the Poles in Philadelphia in 1915 were in unskilled occupations, with only 24 percent in skilled and semiskilled industrial work. The unskilled Poles laborered in a variety of enterprises in the city—as ironworkers, steelworkers, and leatherworkers, and as general laborers in chemical factories, petroleum and sugar refineries, slaughterhouses, and tanneries as well as on the docks and in the railroad yards. One immigrant Pole's job record showed initial employment in a New York sugar factory, then to the brickyards, on to a railroad job in Boston, then a lumberyard, and finally home after the 1907 economic crisis hit. The drive to accumulate savings fueled such mobility, and another Pole responded to his wife's request that he return by vowing that he would work "as long as we have not a thousand roubles." It would not pay to stay just a year in America: "I came in order to earn something."[24]

The mines and forests of the Lake states and Pacific Northwest attracted Scandinavians in large numbers, although Italians, Magyars, Croatians, and Slovenes also found jobs there. Italians were urged on by their government in this job quest, even receiving advice to "remember that you are in a great and free country that is like your country of labor." Although their backgrounds included many occupations in addition to farming, Italian laborers were concentrated in excavation work such as on the Bronx Aqueduct, on construction projects such as building Grand Central Station in New York, and railroad track work ("It would be difficult at the present time to build a railroad of any considerable length without Italian labor," a Maine Bureau of Labor report stated). As historian Rudolph Vecoli asserted, "it was the uncommon immigrant from Italy who did not do his stint working in a *ghenga* (gang) on the *tracca* (track)."[25]

No one expected such work to be easy. "Everyone works like hell," a Finn wrote home from Michigan, and the experiences gave rise to a Polish saying: "America for the oxen, Europe for the peasant." A YMCA leader examining the immigrants' situation in Pittsburgh found that as a rule they earned the lowest wages and worked the "full stint" of hours, including twelve hours daily on a seven-day week at the blast furnaces. Long hours were common for immigrant workers; so was energy-sapping labor. An Irishman recalled a story he was told by a returned "Yank":

> At a place called Watertown near Boston, there was a man who owned sandpits and who employed a lot of men. He used to meet the boats coming into Boston and engage the immigrants. A lot of Irishmen were engaged by him and he used to tell them this was the way to work—here informant made the motion of shovelling very rapidly with a spade he held in his hands—if they wished to get on well in America. Very few were able to endure the work for very long, but he was always able to obtain fresh relays from the incoming boats. In this way he managed to keep the sand pits going at full pressure.[26]

They agreed: you worked hard in America. One had to "sweat more during a day than during a whole week in Poland," a peasant immigrant wrote home. Returnees to Ireland said that they had worked like slaves, and some argued that "if people worked hard at home they would make as much money at home as any one in America." Interviewers with Norwegian immigrants found general agreement that they had to work harder in America than in Norway. Similar comments appeared across the Continent as remigrants recounted their experiences.[27]

Immigrant women also worked hard. A study of Chicago's Polonia in 1900 found that 38.7 percent of all employed Polish women were in the garment trades, with another 7.3 percent in laundry work. Their weekly wages ranged from $3.14 to $5.73 for operators in the sweatshops, down to $2.05 for handworkers and only $1.63 for home finishers. Overall, their average weekly wage was $3.14 for five ten-hour days. And Polish women were paid somewhat less than such other groups as Italians, Bohemians, Jews, Germans, and Irish in the garment industry.[28]

With these jobs also went treatment that was at best indifferent but more frequently hard, cruel, like that given the oxen of the Polish aphorism (although one immigrant pointed out that horses and oxen, in contrast, were idle on Sundays and holidays at home: "Here you do not have any free time!"). A Norwegian got a job digging ditches in Duluth, Minnesota, in a crew of nine watched over by a man with a cane: "If anyone took a break, he was there at once threatening him and warning him that he would be thrown out if he didn't work."[29]

These were "immigrant jobs," "greenhorn jobs." They generally went to newly arrived single men desperate for immediate cash. Those planning to return home grabbed them eagerly. An immigrant once pointed out in a letter to *The Survey* that, when the workers' savings accumulate enough "to bring over their families, they leave the murderous plants and seek better occupations in other trades." But until then they worked in immigrant jobs in the "murderous plants." When a Yale graduate took a steel mill position in 1919, he wanted to sample a variety of work activities and asked the boss about a helper's job in the cast house. "You don't want to work there," he was told; "only Hunkies work on those jobs, they're too damn dirty and too damn hot for a 'white' man."[30]

The men cleaning stills in the Bayonne, New Jersey, refineries also had immigrant jobs:

> Wearing iron shoes, and wrapped in layers and layers of sacking, they enter the still in turns to break out the red-hot "cokes" left by the oil. In a temperature of over two hundred degrees they work furiously—a man can only stand it for three or four minutes at a time—from three to four hours a day. Almost every day someone collapses in the still and has to be rescued, sometimes with his clothing on fire. When they come out after their spell, they strip and throw themselves down in the snow, if it be winter, or dash buckets of water over each other. One man said they looked like "boiled meat."[31]

British coal miners began to find that American conditions were harder, and their lives in America more distasteful, than they had known back home. Though American daily wages were usually higher for skilled workers than in Britain, this was often not true on lower skill levels, and the wage did not always cover added expenses and the problems brought by lengthy periods of unemployment. For eastern and southern European peasants, especially, the financial advantages in the United States were enormous but working conditions remained a target of criticism. The Italian consul in New Orleans visited his compatriots employed on a southern cotton plantation and termed the situation "a complete bankruptcy" for an Italian, "because when he does leave Sunny Side [plantation], after three or four years of honest toil, he is impoverished bodily, impoverished mentally and ruined materially."[32]

It was railroad work, on the *tracca*, that drew the greatest chorus of attacks from visiting Italian writers. One noted that his countrymen began work at 5 A.M., pumped a handcar six miles to work, labored until noon without a break, had an hour for lunch, and worked until 4 P.M., seldom away from the boss's curses. Another young writer encountered his compatriots slaving away fourteen hours a day for the line, putting ties and rails in place: "They work like bulls, like slaves, like prisoners, while the 'boss' kicks them, insults them, tortures them." It went on in broiling sun and chilling rain; "this was the life of these obscure, exploited and despised martyrs of work in this richest of lands."[33]

A newly arrived Irishman found similar conditions when he looked into a foundry and saw workers half-naked laboring in the dark. The Irishman, Frank Roney, soon turned against America after encountering neither conscience among employers nor unity among workers; he concluded that his "exalted idea of man's equality in the American republic was rather mythical." A German in Chicago came to a like conclusion after his experiences in the stockyards: he labored alongside—and eventually lost his job to—children filling sausages and cleaning casings, working ten hours a day in a room flooded with water, foul smells, smoke, and steam. He made only 16 cents an hour, double what the children received.[34]

Despite such conditions, newcomers frequently sought such work because longer hours with more dangers frequently brought more pay than did easier work. More commonly, however, this was the only employment open to greenhorns. One Pole warned his brother, who planned to come to America and earn a living as a writer, that "America does not want writers, only working people." No immigrant in the 1880–1930 years would have disagreed.[35]

At the center of this exploitation usually stood the padrone, or his

Employment agencies, usually run by padroni or their equivalents, welcomed short-term immigrants to America and provided them with what they most wanted: jobs without requirements in either work skills or knowledge of English. Working conditions were often dismal but paydays were regular, and an immigrant who planned to return usually had little choice. This Italian agency served job seekers in Chicago at the turn of the century. Photograph by Chicago Historical Society, DN 204.

equivalent under other names—sometimes simply "boss" or "contractor." He frequently arranged for the immigrants' travel to America through contacts with confederates back home; or he was among the swarms of "vampires" on the docks and hired them on arrival. More commonly he operated through an employment agency. Chicago had 289 licensed employment bureaus in 1908, and 110 of them specialized in supplying immigrant workers; from June 1908 through June 1909 the agencies sent some 40,000 men and women to jobs. That year the Chicago agencies sent Italians, Greeks, and Serbians to railroad section work; Bulgarians, Austrians, and Scandinavians (and most native-born Americans) into construction; and Poles to the logging camps in the northwoods.[36]

An Italian Socialist newspaper described the employment agency's operations: the shop's windows featured posters advertising jobs for 1,000 shovelers, 300 carpenters, 200 hod carriers. Contact had been made with companies building railroad lines, bridges, tunnels, and similar projects, all needing laborers. The immigrants—out of work, desperate, unable to speak English and fend for themselves—gathered eagerly at the counter and were talked to "in the friendliest, most fatherly manner" by the padrone: "He makes them believe that he had rejected two or three hundred Slavs or Greeks in order to reserve the good jobs for the Italians. And what fine jobs! Two dollars a day, nine hours of light, easy work, the purest air, distilled water, free board, Italian boss, low cost of living—an Eldorado! They must decide quickly for few vacancies are left." The men then paid costs of $8 to $12 for the trip to the work site, plus $5 as the *bossatura*, the padrone's fee. From a gang of twelve, the padrone made $108: $60 from his $5-per-man fee plus $2 discount on the railroad ticket paid by each, plus $2 paid him for each laborer delivered to the hiring company.[37]

At the work site the padrone could sometimes make money in other ways, buying $100 worth of lumber to construct sleeping shacks, billing workers $1 a month each to sleep in them, charging for food if he supplied that. Often workers' wages went first through his hands. Added to this were cases of the padrone fleeing with wages or setting up his own bank allegedly to send money home but then absconding with the funds. For all these reasons, the padrone was a frequent target of immigrant complaints and governmental investigations.[38]

Irregular employment, in addition to dismal job conditions and the search for better pay, kept the immigrants mobile. A Pennsylvania investigator admitted that he could make no estimate of the number of Johnstown's Hungarians since they were always moving; only about 60 percent of the city's foreign-born were "permanently located," in fact. The Dillingham Commission found in a survey of almost 4,000 coal miners' households that only 16.6 percent of the immigrants had worked a full twelve months the preceding year, and less than half had worked as long as nine months. This was a life known well by a Finn who described his job forays among the logging camps of northern Wisconsin and Michigan's Upper Peninsula:

> The Flambo camp stopped running in the middle of November. I spent one week going from camp to camp but could not find work. All the camps were full of men. There were not enough beds and I had to sleep on the floor. I went to one camp on Saturday evening and I was planning to stay there over the weekend. But next morning I had to start walking to another camp again to get there before dark. And when I could not find work, I drove to Bessemer. So now I lie here at Lehtonen's. I am not sure whether I can find work before Christmas.[39]

Quitting became one of the most common responses by greenhorns to heavy exertion and degrading conditions, and they trooped out of American industry as fast as they trooped in. Turnover in Philadelphia's Polish areas often ran from 75 to 80 percent; in Pittsburgh a large machine works hired 21,000 men and women through the course of 1906 to maintain a work force of 10,000. The claim of one mining superintendent to have hired 5,000 men in a year to keep 1,000 working was challenged by the operator of the district's largest property; he admitted, however, that hiring 2,000 to keep a crew of 1,000 would not be an exaggeration. Ford reported 416 percent turnover at a plant in 1913, and the following year metal manufacturing industries had turnover rates ranging from 88 to 157 percent.[40]

It was in some ways a symbiotic relationship, despite the unequal bargaining power between the two sides. In the "land of opportunity," the immigrants used their freedom to travel to seek the best-paying jobs where they could save the most money. Loyalty to a company did not enter into the picture. But it was a land of opportunity for employers, too, and they counted on a flexible, unending labor supply. Chicago meatpackers rebutted a union wage demand in 1904 by pointing out that up to 5,000 transient laborers gathered each morning at 7 A.M. to seek work outside the plant gates, but less than 10 percent of these could be hired. No special inducements were needed in such cases.[41]

Labor economist John R. Commons encountered these realities one day when he entered the hiring office in a large factory:

Scattered about were a number of sturdy immigrants fresh from the old country. On that day the manager was hiring Swedes. He said that the week before he had been hiring Poles, and before that he had taken on Italians. It was a good idea, he said, to get them mixed up. He told me of other large firms in that city with similar employment managers and a similar policy. They had an informal club that met usually once a week.

Commons found that managers were proud of being able to forecast the condition, even the mood, of the labor market. If raising wages 10 percent would keep workers calm, they would raise them, then lower them later. They even claimed to have contacts with union leaders who would let them know in advance where they planned to organize. At another establishment Commons observed the hiring officer walking among a hundred men waiting on the sidewalk. He "looked at their feet, sized up their nationality and fitness," and then "picked out ten or fifteen and sent them in." The rest, Commons added, "stood around with serious faces and then drifted away." These conditions—employers adjusting wages to maintain a quiescent and adequate crew, hiring and firing immigrants at will, with an abundance of immigrants desperate for work—were said by Commons to represent "the commodity theory of labor. Demand and supply determine wages. . . . The ebb and flow of the labor market is like the ebb and flow of the commodity market."[42]

AIM: SAVINGS

Commons's report drives home another point concerning immigrant industrial workers, one that complements his commodity theory. "They were all eager to save money," he observed. "That was their main ambition." The thought runs like a main current through the 1880–1930 immigration into the United States. Immigrants came to the New World to acquire savings. This motivation was jarring to many Americans, who held cherished notions of idealists fleeing persecution to finally reach the sheltering arms of the world's greatest democracy. One New Yorker teaching English to East Side Italians asked them why they had come to America, expecting they might reply "liberty" or "democracy"; instead, "in one roar they shouted 'money!' "[43]

The American dollar was their goal. It dictated their every move, with plans for a quick return when enough dollars were collected. The New York factory inspector lamented the boost this dream gave to the use of child labor, for some Italians brought children with them and placed them in the tenement sweatshops. These children were kept from school and stunted "morally, physically and intellectually"—all because of "the desire on the part of these people to earn and hoard up money, with the ultimate view of returning to their native clime." Here was no interest in struggling with nature to create a farm in the Midwest; no long-range dreams to start a business; no hopes to develop a better life in America. "Work was good or bad depending on the pay," a study of Polish immigrants noted. "A 'good work' was a better paid job which made it possible to amass some savings."[44]

Stories of the enormous sacrifices immigrants made to build up savings circulated in the industrial centers and even in the halls of Congress. Common laborers in Pittsburgh were reported to be putting away up to $15 a month; this is consistent with Ewa Morawska's conclusion that the savings by east-central European men in Johnstown averaged $100–200 annually. Italian laborers had the highest savings rate among European laborers, according to a 1907 Bureau of Labor report, putting away $25–27 monthly from railroad work. Floating immigrant workers in the western Midwest and Plains states were reported to have "clear saving" of $1 per day from wages of only $1.25–1.65. An American working in a steel mill found many employees who did not save, but he said that "practically all the 'Hunkies' of twenty-eight or thirty and over saved very successfully"—and these were expecting to return to Europe. One told him: "A good job, save money, work all time, go home, sleep, no spend."[45]

Immigrant savings banks multiplied, often becoming targets for robbery or fraud. Government probers frequently looked into the institutions. Dillingham Commission investigators found, however, that Bulgarians working on western railroads kept their savings in leathern belts, after a Bulgarian bank in the area had failed. Padrone banks were notorious for illegal acts, and Italy finally authorized the Banco di Napoli to handle the return of savings from America. Many funds continued to be carried back by returnees or to be transferred through postal money orders or in other ways. A banker serving Serbians on Pittsburgh's South Side reported in 1908 that he sent back $20,000–25,000 *daily* to the old country. Hungarian postal receipts show that American Slovaks sent home $41.6 million from 1900 to 1912, and one scholar has estimated that the Slovak total for 1870–1914 was at least $200 million. Remittances to Sweden averaged $8 million yearly from 1906 to 1930, making up a quarter of Sweden's balance of payments. The 1897–1902 total entering Italy from its emigrants abroad was estimated at $100 million, and the New York Post Office sent 12.3 million individual money orders to foreign lands in 1900–6, with 50 percent of the dollar amount going to Italy, Hungary, and the Slavic countries.[46]

HOUSING CONGESTION

Closely related to the immigrants' desire to save and their willingness to put up with dismal job conditions was their acceptance of housing that was primitive and congested in the extreme. Some of this acquiescence stemmed from peasant backgrounds, but much arose also from "the desire of employees from the south and east of Europe to decrease expenses," as a government investigator put it. If they crowded together in sleeping rooms, their rent could be sharply reduced; if all went together in a communal cooking and eating plan, or hired a wife or "boss" to handle cooking—the Italian *bordo*, the Bulgarian *boort*, the "boarding boss" system—then costs could be cut even further.[47]

Immigrant housing and boarding were targets of frequent inspections, especially by social workers, visitors from Europe, and U.S. congressional bodies. F. Elisabeth Crowell, of the New York Charity Organization Society, surveyed Pittsburgh and reported that "evil conditions were found to exist in every section of the city," with boarders jammed into corners of a family's single room, privy vaults overflowing, and thick smoke and dust hanging over it all. But "every phase of the situation," she lamented, "was intensified by the evil of overcrowding." Similarly, the manager of New York's United Hebrew Charities warned of chronic poverty in the city's Jewish community, "appalling in its immensity," caused partly by "horrible congestion" and immoral behavior stemming from these conditions. And an Italian university student who worked on a railroad crew in Indiana wrote of the airless boxcars housing the men, the vermin on beds and the floor, the old coats or horse blankets used for bed coverings. He found the laborers transformed into "the gaunt, pale, emaciated remains of a former healthy manhood."[48]

Government inquiries noted the close identification of foreigners with slums: immigrants made up 95 percent of New York's slum population, 91 percent of Philadelphia's, 90 percent of Chicago's. The Dillingham Commission showed special concern to immigrant housing, examining numbers per room, rents, home ownership. In Pittsburgh, for example, the commission discovered that, overall, 56.9 percent of the households headed by immigrants kept boarders or lodgers. This figure was skewed, however, by the extremely low percentages for such groups as

Bohemians, Moravians, Jews, and Irish; on the other hand, among Serbian-headed households 90.3 percent kept boarders or lodgers, among Romanians 89.3 percent, among Croatians 81 percent, and among southern Italians 70.6 percent. Congestion per room, the commission found, was considerably greater in foreign than in native households.[49]

Congestion met the immigrants as they arrived and was seldom a stranger to them during their years in America if they planned to return home. The density of population was so great in the "Polish Downtown" of Chicago's Polonia in 1900 that, if it was uniformly applied over the entire city, Chicago's population would have reached 41.5 million—instead of its actual 1.7 million. The reality of it all hit Stoyan Christowe after he traveled from Bulgaria to St. Louis and presented himself at his uncle's abode on Plum Street:

> There were six men in the flat at the moment and they worked days, sharing the six beds with a like number of men who worked nights. In other words, there were twelve men living in the two-room flat. The beds, placed lengthwise along the walls in the room overlooking the street, were never given a rest or an airing. There were no sheets, and the blankets and comfortables were so filthy with coal dust and grease from the roundhouses where the men worked that they looked like tarpaulins.[50]

In coal mining areas the immigrants sometimes lived in deserted pigpens and cowsheds: "You might call them outhouses," one critic said. A manufacturer told of seeing the homes of Italian and Hungarian miners at Honey Brook, Pennsylvania, where the huts were seven feet high, "built of slabs and rotten planks and poles, and I supposed when I saw them that they were places where these people, the miners around there, kept their pigs or something. I didn't really suppose, to look at them, that they were the habitations of human beings." Similarly, a Knights of Labor official encountered a settlement of Hungarian brick workers near Detroit: it had 127 persons living in a building ten feet by fifty feet, including five families cooped into a single room, "eating from one common kettle of food and sleeping in one common bed."[51]

Even food supplies were often sacrificed in the immigrants' desire to save. Italians and Slavs planning to return home were sometimes found to be skimping on food to such an extent that they lacked the strength for heavy work. One Lithuanian lived on ten cents a day, then went further in his quest for savings: by helping his landlady he was freed from paying room rent. Macaroni cooked in rancid lard and covered with rotten tomato sauce formed the daily diet of some Italian track workers who were visited by one of their countrymen, and the head of Pittsburgh's Department of Charities came upon a group of Italian pipeline workers enjoying a feast made up of a sheep that had died of hoof rot several days earlier. The men purchased it for $1.00. "They had quite a banquet off of this sheep, and invited me to partake of it, too, which I declined with thanks."[52]

ASSIMILATION DIFFICULTIES

The desire for a short, profitable stay in America—with as few expenses as possible—combined with ethnic clustering in the slums and on railroad section crews to isolate the immigrant. Though isolation has been common among newcomers in all lands in all eras, the situation was clearly worsened when immigrants arrived with plans already made that they would *not* become Americans. Repatriation might still take a long time to occur; reports tell of Italians who lived alone, in temporary housing, for fifteen years before heading back. But if they resided in an immigrant colony during this time, and worked only among immigrants, they learned little of life in the United States. A Norwegian admitted that during his stay, "I often had to pinch my arm to realize that I really was in America." Such persons considered it impractical to devote time and money to such activities as learning English, attending citizenship classes, or joining American organizations, even if time and money were available. They simply did not plan to become Americans.[53]

Not only U.S. officials had troubles with these immigrants. Leaders in ethnic communities also faced problems in securing commitments from them. A Hungarian minister in Cleveland discovered that few were willing to answer his invitation to become regular, paying members of the congregation; they told him "they had come to America for only a short time, and would soon go home; meanwhile they were paying church taxes at home." An almost identical response came from an Italian immigrant who was pestered to give more to the local parish: he answered that he had come to America "to work, make some money and go back home. When we return to Italy, there we will attend mass."[54]

Knowledge of English became a center of controversy in these conditions. Americans generally felt that any person living in the country should learn its language; immigrants planning to return home, however, could justify avoiding English and could usually survive without it. A study of 33,000 immigrants who went to work in Detroit in 1915 found that 75 percent did not know English, a higher percentage than found overall in Dillingham Commission inquiries. The commission's survey of 246,673 foreign-born employees revealed that 44.4 percent of the males and 61.4 percent of the females could not speak English. The Dillingham investigation found that 66.5 percent of the Greek men did not know English, 56.5 percent of the Poles, 56.4 percent of the Russians, 53.6 percent of the Magyars. In contrast, only 5.3 percent of Swedish male employees and 12.5 percent of the Germans could *not* speak English.[55]

This lack of English knowledge, especially among immigrants who had spent years in the country, rankled many Americans. Congressmen in 1888 questioned Cipriano Auletta, just arrived from a seven-month return visit to Italy and hoping to get reestablished in the New York Street Department job he had held earlier for "four or five years":

Q. Do you speak English?—A little.
Q. You don't understand hardly any English?—A little bit.
Q. You have lived in this country four or five years?— A. Yes, sir.
Q. Why didn't you learn English?—I couldn't do it. . . .
Q. Do you know what kind of a government we have here; is this a kingdom?—A. The president is the head man, just like the king or the emperor.

The same investigators heard a New York reporter describe what he found among Hungarians and Italians in the Pennsylvania coal regions: "None of them spoke English, and they were just as foreign as they could be abroad."[56]

Similarly, a Pittsburgh judge faced a young Slav who could not speak English after four years in America. "Four years, . . . and you cannot talk English?" the judge asked, incredulous. "Don't you know that you ought to learn English that you may know we have laws and ordinances which must be obeyed?" The Immigrants' Protective League of Chicago was bothered by the request for aid from a Czechoslovak who had worked ten years in two industrial plants but still needed an interpreter to make himself understood. And when immigrants returned permanently to Europe proudly flashing their U.S. citizenship papers—which let them avoid the Austro-Hungarian military draft—many still could not speak English. U.S. minister Townsend, who discovered this situation, called it "the crowning disgrace to our citizenship, . . . they having spent their time while in the United States, among the members of a foreign colony, where their native language is almost entirely spoken and they have not the smallest conception of the Constitution of the United States or the nature of the oath of allegiance." Such protests led to a 1906 law that required speaking ability in English before citizenship could be granted.[57]

Most remigrants did not seek U.S. citizenship, however, and this also stirred controversy. Congress linked the citizenship problem to the immigrants' brief stay, as when Angelo Salimarde of Portenzo was questioned regarding his return to Italy:

> Q.   You would rather be in Italy?—A. Wherever I find work I have got to stay.
> Q.   You do not intend to become a citizen of the United States, and to stay here, and to remain here forever?—A. No; I shall not become a citizen of America; I prefer to go home in two or three years; I am going home again.[58]

The Dillingham Commission would later discover that only 57 percent of adult foreign-born males were citizens, a percentage that declined sharply among industrial workers even after five years' residence. When such persons were allowed to vote, the outcry by nativist critics was enormous. "A man who can not read his ballot does not know what he is doing at the ballot box," argued the commissioner-general of immigration in 1901. Mounting pressures against alien voting led most states to adopt restrictions; only seven states permitted noncitizens to vote by 1914.[59]

Immigrant leaders who sought permanency for their groups within the United States were often painfully aware of the problems this lack of citizenship caused. A Slovak priest urged his parishioners to apply for U.S. citizenship to quiet nativist charges that Slovaks "were exploiting America by staying only long enough to earn their 'fortune' and then returning home." Soon the National Slovak Society began requiring its members to apply for U.S. citizenship as soon as their five years' residence requirement was met.[60]

The impermanence had other results that hurt the immigrant community. In his examination of schooling differences in Providence, Rhode Island, among Irish, Italians, Jews, and blacks, Joel Perlmann noted the close relation between the Italians' lack of citizenship, their poor school attendance, and their high rates of return. While conceding the existence of many other factors, he speculated that Italian children may have been influenced "by growing up in a community in which there were unskilled, unattached young men working for relatively brief periods in the United States," their presence discouraging youngsters from going to school.[61]

UNIONIZATION AND REMIGRANTS

Many of the same goals that discouraged short-term immigrants from learning English, becoming U.S. citizens, and adapting to American life worked to keep them out of labor unions. Several aspects of their lives steered them away from this direction. Coming from peasant backgrounds, most immigrants had no previous connections with unions. Rightly or wrongly, *union* was often seen as synonymous with *strike*, and strikes meant no work, no wages. Belonging to a union also meant paying dues, an unpleasant thought to workers for whom any new expense was to be avoided. Also, the bulk of those arriving in the years 1880–1930 went into jobs that were not primary targets of the craft unions then rising to dominance in the American union movement. As specialization was pushed further and further by industry, reducing skilled positions while opening up vast areas to the unskilled, craft unions turned away from those regarded as infringing on their territory; in A. T. Lane's phrase, "solidarity had become a victim of modernization." Workers would sometimes stand together, and often did, but as members of distinct groups rather than united in different skill levels.[62]

The size of their wages compared to what they had known earlier in Europe worked against the union agitators' arguments that they were poorly paid. Payday every two weeks in dollars was a grand step forward to peasants who had earlier labored long and hard before receiving a kopeck or centissimo. And with many of them harboring a desire to save a specific amount quickly and return home, unions could be seen as a roadblock in their planned itinerary. "It is solely the dullards and *strikers* who come back without savings," an Italian claimed. Robert F. Foerster listened to such statements and concluded that the Italian's behavior in the United States did not mean that he was hostile to other workers when he left a job that was entangled in a labor dispute; rather, this behavior reflected his single-minded drive to earn money. "His traits are rudimentary still and a sense of oneness with other toilers has simply not found a place among them," Foerster stated.[63]

Unions, moreover, did not always actively seek out these immigrants, despite their numbers which brought "nothing less than an ethnic recomposition of the American working class." To reject out of hand such a large potential membership may seem shortsighted in retrospect, but the fact is that unskilled workers, whether foreign- or native-born, were generally not considered union material after the decline of the Knights of Labor in the mid-1880s. Immigrants came to realize this, and a Polish humanitarian society's pamphlet of advice for those emigrating in 1908 warned that American trade unions were opposed to Poles, leaving for them the worst, most dangerous, and dirtiest jobs. The Dillingham Commission's investigation at the same time found union membership among only 5.9 percent of the Slovak bituminous coal miners who had been in America for less than five years, and only 8.1 percent of the Magyars, 13.1 percent of the Poles, and 19.1 percent of the southern Italians.[64]

Lacking a long-term commitment, these immigrants often rebuffed those seeking to enlist them in broader campaigns. They suffered their own maltreatment in silence rather than fight for justice. "These creatures are willing to take anything offered them, because they do not intend to remain, and will sacrifice anything to acquire a little fortune," the Brass-Workers national leader asserted contemptuously. Finns working in a Colorado mine drew a similar complaint from a coworker, who said that they were "ignorant of the language and ways of working in this country, and will take from the bosses any insult they may offer, and are willing to accept any usage in the company's boardinghouse." The central European peasant in America, it was said, "kissed the hand of the boss who sent him to work." Ultimately, then, the lower levels of America's booming industries were filling up with persons who willingly endured lower wages, coarse treatment, and poor conditions. They avoided friction with the boss so the paychecks would not stop coming. Because of this, they were widely regarded as a retarding influence in the drive for better conditions in the nation's workplaces.[65]

Immigrant strikebreaking flourished. Not only were foreign-born laborers ill-informed about unions and desperate for wages, they were also poorly equipped by language and literacy to learn details of labor disputes. Foerster conceded that Italians were often strikebreakers and cited a long list of incidents. Though immigrant skilled workers could frequently be deflected from serving as American strikebreakers, padroni employed by corporations could go straight to the docks to recruit replacements from among the unskilled new arrivals. The Austrian consul in Pittsburgh admitted that employers preferred Slovak workers because they would not strike, clinging to their goal of earning money and returning home. This view was seconded by the brother of a prominent coke manufacturer: peasants flocking to America "never grumble about wages, and take what is given them by the company stores without murmuring, and . . . never strike." The temporary migrant stood out sharply in this legion of uncomplainers. The massive 1919 steel strike was supported by thousands of immigrant workers, but it was reported that immigrant employees planning to go back to Europe were still working.[66]

It did not take long for reaction to build against such workers. A reporter covering Pennsylvania's mining strikes testified in 1888 that he saw Hungarians, Poles, and Italians "marched up to the shanties" from the train at the Highland mines in the Lehigh region; they were blamed with "breaking down the strike" there.[67]

Recruitment of immigrants to break strikes was sometimes blatant, but often the onrushing tide made recruitment unnecessary: they arrived regardless. The *Chicagoer Arbeiter-Zeitung* was both pro-union and pro-immigrant and was therefore in a quandary as the influx began to affect the city's labor market: "We are not enemies of immigration and hence cannot choose to fight it; but we must still raise the question: What should be done to lessen, or eliminate, the decrease in wages resulting from the huge labor supply?" Given Chicago's scarcity of jobs, the newspaper asked, "What, then, can the new immigrants do save offer their labor below the established pay scale?" It feared the result: Chicago's established workers would be forced to give way to the cheaper immigrant labor.[68]

To be sure, unions took great steps to assure their own failure. New Immigrants were deliberately excluded, at least up to 1900, by such building trades organizations as the Plasterers, Carpenters, Painters and Decorators, Stonecutters, Bricklayers, Masons, and Hod Carriers. Their policies were often accompanied by antiimmigrant statements, many by union leaders who were themselves immigrants. Samuel Gompers of the American Federation of Labor (AFL) was most famous for this—he being a Dutch-English Jew—but there were others, including the Italian official of the Boot and Shoe Workers who asserted in 1898, "We haven't room for any more immigrants." Sometimes contradictory signals were given, as when the AFL criticized the "influx of foreigners" during its recruitment drive in the steel mills in 1912–13. Even W. Jett Lauck, head of industrial investigations for the Dillingham Commission, thought that immigrants were rejecting unions because of this negative community response. Historian Robert Asher examined union failures among the New Immigrants and blamed nativistic hostility, lack of provision for extra time and money to organize non-English speaking employees, intraunion conflict sparked by the radicalism of many of the immigrant union agitators, and the immigrants' resentment at their exclusion or second-class treatment.[69]

All these factors were important in the frustrated union drives among immigrants; but all were also capable of being changed. Improvements began to appear. John R. Commons was surprised in 1907 when he found New Immigrants joining unions: "Such a sight would have been unlikely a dozen years ago." Of course, the very conditions that brought immigrants flocking into industry's lower ranks eventually made it imperative that they be organized, as indicated in a Lithuanian's comments during the Chicago stockyards strike: "Because those sharp foremen are inventing new machines and the work is easier to learn, and so these slow Lithuanians and even green girls can learn to do it, and then the Americans and Germans and Irish are put out and the employer saves money, because the Lithuanians work cheaper. This was why the American labor unions began to organize us all." Poles became union members in that stockyards dispute; Italians largely remained outside and helped break it.[70]

These conditions were reproduced elsewhere, and unionism began to spread, somewhat tentatively, among members of the New Immigration. Jewish and Italian radicals made breakthroughs in the garment trades, organizing their own groups when the AFL unions stayed away. Italians working on the New York subway, as well as Italian hod carriers in the city, were brought into unions.[71]

A major reason for these advances in unionism also came from a change in the immigrants themselves: rather than returning to Europe as planned, large numbers—a majority of virtually every group—eventually decided to remain in the United States. And when wives and children began to join them, job conditions they could accept as short-term migrants became unacceptable as permanent residents. Further, union leaders began to change their organizing techniques, and an analyst of the United Mine Workers' growing success in the anthracite fields noted that the union had started to use immigrants as organizers, elected leaders from among immigrant groups, printed materials in their own languages, and begun enforced dues payments. The New Immigrants were inclined toward passivity in union activity, one student of anthracite mining admitted, "but as they become more Americanized they gradually take a more active part."[72]

More than longevity in America was involved in this turnaround, as shown by Victor Greene in his major study of Slavs in anthracite mining, *The Slavic Community on Strike*. Greene charted the rise of Slavic community consciousness, which grew despite union incompetence, the disarray left by competing unions, and the immigrants' own reluctance to get involved. "Thus when the Slavic locality went on the march," Greene found, "it did so with a terrible ferocity and unity." All members of the community, particularly women and children, were involved. It was these cohesive elements within eastern European groups that carried the day in the anthracite fields. "Once the community approved of the strike, it demanded conformity of its members," and few would challenge this, "for the Slav's cultural identity was at stake." The result: "the secure establishment of the labor union in the anthracite districts."[73]

By the time the Dillingham Commission conducted its investigations, union membership in anthracite was far ahead of other eastern U.S. mining: 77.5 percent of the Pennsylvania anthracite miners surveyed belonged to a union, and even among those in the country less than five years 71.2 percent of the Lithuanians and 58 percent of the Poles held memberships. Slovaks were also active in Pennsylvania mining unions.[74]

After the outbreak of war in 1914, New Immigrant steelworkers were successfully brought into the Amalgamated Association of Iron, Steel and Tin Workers, eventually playing a major role in the 1919 steel strike. The virtual cutoff in immigration and emigration, war enthusiasms, and a change in union recruiting tactics made them fervent believers in the need for united action.[75]

Not all group protests by the New Immigrants signified that they accepted the American union movement, however. For example, Hungarians' spontaneous outbursts against wage cuts have also been linked to their concerns over saving large amounts to carry home. As a Hungarian historian has argued, "they were still unable to integrate their individual aim of returning to Hungary with the collective struggle for the realization of long-term goals in America."[76]

A HARSH ENVIRONMENT

It all showed their vulnerability—these greenhorns far from home, without skills, without English, without citizenship. They were generally shunned by labor unions; employed in the hardest, dirtiest sectors of American industrial life; and they dwelt in shanties or congested tenements. It was life in the raw in America, and immigrants had few protections against the rawness.

This became evident in their declining physical condition. An Italian doctor argued that Calabrians and Sicilians who had gone to America became, after six months in New York's slums, "pale, flabby, under-sized creatures." In fact, Italians had a death rate in New York of 36.43 per thousand, compared to the Germans' 12.13, the native-born Americans' 13.98, and the average for all groups of 18.71. Tuberculosis was called "the Irish disease" by American social workers, who labored under the theory that certain ethnic groups were predisposed to it. This bias led health workers to ignore the high tuberculosis rates in an area of New York's Lower East Side dubbed the "Lung Block." But when immigrants were housed in better areas, and when reformers rebuilt the "Lung Block," the theory had to be jettisoned as tuberculosis rates declined sharply. It was the environment, not the immigrants, that caused the disease.[77]

Pittsburgh's smoke was world famous, and worried Galicians wrote to their children, "People say that in that town where you are there is a big stench, the whole town is covered with smoke as with clouds. . . . We pity you very much that you have no health there now, and I wrote you already to move away from that Pittsburgh. . . . There in Pittsburgh, people say, the dear sun never shines brightly, the air is saturated with stench and gas." A Pittsburgh doctor estimated that as many as 50 percent of the young foreigners who came to the city caught typhoid fever within two years, partly because their earlier experiences in rural communities did not prepare them for the fact that water could be contaminated.[78]

Within the workplace these immigrants faced daily challenges far beyond tuberculosis or typhoid. Crystal Eastman's path-breaking study traced the causes and results of industrial accidents in Allegheny County (Pittsburgh) in 1906–7. She found large numbers of cases flowing inexorably from a system that employed "greeners" and placed them untrained in dangerous areas without experienced workers at their sides. Of 410 fatal work accidents (causing 501 deaths) over twelve months for which she could determine responsibility, in 132 of them the victim was obviously to blame at least in part. But she noted how complex many of these incidents were, and how inadequate any easy assignment of blame. Such a case was that of a seventeen-year-old Croatian, recently arrived and newly hired, who was electrocuted "by fooling with a switch with wet gloves on, watching the sparks fly." There had been no electric switches in his village, one could assume, and it is probable that little training was provided before he began his work around high-voltage lines in Pittsburgh.[79]

Eastman could seldom accept simple causal explanations for industrial accidents. "Ignorance covers a large share of these cases," she agreed. But what kind of ignorance? Much was really the ignorance "of young boys, of those who are 'green' at their job, of the tongue-tied alien, who finds himself for the first time a part of swift and mighty processes." One incident involved a man on his first night on the job; another had been working only three days, and nearly all twenty-two of the "greeners" killed were foreigners. One Slav who had worked fourteen days as a trestle laborer did not understand when three other workers ran to tell him to get out from under a car; he was killed as the brakeman signaled the engineer to come ahead. The easy condemnation of immigrant "ignorance," Eastman showed, could cover a wide range of culpability by many persons—including the entrepreneurs who made the basic decisions in American industry.[80]

Despite the fact that only 132 of the 501 fatalities could be blamed on the victim, survivors assumed almost the entire burden of the loss. Eastman found that most survivors who received anything from the employer got less than $100; in 149 cases this meant that the loss would be felt back in Europe, where dependents waited for regular checks from family members working in Pittsburgh. Pennsylvania courts further assured that the poverty would be transferred abroad by ruling that survivors in Europe could not bring suit to recover damages in Pennsylvania job accidents.[81]

Another major area of immigrant vulnerability lay in the United States' frequent business downturns, which cost thousands their jobs and threw them into a society that made few provisions for helping the destitute. Records of charitable agencies bear out the devastating impact these recessions had on the immigrant. The head of Pittsburgh's Department of Charities testified in 1888 that three-fourths of the paupers in the city poorhouse were foreigners and 90 percent of "regular" outdoor relief went to foreigners.[82]

One Pole claimed that before elections in America there were always periods of unemployment, and he knew: as an unskilled factory hand he lost his job in one of these and soon used up all his savings. The 1907 Panic swept chillingly through immigrant life in the steel mill center of Granite City, Illinois, first bringing dismissal of recently hired immigrants, then of the previous arrivals, and finally the company simply gave preference to Americans for remaining positions. Immigrants and the native-born had earlier worked out a modus vivendi in their separate Granite City housing areas and job classifications, but as the Panic worsened the native-born were seeking even the unskilled jobs, and the Tri-Cities Central Trades and Labor Council voted to ask manufacturers "to employ American labor in preference for foreign." This occurred as the Italian Commissariato dell'Emigrazione, for the first time, sought as the Panic deepened to dissuade emigration to the United States by those without assured jobs.[83]

Letters sent back to Poland told what the downturns meant: "You write that there is poverty in the Old Country. There is no greater poverty than there is in America, because all the factories are shutting down," a couple in Brooklyn wrote. A letter writer in Jersey City said that he did not want to "talk anyone into coming to America. Here one can obviously and more quickly earn something than one can in Europe, but who can count on that?" From Chicago came the admission, "When one does not work, one does not have anything. And right now my husband is not working."[84]

It was this uncertainty, hanging over immigrant and native-born alike, that sent messages to Europe that life in America was not always filled with abundant employment and regular wages. An Irishman recalled that those returning described American life as "very trying on a person's nerves, and there was always the fear that one might lose his position and become destitute, and destitution in America made life impossible." The recurring economic downturns—especially in 1893 and 1907—also cut off the upward mobility that had seemed to be the destiny of many. Immigrants were forced to continue accepting positions at the bottom of the pile. There was often extreme hardship for those immigrants whose liabilities extended beyond mere lack of skills—such as Gaelic, Polish, or Slovak speakers who could not adjust to English, and those not physically robust. They lived on the edge of disaster.[85]

New York's *Jewish Daily Forward* carried many letters from readers who had experienced the trauma of being thrown out of work in America. One came in the 1907 Panic's aftermath, from an unemployed man who had earlier fled the Russian army after hitting his superior but now survived in New York on only five cents a day: "One goes about with strong hands, one wants to sell them for a bit of bread, and no one wants to buy," he wrote. "They tell you cold-bloodedly: 'We don't need you.'" He talked of ending it all but pleaded, "had [I] known it would be so bitter for me here, I wouldn't have come. I didn't come here for a fortune, but where is bread?"[86]

Where is bread? Many immigrants raised that question. And for many this issue, and several others equally fundamental, strengthened their determination to return to Europe.

CHAPTER 4

Leaving the Land
of Bosses and Clocks

An Irish story, recalled by an elderly county Mayo man some years ago, told of the emigrant who traveled from Ireland directly to a friend's home in a Pennsylvania coal mining district. Taken aback by the grime and crudeness of the mining camp, in what had been touted as a land with gold in the streets, the visitor could only exclaim, "And you mean to tell me this is America." Dejected, he changed his plans and went back to Ireland.[1]

There is bitter truth behind the outlines of this Irish tale, for the massive recrossing of the Atlantic was pushed and pulled by a myriad of causes, much like the original decisions to go to America. Many stories of return were filled with hope, for dreary lives at home had been buoyed by expectations of just what would be brought back from the New World; but other return trips were grounded in failure and discouragement. All could be found within the mammoth movement homeward; 3,078,403 returned to Europe during the 1908–23 period alone, when the U.S. government kept records on the subject. And there were thousands of others going back, before and after.[2]

These massive numbers drew attention. One writer in 1920 reported that the "outward drift" from the United States had become "the most significant feature of the immigration movement." And she added, "Without it the record of arrivals is as incomplete and misleading as the debit side of a cash account without the credit side."[3]

Put another way, ignoring this movement would be like telling the story of Pennsylvania anthracite, and its importance to the nation's industrial machine, without taking note of the mining camp degradation that confronted the Irish visitor. An honest history of the populating of the continent must include both. And though an Italian was so over-joyed at the bounty coming back from the United States that he told parliamentary investigators, "The portrait of Christopher Columbus should be carried with that of Jesus Christ," an honest account must also include the comments of another immigrant, from Minsk, who wrote to the New York Yiddish newspaper *Forverts* in 1902:

> Where is the golden land, where are the golden people? What has happened to human feeling in such a great wide world, in such a land which is, as it is said, a land flowing with milk and honey? When in such a rich city like New York on 88 Clinton Street a woman is dying of hunger, of loneliness, and need—that can only say: "Cursed be Columbus, cursed be he for discovering America."[4]

Such conflicting judgments about America were frequent; Columbus was the focus of both toasts and scorn. A writer heading eastward across the Atlantic in 1905 encountered these contradictory reactions as he interviewed passengers in steerage, probing to discover why they had turned their backs on the glorious, free land of America. He ultimately divided them into two broad classes: "those who go home because they have succeeded, and those who go home because they have failed." Then and now, however, other students of immigration have contended that the wide variety of causes cannot be made to fit into such simple categories. Finland's government inspectors discovered as much when they quizzed those returning in 1918: major reasons given included homesickness, rejoining family, politics, fulfillment of economic objec-tives, and unemployment.[5]

Modern investigators have found several major reasons behind the returns. Francesco Cerase, who interviewed Italians who had gone back between 1920 and 1950, reported returns of failure, conservatism (bringing back savings to better a situation in a traditional setting), in-novation, and retirement (stemming from illness as well as old age). Another student of Italian remigration, Dino Cinel, took only a slightly different tack: he listed returns of failure, retirement, investment, and "ambivalent returnees" (those uncertain of which side of the ocean was preferable, who often traveled back and forth over a period of years, never quite happy in either place). Finns' repatriations have been grouped by Keijo Virtanen into "general factors," such as the state of the economy, and "personal factors," considered more significant in return than in the original emigration. Theodore Saloutos' studies of Greek returnees led him to argue that the major reasons for remigration in the years just before and after World War I "were a combination of patriotism, idealism, fulfillment of objectives, unhappiness with living conditions in this country, a feel of discrimination—especially on the part of the southern and eastern Europeans—homesickness, a desire to return to one's family, and other personal reasons."[6]

Whenever interviews or questionnaires were used, however, individual remigrants often listed a wide variety of reasons behind their returns, as if they themselves were not quite certain. After investigating earlier Finnish data, Reino Kero found that "a large proportion . . . could not explain the reasons for their returning to Finland." He argued that problems in adapting to life in America were probably most important in these.[7]

Surveys of evidence from the 1880–1930 period, as well as more recent studies, suggest that most explanations of remigration can be grouped under these headings: (1) Success; goals attained in America. (2) Failure, through injury or other causes, to reach goals. (3) Homesickness, nostalgia, and patriotism, including the various calls of relatives and family obligations (caring for elderly parents, saving the family farm). (4) Rejection of the United States, often for political or religious reasons, although inability to assimilate must also be included. These varying reasons for remigration are examined, along with the role of European governments in encouraging returns, in this chapter.

SUCCESSES

Without a doubt, many immigrants returned because they had succeeded in America. The Finn who predicted that he would go home as soon as "the pockets [were] full of money" spoke for legions. And though a variety of explanations, including failure, appeared among those returning to Szamosszeg, Hungary, an investigator found that "more considered that they had fulfilled their purpose for going"—that is, they reached their savings target. Three to five years was the most frequent length of stay in America to reach the immigrant's goal, although many stayed longer and some, less. Slovaks reportedly set $1,000 as the "fortune" to be amassed before they would return, and among the workers in a 1919 steel mill pit was "a quiet-eyed Pole, who was saving up two hundred dollars to go to the old country." But interviews with other Poles who returned after World War I turned up many who were much more successful, including one who left the United States with $6,000 in his money belt—and on the ship discovered more: a vest with double lining sewed up with banknotes. Immediately he encountered a Croat running wildly and yelling, "Has anyone seen my vest?" It was returned to him. Such funds carried in belts, bags, clothing, and pockets formed an important portion of the transfer of American wealth across the ocean.[8]

Interviews with returned Finns and questionnaire data disclosed the fact that, although these immigrants had performed some of the hardest drudgery in American capitalist enterprises during the 1880–1930 years—in such jobs as logging, mining, and steel mill work—they were still overwhelmingly positive about their achievements. A 1934 study found that 40.3 percent (255 persons) reported good results in America, 17.3 percent (109) had "quite good" results, and 16.4 percent (104) had a "fair result." Only 18.5 percent reported a bad result. Later studies uncovered similar findings.[9]

It can be assumed that the experience was a success for most, at least in part, because some monetary objectives were met. And these successes called for a different sort of party back in Europe than the mournful rituals that had taken place earlier when the emigrants had departed for the United States. In Ireland a sort of reverse "American wake" was held for the person returning. "When I came home they were as glad to see me as if I came from the grave," a returned Irishwoman recalled. Others described the big day when a group disembarked:

> They were met in Galway by friends and relatives and the neighbors on their arrival home would assemble to greet and welcome them. Everyone would be interested in what they had to say and many questions would be addressed to them about conditions in America, and enquiries made about relatives and friends there. People would come from far and near. . . . A party, singing and dancing would be given for them at home in a few days.[10]

The New Immigration was quickly marked by its high return rates, rates American critics began to point to as another reason to exclude the southern and eastern Europeans from entry into the country. Two veterans of the Dillingham Commission's work, Jeremiah Jenks and W. Jett Lauck, noted that, after the Panic of 1907, 91.1 percent of those returning to Europe were from the New Immigration. A recent commentator concluded that this transient or temporary immigration distinguished the New Immigration from the Old.[11]

But this return flow also reflected the changing patterns of late-nine-teenth-century immigration for most groups. Even such Old Immigrant nationalities as the British and Swedish had shown a shift toward single, younger males in the streams heading toward America, moving now to industrial jobs rather than to farms on the midwestern prairies or small towns across the hinterland. And it was by and large these young men working the "immigrant jobs" and living in American railway boxcars and cramped tenements who, in a few short years, headed home with their savings. German evidence indicates that the remigrant flow had been heavily male for years. These were not the stuff of stable immi-grant communities abroad. Not only were more men emigrating to America, but they were usually hired for jobs that gave fewer oppor-tunities for adapting to American life. Women who took employment generally worked in the service sector, where interaction with Ameri-cans was more likely and assimilation could often proceed more rap-idly; it is not surprising, then, that women were less likely to remigrate. Studies in Finland and Sweden clearly show this gender differential, which is reinforced by evidence from other European countries.[12]

Statistics reflect this difference for both New and Old Immigrants. The young males stood out: 72.3 percent of Poland's return from 1908 to 1914 was male, and 87 percent of the overall return was in the 15–45 age group. An Italian scholar calculated that, for the typical years of 1905–6, there were only twelve women returning for every 100 men. Italy's Commissariato Generale dell'Emigrazione found the male return percentage growing year by year, rising at the end of the war in 1917 to 92 percent. The typical Croatian repatriate in the 1900–14 period was described as generally male, age fourteen to forty-four, a common la-borer who had spent no more than five years in the United States and who sometimes returned to America again. Among Poles, a recent study has shown that 70 percent of those who returned had worked in U.S. industry as unskilled workers; they stayed less than ten years abroad.[13]

Similar generalizations could be made for other groups as well, and a Finnish scholar has concluded that immigrants most likely to return were those who seemed to be "adrift, constantly exploring their chances both at home and abroad." Although most remigrants went singly, this did not necessarily reflect their marital state: a Swedish researcher ex-amined a sawmill district in which 74 percent of the *married* Swedish men going to and from America both went and returned without their families—shedding an interesting light on the migrant labor strain in remigration.[14]

TRAVELERS AND THE STATE OF
THE ECONOMY

If the journey to America was based heavily on the expectation of finding employment in American industry, it was therefore vulnerable to the vicissitudes of that industry. The label "migrant industrials" was fastened on these immigrants by an American scholar, but it was contemporary Italians who called the United States "the workshop." Italians flocked to this land of labor mainly in March, April, and May, and their heaviest returns were in October, November, and December, when layoffs were often most numerous. And the workshop could close, as it did at times, abruptly, sending throngs eastward across the Atlantic. One remigrant in late 1894 was a Pole who encountered many of his compatriots "running away from America. The stagnation existing there has now driven them out of their 'new homeland,'" he said. Remigration data revealed that a large proportion of those returning had been in factory work, mills, or mining, occupations especially vulnerable to the boom-and-bust nature of the American economy.[15]

Economists have long noted the close relation between these economic downturns and soaring rates of return: for example, in 1893 there were 28 remigrants for every 100 immigrants into the United States, but as the financial depression took hold in 1894 the rate climbed to 61 for every 100, and further in 1895 to 79 per 100. Using Italian government statistics, the Dillingham Commission spotlighted Italy's returns in comparison with the state of the American economy. These showed an average yearly return of 436 going back to Italy for every 1,000 immigrating into the United States from 1887 to 1907, rising sharply in the panic years of 1894 (to 848) and 1904 (765). Although it did not have Italian figures showing the impact of the recent 1907 Panic, the commission studied American immigration records covering 1 July 1907 to 30 June 1908 and found that 135,247 Italians were admitted to the United States while returns to Italy numbered 167,335—or 32,088 higher than the incoming total. Studies of German and Finnish return movements also demonstrate that periods of U.S. economic trouble generally stimulated the greatest repatriation.[16]

But, independent of economic conditions, massive waves of immigration were usually followed by large numbers returning a few years later, like an outgoing tide. These would include persons who reached their American goals and returned or were affected by conditions not directly tied to the business cycle. This seems to be what British geographer

Ernest G. Ravenstein was referring to in his 1885 theoretical list of laws of migration: "Each main current of migration produces a compensating counter-current." German historian Günter Moltmann contends that there were two determinants affecting the return rate: "(1) one constant, conforming to emigration trends but more steady, and independent of external factors; (2) one variable, dependent on business cycles or other external factors, stronger or weaker as compared to emigration trends in the opposite direction." Finnish scholar Keijo Virtanen categorizes them as either "general factors" or "personal" or "individual" factors and argues that they are complementary, although personal factors are more significant in returns.[17]

With the exception of Ravenstein, it is the more recent scholars such as Moltmann who have noted the existence of a return lag after a heavy surge of immigration. Contemporaries generally argued that remigrants were responding to shifts in the U.S. economy. Herbert Francis Sherwood's investigative trips across the Atlantic put the blame on unemployment as the major cause of returns: for example, of 400 New Immigrants interviewed circa 1911 en route home through a North Sea port, 104 told Sherwood that they were out of work, by far the largest category. "While sickness and visiting contribute to the passenger lists of the third class," Sherwood concluded, "the chief factor in filling and emptying the cabins is clearly the state of our labor market."[18]

The lag before immigration actually subsided, as news came of American economic troubles, was studied by a Polish contemporary, Leopold Caro. He suggested that the falloff in European emigration after an American financial panic was largely due to stories told by returned emigrants. Their dire tales, rather than economic reports from the authorities, had the most impact. The likely accuracy of Caro's assertion was revealed in a letter from Tomasz and Antonina Barazczewski in Poland to their brother Stanisław in the United States in 1908: "We know that in America it is no longer as it used to be, because a multitude of factories have stopped work. Many of our people have come back under their native roofs." Thanks to returning emigrants such as these, Europeans soon learned the condition of American industry.[19]

Immigrants on the scene working in U.S. industry learned its condition immediately, of course, and often painfully. When the Panic of 1907 hit, railroad construction gangs were quickly laid off, steel mills cut their forces, mines and tanneries simply closed. Pittsburgh's manufacturers discharged some 15,000 Italians, Hungarians, and Slavs in

November that year, and special trains had to be put on to handle the massive exodus as immigrants from all around the country converged on the Port of New York en route home. Europe's ports were soon thronged as the reverse tide hit its shores, with Germany forced to put on 104 special trains to handle the traffic eastward from Bremen as the Panic deepened. Croatian newspapers began running long lists of those returning, and Croatia's major travel firm was bringing home 500 per week in late January 1908, and seldom less than 400 weekly during succeeding months.[20]

When the Panic reached the steel mills of Granite City, Illinois, furnaces began to close until the city's economic life was at a standstill by May 1908. Some 2,000 Bulgarian, Macedonian, Romanian, and Greek steelworkers left in early December 1907, many having saved large amounts before the layoffs came. The January–June 1908 return total from the area was estimated at 5,000–6,000. For those who could not afford a return ticket—recent arrivals, in the main—the disaster worked much hardship. Extensive charity work began, with the major steel mill eventually providing food; the immigrants' main boarding-house area, "Hungary Hollow," now became known as Hungry Hollow. One Granite City immigrant shot himself in despondence over not finding work. A labor agency took $5 apiece from 600 desperate men for jobs which, unfortunately, did not appear.[21]

These were the hammer blows of the American economy. They hit different groups with varying impact, and a Hungarian study found that those who failed were even less likely than others to return home, ashamed of their plight. Economist Harry Jerome, writing in 1926, observed that Italian immigration was unusually sensitive to industrial conditions in the United States. He cited statistics showing that almost 70 percent of returning emigrants declared their occupation to be laborer, and only 12.3 percent said they were skilled workers. It was those in unskilled positions—last hired, first fired—who suffered immediately in a financial panic. The Commissariato dell'Emigrazione warned that the most fluctuating, variable portions of Italy's citizenry in America were the unskilled, who returned home in masses during times of layoffs. Jerome went beyond the Commissariato's statistics to point out which groups were most vulnerable to shifts in the U.S. economy: males more than females; the foreign-born more than the native-born; the unskilled more than skilled, professional, or even "no occupation" groups. It all added up to an enormous stimulus for return by young male industrial workers.[22]

BIRDS OF PASSAGE

Some who saw jobs disappear went home with little bitterness: the trip to America had already become a habit for these "birds of passage." They sailed away as they had done on earlier occasions, to return again when word arrived that jobs were plentiful. Germans called them *Pendler*—as one who goes back and forth like the pendulum of a clock. The large numbers of Italians flocking to Argentina for harvest labor employment each year, and then returning home, were known as *golondrinas* (swallows). As with other types of migrants, the birds of passage had been around for generations, but the steamship became a midwife that stimulated their proliferation. The changing nature of immigration because of this transportation revolution was nowhere better revealed than in the appearance of "reverse" birds of passage during the economic doldrums of the 1870s: American skilled workers began crossing over to Britain for temporary work when they could not obtain employment at home.[23]

The birds of passage produced dramatic stories that often attracted public notice. Early accounts told of artisans from Britain, especially, coming to work at skilled American jobs and then returning at the onset of bad weather or layoffs. Some U.S. potteries imported Englishmen before the 1885 Contract Labor Law forbade it, and other accounts reported silk weavers going to Paterson, New Jersey, and British quarry workers, stonemasons, and other artisans making regular and repeated trips to and from the United States. Alexander MacDonald, head of the British Miners' National Union, told in 1873 of "hundreds of youths in Scotland . . . [who] go out for the run in the summer season in the United States"—making up to £20 ($97.20) before heading back home in the fall. A Lancashire bricklayer commented as he left New York in 1887, "I goes 'ome every year and takes five 'undred dollars with me."[24]

Such cases excited anger among American workers and prompted a congressional investigation in 1888. Other evidence indicates, however, that the repeated crossers were but a minor proportion of total return migration. An examination of six Finnish areas before 1930, for example, showed that four-fifths of those who returned from America had made only a single trip abroad. But villages differed, depending on access to trade and migration routes, emigration traditions, and local conditions: Ewa Morawska examined return migration to two central European areas and found that 34.5 percent of those in one community and 40 percent in the other had made more than one trip to America. Still, the Dillingham Commission reported that only 17.5 percent of foreign-born bituminous coal miners had made one or more trips abroad since their first arrival in the United States. According to port records for 1899 to 1906, 11.9 percent of all incoming Europeans had previously been in the United States.[25]

Several famous cases put birds of passage into local spotlights. An Irishwoman who recrossed the Atlantic six times became known locally as "the Atlantic swimmer." Family stories are told today of ancestors making two, three, or four trips, but then there was Juho Antinpoika Paavola of Finland, the earliest known emigrant from Elimäki, who went to America in 1888, 1891, 1897, 1899, and 1902 and never settled permanently back in Finland. And there was the Greek reported by Theodore Saloutos who made "about thirty crossings"—fifteen round-trips—beating out a countryman with only eighteen, or nine round-trips. But the international birds of passage crown (U.S. division) apparently goes to a southern Slav, Ivan Modrica, famous for making seventeen round-trips to America. It was cases such as these to which the Cunard Line steerage chief referred when he told congressional investigators about passengers who "are going backwards and forwards all the time. We have passengers coming backwards and forwards; they come back with us, and we treat them well, and if they are not satisfied with the treatment we give them they go to other lines."[26]

Some Americans interpreted the birds of passage as evidence that the economy had developed a sort of safety valve. "That recent crisis [1907] came without warning, almost overnight," the National Liberal Immigration League noted in arguing for continued unrestricted immigration, "yet quietly and doing no damage either to our social or economic fabric a half million foreigners promptly returned to their homes abroad."[27]

AMERICA CONDEMNED

Many immigrants viewed the increasing returns not as a reason to celebrate the American economy but as grounds to condemn it. Some European observers charged that there would be even more returns if not for the shame that prevented some immigrants from going home; better to hang on and hope for improvement than return in disgrace. And many who went back were seemingly "worse than when they came, for many had failed and were broken in spirit," Edward Steiner observed after his steerage interviews.[28]

Embitterment against America often followed, as with the Irishman who had arrived in Cleveland just in time for an economic depression. His brother was already there but had lost his savings when a bank failed, and only because a sister was married to a still-employed policeman was the Irishman able to remain alive—barely—until he could make his way back to Ireland. "He hates to talk about it, and he even hates the Yanks that come home," a friend later recalled; "he said America ruined his life." Another told of returning Irishmen who were so destitute when they landed that they had to walk all the way home to Kilkenny from the Dublin docks, some seventy miles. They were not proud of their time in America.[29]

Pride was also missing from those ground up by American industry or ruined by tenement conditions. "They escaped from America," a Pole concluded after seeing the emigrants crossing following the 1893–94 panic. Many who went back to Ireland were described as "old people long before their time," broken in health, surviving only briefly on their home soil; others kept their ill health a secret if they could. When Emily Balch toured the Slavic regions of Europe, she encountered much unhappiness with what American industry had done to the emigrants. Complaints seemed to increase as she headed south from Austria, and nowhere did she hear "so often as in Carniola [Austria] that men returned used up or hurt. Everyone seemed to be struck by it," Balch noted. "This is probably because they work in America largely in the most dangerous trades, in mining and iron works especially, but I think it is largely the pace that kills."[30]

Other travelers on returning ships were repeatedly struck by the large numbers of injured, broken, or ill immigrants on board and the multiplicity of widows. One American was surprised that more than a fifth of those coming back on the steamship *Canopic* were sick. Steiner looked at returning Polish women who seemed crushed (their cheeks pale and pinched, their skin severely wrinkled) and asked himself how it could be otherwise: "They had lived for years by the coke ovens of Pennsylvania, breathing sulphur with every breath; their eyes had rarely seen the full daylight and their cheeks had not often felt the warm sunlight." Steiner also interviewed a Bohemian woman who had worked for five years in a mammoth New York cigar factory. Now she had a hollow cough and glowing cheeks, because in those five years "she had to bite the end of every cigar, she swallowed much tobacco juice, and breathed in much tobacco dust." Her skill was such that she earned $20 a week, Steiner added, "but she had ruined her health, had spent all her savings for medicine and now was going home to die." The theme was a frequent one on eastbound ships.[31]

American social workers may initially have called tuberculosis "the Irish disease," but back in Connacht it was referred to as "the American sickness." The Italian government kept statistics on the health of both emigrants and those returning, and the results constituted a sharp condemnation of conditions in the United States. Robert Foerster contended that "no one who reflects that the eastward journey overseas is made much less often than the westward can fail to be impressed by the far greater numbers of sick Italians reported by the ship physicians for the eastward journey, especially from the United States." He noted that in 1910 Italian ships carried 857 persons having tuberculosis—but 841 of these were on the return trip, 700 of them coming from North America. This was in addition to other sicknesses such as syphilis and the large numbers of returners who had been injured in industry. They called America *la terra del dollaro e del dolore*—land of the dollar and of sorrow—and the tragedy of the remigrants' health was behind creation of new hospitals in Palermo, Genoa, and Naples. An immigrant writer argued that consumption had been unknown in Italy twenty-five years earlier, but the number of cases in southern Italy was rising sharply "due largely to the returned immigrant."[32]

Italian public health officials were worried. They found 0.07 cases of tuberculosis per 1,000 emigrants leaving Italy in 1909, but 9.71 cases per 1,000 among those returning. When they later surveyed the period from 1903 to 1923, they discovered that 7,487 cases of tuberculosis had been brought to Italy by those returning from the United States. Both Italian parliamentary investigators and the head of the Italian public health service agreed that tuberculosis flourished in the Mezzogiorno largely because of returned emigrants. Their statistics also reveal that the general sickness rate was often doubled, trebled, or quadrupled among those returning, compared to westward emigration.[33]

Other countries reported similar findings, and Kero's studies of Finnish remigrants led him to estimate that about 10 percent of those returning were sick or injured. Swedish medical experts told parliamentary investigators of returnees with broken health, some from consumption, others from neurological or mental diseases acquired in America.[34]

Looming behind these health problems, the missing limbs and diseased lungs, were the conditions of labor in America. A leading Hungarian-American newspaper, *Szabadság* of Pittsburgh, featured in its yearly almanac a chapter titled "Fatal Accidents and Mine Disasters." It had plenty of material to chronicle—cave-ins, explosions, haulage accidents—and one recent estimate is that 25 percent of the New Immigrant workers in Carnegie Steel's South Works in Pittsburgh were killed or injured in the 1907–10 years. Immigrants struggled against such conditions mainly by quitting but also by forming their own mutual aid societies, often a carryover from home.[35]

Mining in particular was a story whose chapters were always filled with disasters, such as the string of mine explosions and cave-ins in Pennsylvania bituminous districts which killed hundreds of immigrants—100 Hungarians and 120 Slovaks in the 1907 Jacobs Creek disaster alone, bringing calls for a Hungarian government inquiry. The Darr Mine disaster that year wiped out the entire membership of one of the immigrant benefit societies.[36]

Company payments to accident victims were small, and immigrants soon drew the conclusion that American industry was callous and uncaring about human life. The emigrants' unhappiness was recalled by a county Donegal woman, who judged that if ten men were killed on a job in America it meant little: "Just get them away out of the road and go on with the work. A living man was alright but a dead one was no good to anybody," she said. "That was the way they always looked on it in America." Another Irish observer of the immigration scene agreed that anyone hurt or sick in America should return home, "for if you could not work in that country there was no value on you." This return of the sick and injured was explained by an American writer, however, as simply demonstrating "that a portion of the normal eastward movement is a self-elimination of the unfit from our working forces."[37]

Were they unfit? The records reveal no returned immigrant who felt this way. Sent to lure Europe's workers away from the rising socialist movement spreading rapidly amid the ruins of World War I, a member of the American Labor Mission received a different answer from a group of returned Italians: America, they told him, had ruined their health and exploited their labor.[38]

This theme ran like an undercurrent through return migration. America had taken their labor and left them useless, some charged; it was not the "golden land." A Hungarian in a steel mill was asked by a native worker whether he liked the country:

"America, all right," he said.
"Good country?" I pushed him a little.
"Mak' money America," he explained; "no good live. Old country fine place live."[39]

The worker's skeptical frown—often a scowl—was frequently present when talk turned to working conditions in the "conscientiousless" United States. Amy Bernardy followed her Italian compatriots to the New World and was aghast at what she saw, as the "poor intelligent illiterate" was taken by America and bathed and tempered in its metal bath, hammered on its red-hot anvil, "and then when it can no longer use him it sends him back" in terrible condition—no longer good for America, but spoiled for Italian rural life. The idea also appeared in a Lithuanian newspaper in Chicago, which admitted, "we came to America and did not find a better life," for the immigrants were given the filthiest, most dangerous jobs. "Let us return to our Fatherland and live there," it urged.[40]

High on the list for condemnation, after unsafe working conditions, was the driving of workers in the American system—relentless, shoving, pushing, threatening. Peasants had been raised with different manners and a different pace of daily and yearly work. Gone now were the special holidays and festivals that dotted the work year in Europe; vanished as well were name days and wedding feasts when work was not allowed. And notably absent in the day-to-day handling of employment in large American concerns or labor gangs was consideration for individual problems: an illness, a need to visit a relative, a family problem that took someone away from work for a day.

Now there were supervisors who used fines or dismissal as weapons to enforce the speedup. Herbert Gutman stressed the personal costs of the peasant's transformation to wage laborer, and angry reactions by immigrants are not difficult to locate in the industrial records of the era. Many returned to Ireland to take up fishing again because, it was said, "they preferred that free life to bosses and clocks." One remigrant said that he was glad to be back where work was hard but free and easy, for "there is no clock or watch or boss to watch you here." Clothing workers on New York's Lower East Side wrote to a newspaper to complain of their employer in a raincoat factory, where a thirteen-year-old boy—earning $2.50 weekly—arrived ten minutes late one day and was docked two cents. "Isn't that a bitter joke?"[41]

With only slight costs involved in replacing an unskilled factory worker—a large firm determined the replacement cost to be $8.50 in 1915—employers had little incentive to worry about individuals or even to know exactly how many employees they had. Anyone not showing up was immediately replaced, with no effort to determine why he or she had not appeared. The best means of keeping workers produc-

ing steadily was absolute power by the boss; thus the immigrant loath-
ing for "bosses and clocks."[42]

"A GODLESS LAND"

Those trying to follow their religion faced additional problems that
soured them on America. "America has robbed me of my glory," be-
wails a Jewish immigrant father in Abraham Cahan's short story "The
Imported Bridegroom" after he discovers his daughter's fiancé eating
non-kosher food in a gentile restaurant. This theme runs through the
realist fiction of Cahan, a turn-of-the-century Lithuanian Jewish writer
who would become best known as editor of the New York *Jewish Daily
Forward*. More recently, Jonathan D. Sarna has examined Jewish return
migration and, in explaining why it was larger than previously recognized, notes that many Jews were simply discouraged at the obstacles to
practicing their religion. America was "a Godless land," filled with im-
pieties and heresies, causing rabbis especially to have a high rate of
return. Records of the Association of Jewish Immigrants of Philadelphia
document a case of a Jewish immigrant asking for money to go home
simply because he could not observe the Sabbath in the United States.[43]

Other groups also worried about preserving their religion, their
church, in a land overloaded with contrary pressures. Religious leaders
were often scarce, and totally absent was the guidance of a government-
supported church. Many missed this. A Pole wrote home from upstate
New York that "there are no churches here nor any Lent. It is nothing
like we have it in the old country." And a Swedish immigrant complained that "instruction in religion is entirely absent in American
schools," which meant a dismal future for the nation. Sweden was
ahead on this, he added, because it had "the advantage of having the
state church control the preaching of Christianity and the confirmation
of children. I wonder when this will become law in America?"[44]

Catholics, depending on tangible objects for the mass and other rituals, suffered especially in the American hinterland that lay beyond the
large cities. A "Yank" coming back to Ireland told the crowds at home
that "there were places where it was impossible to go to Mass on Sundays owing to lack of facilities," and, he added darkly, "there were
places so lonely that you would scarcely know what day of the week it
was." People traveling between two Italian communities tied together
by immigration and return migration—Roseto Valfortore, Italy, and
Roseto, Pennsylvania—put their disillusionment into a song:

What can we find in America?
Mountains of gold and mountains of work,
A gold cross, but still a cross,
A diamond cross is still a cross.[45]

Beyond the elements necessary for religious practice were the ideals of religion, which many also found lacking in the New World. Lynchings of Negroes held out warnings for immigrants, who after all were also a different, easily identifiable group. "Truth and justice are very little respected in America," a Swede reported to the Swedish Royal Emigration Commission, and he mentioned lying newspapers and unpunished crimes as well as attacks on Negroes. And when Edward Steiner sat down with thirty returned emigrants in Cetinje, Montenegro, to talk about America, most complaints centered on their treatment in the Land of the Free: being cheated by employment agencies figured in 80 percent of the complaints; money lost through bribes to Irish-American bosses to obtain work, 36 percent; rough treatment by bosses, 72 percent; robbery by railway crews in Montana, 80 percent; made drunk and shanghaied, 15 percent; theft of money and tickets before departure, 40 percent.[46]

Curiously, the advice sent back to prospective emigrants about what to wear, what to say, and how to act in America sometimes contained forewarnings of the treatment greenhorns could expect. Frank Paczkowski told his parents to prevent his sister from bringing a dress that comes to midcalf; she would look like someone from the Kujawy district, he complained, "and secondly, the American children would throw rocks at her."[47]

German workers especially began to feel that things might be better back home. In the winter of 1883 Paul Grottkau, editor of the *Chicagoer Arbeiter-Zeitung*, was on a citizens' association inspecting Chicago's tenement districts. A friend noted that when he returned from the tour he was pale, not well, greatly excited: "He said that he would never go out to see such terrible things again. He knew a good deal of Berlin and her misery, but such a condition of affairs did not exist there, not even in the poorest quarters." Indeed, at home the reformers of the Bismarck era were beginning to focus on Germany's working class— hoping both to cement their loyalty and discourage emigration—and German workers abroad were well aware of those improvements. Radical immigrant leaders Michael Schwab and August Spies, anarchists later convicted in the Haymarket bombing, were among those who found Chicago's living and working conditions even worse than in Germany. "I never saw there such real suffering from want as I have seen in this country," Spies wrote. "And there is more protection for women and children in Germany than here." Isaac Hourwich, in his analysis of the 1911 Dillingham Commission report, agreed that Germany was better in many areas, such as workers' protections against unemployment, the new workmen's compensation system for job accident victims, and factory sanitation.[48]

All this made working conditions in America less tolerable, the decision to return easier. No wonder some remigrants vowed that from then on they would never let their family members go to America; one repatriated county Kerry man even said that he would take his children to the tide and drown them rather than let them emigrate.[49]

HOMESICKNESS

Pure nostalgia drove many back, often the same love and concern for home and family that had propelled them abroad in the first place, when their goal was to earn funds to preserve the homestead. Guilt over the fate of parents left behind runs through many letters. Edit Fél and Tamás Hofer have described Hungarian peasants from Átány who became so homesick that they left America before six months were up, arriving home without the money they needed to expand their farm. These ties must have been strong, Caroline Golab has written, to compel such a high rate of return among Italians and Slavs. Some investigators have even deemed homesickness the major cause of return, ahead of unemployment and illness. This was the case with Virtanen's examination of questionnaires filled out by 937 returned Finnish emigrants, which showed that 21.3 percent claimed homesickness as a major reason for return—ahead of unemployment, with 14.5 percent. In a Norwegian study, 19 of 33 pre-1930 remigrants interviewed put homesickness at the top of their list for reasons to return, one of them observing that "an emigrant has always one foot in each country, but his heart is in the mother country."[50]

The thought echoes through the tales and folksongs of return migration. A Pole wrote to his wife that she should not be surprised that he looked so sad in the photo he had sent home: "I have not yet been happy in America! I am always sad and lonely and I look forward to the day and the hour when God will assist me to get to my dear wife and my dear children." Another Pole told of his head aching at work as he thought of home: "Now I know what a Mother is." An Irishwoman who had crossed "the pond" in 1892 admitted years later back in Ireland that she had never been happy in America: "I never got up a morning in it but I thought how nice it would have been to be rising in Ballighan and seeing the sun on top of the Cruach."[51]

Hundreds of miles eastward in the Hungarian village of Bükkszentkereszt the same thought was expressed in a song:

> I boarded the ship on Tuesday morning
>   Going back to Hungary.
> God bless America forever,
>   Just let me get away.

Far off in Cleveland, Ohio, another Hungarian sang:

> God bless these Hungarian hands
>   The feet that have roamed America far and wide.
> O God, where is my homeland?
>   Does my mother still weep for me?

And the nostalgia dripped heavily from a song originally published in a Norwegian-American newspaper in 1846 but reprinted in 1925 at a time when return migration was high; the last verse confessed,

For many a man has gone to America; but many a man has come disappointed away.
But even should you find there gold abundant as the sands of the sea, one thing you will never find—a fatherland.[52]

Statistics provide documentation for the power of family ties. Half the Finns going home were married, but in the westbound movement going to America three-fourths had been *unmarried*; that is, many of those returning were going back to spouse and children. Conversely, the presence of wives in America was crucial in discouraging immigrants from returning to Europe, a reality noted by the Immigration Restriction League. The pull of home was also demonstrated in the fact that about 80 percent of those returning to Sweden's Västernorrland country from 1875 to 1913 went back to their original parishes, a finding generally paralleled in other European countries. Scattered Irish evidence suggests also that many single women returned with dowries, preferring to find a husband in their homeland, which they easily did.[53]

Others came home because they were sent for, or because they had

inherited land. Money from America obviously provided a boost toward economic success in such a situation, but if it was missing the
obligation to return was still unavoidable: "Paddy McGuire came home
from America and stayed. He had to come for all his other brothers
went away and he had to come to look after his father and mother.
When he came home he began his old life again working the wee bit of
land. He had some money saved and that helped him along."[54]

What is apparent in many of these stories is that large numbers of
immigrants failed to adapt to American life. Homesickness overcame
them, or pleas from their families overpowered the search for wealth in
the United States. The idea ran through the verses of a Polish folksong
that describes the return of a foundry worker going first to New York
and the shipping agent, boarding the ship to cross the Atlantic to Hamburg, then on to Berlin, Kraków, and at last home:

> And my children did not know me,
> For they fled from me, a stranger.
> "My dear children, I'm your papa;
> Three long years I have not seen you."[55]

GOVERNMENTS SEEK RETURN

From overseas came other appeals to return, appeals that used homesickness and patriotism but often had other goals than reuniting families. These were directed and financed by European governments and
religious bodies and included pamphlets, tours by officials through the
emigrant colonies abroad, financial support for pro-return organizations and newspapers in the United States, even entreaties through
verse. One of Hungary's leading poets sent his message "to the American Hungarians," urging them to return once they became wealthy and
"be truer patriots than we have been." Emil Ábrǎnyi's poem closed
with an appeal that sought to do more than moisten eyelids:

> If rude foe would our nation's life molest
>   Would you remain away when duty calls?
> No, no! I know, with eager zeal you'd heed
>   The nation's call, and you will cross the seas
> To join your brethren here, to fight, to bleed,
>   To die for Magyarland's sweet liberties![56]

Such calls went out across the Atlantic often during the years of mass immigration. In part they reflected the transformation of the modern state, taking on new views of government responsibilities toward the people. These pleas were launched most fervently from two lands suffering enormous losses through emigration, Italy and Austria-Hungary. But, though politicians under both regimes argued about their compatriots overseas, internal political conditions dictated that efforts of each government would follow a distinct path.

In Italy a gnawing apprehension over the exodus ran through the nation's political debates, fueled by hopes that emigration and remigration would somehow solve the chronic problems of the south. And this apprehension was rapidly paralleled by a sincere concern over treatment of Italians abroad. At times emotions were raised suddenly, dramatically, over the issue, as occurred during the rush home in America's 1907 financial panic, when New York was unable to house the thousands pouring into the port: six repatriating Calabrians were found asphyxiated, their bodies piled on two beds crammed in a tiny room. But other worries appeared throughout the period: the high disease rate among Italians in the Americas, rough handling and cheating both on the docks and at the hands of padroni, bankers who vanished with Italians' hard-earned savings, employment agencies that took money from desperate immigrants but did not provide jobs. Italy's far-ranging parliamentary debate on the subject in 1900 brought pleas to protect the emigrants from exploitation by both American trusts and padroni, and to care for them aboard ship. A Socialist contended that Italians were worse off in America than Germans or Dutch because the Italians' plans to return home blocked their quick acclimatization. The Italian was always in an inferior position vis-à-vis other immigrant groups, critics charged; their labor drew the scorn of Americans as well.[57]

And so Italy moved to establish protections for its people overseas, building on the pioneering efforts of Italian Roman Catholic groups already operating in America. As early as 1891 the Italian government provided an annual subsidy for the Italian Home in New York City, which included a small hospital, relief bureau, immigration bureau, and free school. When it became clear that the institution did nothing about padrone exploitation, however, the subsidy was dropped. In 1894 an agreement with the United States led to establishment of an Italian emigration office on Ellis Island, to provide the newly arrived with information on employment opportunities. But other protective programs continued, until by 1921 the Italian government was paying subsidies to fifty-eight Italian organizations and twenty-seven foreign-based units to assist immigrants, spending almost $200,000 a year.[58]

Rising numbers of remigrants, however, caused the Italian government to also provide shipping assistance for homeward-bound indigents, widows, orphans, and the disabled. Free passage for such persons aboard steamship lines serving Italy was required by the 1901 Emigration Law, at the rate of ten adults for 1,000 tons registered, and one for every 200 additional tons. Aid for remigrants was also given through New York's Casa per gli Italiani.[59]

The Italian government soon became caught up in other debates centering on the immigrants, increasingly focusing on those who returned. Were they still citizens of Italy? What if they had been pressured into adopting American citizenship? In view of the fact of Italian overpopulation, were the emigrants remaining in North or South America to be lost forever—or could some part of their loyalty be retained? As this debate broadened, Italian statesmen and writers began working harder to encourage emigrants to remain loyal even while overseas. A 1913 law addressed the citizenship issue: whereas those taking foreign citizenship lost their Italian citizenship, they could regain it without cost by renouncing foreign ties and living again in the homeland, or by simply residing two years in Italy.[60]

Retaining the loyalty of those who remained overseas was not handled as easily, however. Repatriation was an advantage for the nation, a deputy argued in Parliament, so the loyalty of Italians abroad must be kept strong "in order to facilitate their return." Now the matter was not simply to wait for them to disembark in Naples but to foster the goal of return within Italian colonies abroad. One way to foster this ideal was to act through Italian schools in the United States. The objectives of one such group, the Istituto di San Raffaele, may well have paralleled those of many similar organizations: "The purpose of the Society of San Raffaele is to keep alive in the hearts of Italians the Catholic faith and with it the sentiment of nationality and affection for the mother country."[61]

The Istituto Coloniale, another organization that worked to retain the loyalty of Italians in the New World, held immigration congresses in 1908 and 1911 at which delegates from Italian communities abroad sought both government aid for their schools and representation in the Italian Parliament. Neither was forthcoming, but dreams of a "greater Italy" were energized and eventually taken up by the Nationalists. Building on earlier ideas of seeking room for Italy's peoples through expansion around the Mediterranean's rim, the Nationalists saw their ideas reach temporary fruition through Mussolini fascism. As George Gilkey concludes, "in emigration were many of the seeds of ultra-nationalism and imperialism."[62]

Austro-Hungarian policies, to the contrary, were rooted in the heterogeneous conglomeration of peoples jostling for space and power under the dual monarchy's umbrella. Divided after World War I to create part or all of Austria, Czechoslovakia, Hungary, Poland, Romania, Yugoslavia, and Italy, the Austro-Hungarian empire contained an even wider array of ethnic groups—Slovenians, Croatians, Bosnians, Albanians, Ukrainians, Serbs, Moravians, Rusyns among others.

Under the 1867 compromise between the Hapsburgs and the Magyar rulers, major political controls were divided and the Magyars became supreme in Hungary. This arrangement presumably eased certain ethnic tensions, but it also presented the Slovak question to Hungary—an issue that would take on new dimensions as thousands of Slovaks emigrated to America and returned with ethnic pride and ethnic visions for the future. The Hungarians launched an "American Action" program, using threats, mail seizures, assignment of loyal religious leaders abroad, bribes, and bonuses to assure that Slovaks, Ruthenians, and other non-Magyars in America were kept friendly to the Budapest authorities. Emigrants were to be protected, the prime minister told the Hungarian House of Deputies in 1902, with the aim "to keep the Hungarians in America good Hungarian citizens." The new bureau he was proposing, he said, "will thus hold the emigrants in its power." But, significantly, a year later the prime minister relayed gloomy reports that non-Hungarian-speaking emigrants "have come under the influence of bad-intentioned leaders, and have become corrupted from the national point of view."[63]

Immigrant newspapers in America received close scrutiny, and those journals supporting the regime were subsidized—$100 per month to the *Illustrovani List* in New York City at the time of World War I, for example; $50 monthly to a Slavic weekly there, while a Polish newspaper received $700 and a Romanian newspaper $600. The challenge to Budapest from emigrants and their press overseas was formidable, and a 1908 study of Hungary's ethnic problems noted that there were more Slovak newspapers in America than in Hungary. These newspapers, clubs, and societies "do all in their power to awaken Slovak sentiment, and contribute materially to the support of the Slovak press in Hungary," the study warned. The regime reacted by seizing unfriendly newspapers mailed home. The ultimate goals of the authorities can be seen in an announcement on the front page of a Ruthenian immigrant newspaper in 1911, published by the St. Raphael Society for the Protection of Ruthenian Emigrants from Galicia and Bukovyna: "Dear Countrymen! Do not forsake your homeland for always! When fate forces you to emigrate, at least don't sell your lands, so that you will leave something to come back to. Go for the sake of making money. Be thrifty and don't lose your savings on drinking. Return with the money earned and use it to improve your farms/households."[64]

Prospective emigrants were provided with literature that criticized life in the United States, warning that in America it was even illegal to urinate on the street. Hungarian officials paid visits to Pennsylvania anthracite districts and other centers of Austro-Hungarian immigrant life, both to investigate living conditions and to ascertain support for the regime. Churches were placed under close control. The regime dispatched priests from Hungary rather than permitting the Catholic hierarchy in the United States to fill such appointments. Even nuns were ordered overseas from Galicia and Bohemia, selected by the Budapest authorities with an eye to keeping pan-Slavism in check.[65]

Such actions may have helped assure the Slovaks' loyalty, but enough contrary signs appeared over the years to keep the authorities at home always on edge. As early as 1895 the consul in Pittsburgh reported that Slovaks were agitating against everything Hungarian; on returning they would become apostles of dangerous ideas. Slovak nationalism spread through American settlements, producing a hybrid sort of "central dialect" that helped calm the earlier debate over use of the East Slovakian dialect. And whereas the prime minister before 1903 had sought a guarantee of free passage for those wishing to return, an opposing idea suddenly appeared: delegates to a national conference that year said that because of the ethnic situation in Upper Hungary they did not want the return of some 90 percent of the emigrants (but the Hungarian Manufacturers' Alliance unanimously called for the government to take whatever measures possible to bring back Hungarian workmen from abroad; employers needed workers). In 1907 the Hungarian president approved a law that only Hungarian speakers should return, with no Slovak elements allowed back because they would disturb the country's inner peace. No evidence was found to show whether this law was enforced, although the government did authorize free return trips for up to 500 destitute Hungarian emigrants a year. But any male returning without a beard was assumed to be a pan-Slavic radical. Remigration was becoming complicated.[66]

In her study of the Slovakian issue in Austro-Hungarian immigration politics, Monika Glettler concludes that there is no evidence that money was actually sent back from overseas for pan-Slavic agitation or that American-Slovak newspapers circulated widely at home. In fact, she notes, because Slovaks generally held lower-level jobs in America, their own limited backgrounds and the daily pressures of work and saving largely immunized them against intellectual currents. That Hungarian church and state authorities were worried can be seen, however, in the enormity of the surviving cache of "America Action" records.[67]

Other ethnic groups also confronted the dual problems of protecting their people in America and encouraging their return. A Kansas City pastor of a Croatian church wrote to the Croatian Diet in Zagreb: "All the nationalities immigrating here are better organized than the Croats, and their home governments take care of them through consulates. Immigrants are also supported on the other side, and help is given to them at once." Although most immigrants came from southern Europe, he added, these were the least protected in the United States, and even the Austro-Hungarian consul—who should have been looking after Croats—gave more attention to his own banking and ticket business. The Croatian regime eventually established a fund, from fees paid by each person emigrating, to help indigent Croatians return home.[68]

Poles faced unusual difficulties because until the end of World War I there was no Poland, no separate government of the Polish people. Neither Prussia, nor Russia, nor Austria-Hungary showed concern for treatment of Poles abroad. Church and private groups had to fill in, and the mushrooming Polish immigrant population in America was soon served by hundreds of Roman Catholic parishes and organizations. In 1891 St. Joseph's House was founded in New York, run by the Polish Roman Catholic Union; twenty years later the Polish National Alliance started Emigration House there also, and it had emissaries on Ellis Island from 1905 on. A visiting Polish politician after World War I looked with approval on these institutions, especially the large number of churches serving Polish immigrants. The church, he noted happily, saved Poles in America from assimilation; it retained their Polish consciousness. There were also nonchurch institutions aiding Poles abroad, such as the Polish Emigration Society, of Kraków, launched in 1909 to aid needy Poles outside Austria-Hungary.[69]

In 1908 the Greek government began providing money to help penniless Greek emigrants return, and at the same time it publicly criticized conditions in America. Greek periodicals had articles on the sorry conditions left at home by the departed emigrants, the empty fields, children without fathers, churches without worshipers. In Sweden, an antiemigration group in 1907 sought creation of a national labor exchange to draw the emigrants back to jobs at home, and Crown Prince Gustav was urged to visit Swedish settlements abroad to whip up interest in return. It was also suggested that a Swedish ship call at U.S. ports several times a year to transport Swedes back. Finnish newspapers conducted campaigns to bring about more remigration, but organizational efforts had to await formation in 1927 of the Suomi Society and the Overseas Finns' Association. By then the tide of emigration had slowed; two years later the onslaught of the Great Depression in America would send thousands fleeing eastward without any prompting from the homeland.[70]

The immigrant church was thus in a position to become embroiled in American controversies beyond those stimulated by foreign government intervention. Evidence regarding the effectiveness of churches in spurring remigration is incomplete or contradictory, however. What is clear is that European church leaders were worried about their flocks overseas. Although one Polish immigrant assured his brother-in-law at home, "You do not have to worry about God in America," the priest at Miedzybrodzie in Galicia could lament that people from his parish who went abroad were not attending church, were eating meat on Fridays, were losing both their purity and their rural simplicity. But they remained Catholics, he admitted.[71]

Achieving success in America or suffering failure, large numbers of European immigrants decided that the best decision was to return home. Although many had reached their goals, it is evident that the traditional explanation for reemigration—that Europeans returned home as they had always intended —is not sufficient. Many reasons explain the return journeys, and if anger at "bosses and clocks" speeded some departures, nostalgia for waiting families pulled others home like a magnet. Americans were increasingly angered by the tactics of European governments and church officials, as they were upset at the growing exodus itself. Some charged that it was this outside intervention—not factory dangers, not love of home, not reaching savings goals—that was responsible for the immigrants' round-trip. Resentment was growing, and many in America considered return migration an affront to national well-being.

CHAPTER 5

Politics, Unions, and Postwar Americanism

The spectacle of immigrant priests prowling through tenement districts, urging their parishioners to return home—also urging them to avoid learning English, to reject citizenship—sparked a rising chorus of anger from many elements of the American population. That the picture was exaggerated much of the time did not diminish its impact: there was some truth to it, and the existence of large numbers of foreign-language newspapers as well as foreign-language churches and schools gave increasing visibility to the immigrant colonies. The foreigners could not be missed, not by sight, nor sound, nor—if truth be told—smell. Many among the native-born felt they were losing out. They were being displaced.

The question of the immigrants' assimilation was addressed by two Dillingham Commission investigators, Jeremiah W. Jenks and W. Jett Lauck. In the process, they noted the integral role that return migration played in the growing controversy:

If an immigrant intends to remain permanently in the United States and become an American citizen, he naturally begins at once, often indeed before he leaves Europe, to fit himself for the conditions of his new life, by learning the language of the country, studying its institutions, and later on by investing his savings in America and by planning for the future of his children in such a way that they may have advantages even better than his own. If, on the other hand, he intends his sojourn in this country to be short, a matter of a few months or a few years, naturally his whole outlook upon American institutions and American life is changed. He will wish to secure in America that which will be of chief use to him after his return to his home country. . . . The acquisition of the English language will be of little consequence. . . . Naturally, the chief aim of a person with this intention is to put money in his purse . . . not for investment here but for investment in his home country.[1]

The controversy's main segments continued to shift and change. These included natives' fears of job or wage loss, repugnance at the newcomers' living conditions, patriotic stirrings, and often a scarcely concealed racism. Union leaders were angered at the reluctance of temporary migrants to join their movements, while industrial leaders after World War I stood aghast at the scenes of workers leaving the country. And a new wave of attacks on the cities in the 1920s targeted the immigrant, especially those planning temporary residence; in the process, these rural eruptions encouraged many among the foreign-born to turn their backs on America. These issues are taken up in this chapter.

THE UNDESIRABLES

The oratorical linking of New Immigrant groups, many of whom were dark-complexioned, with the Chinese was an early warning that Americans' acceptance of the newcomers would proceed only with difficulty. The Chinese also had a popular image of being only short-term sojourners. In an 1890 investigation, a congressman inquired of a New York public works inspector whether the Italian could be "put down as a superior sort of chinaman." The inspector answered that "as between the class of Italians that have come over here the last ten years, there is not much of a choice." The *Chicago Evening Journal* complained that "these Italians, like the Chinamen in this country, are aliens, not citizens," and charged that those who import "cheap and ignorant Chinese, Polish and Italian laborers to compete with better men are public enemies." Slovaks were compared to the Chinese by the U.S. consul in Budapest: they took cheap wages, they had no intention of remaining in America, they kept to themselves.[2]

Emphasis was increasingly placed on differences between broad ethnic groupings, the so-called Old Immigration from northern and western Europe and the New Immigration from the south and east. A State Department statistician cautioned in 1887 that regarding the new influx of peoples, especially laborers, immigrants from one nation might be far more desirable than those from another. Going further, a U.S. immigration inspector announced shortly afterward that the United States was "now receiving installments of the ignorant and degraded, a class that is little superior to the Digger Indians of the West."[3]

Americans from various walks of life joined in the criticism, many of their arguments having little to do with return migration but centering instead on supposed racial differences or the recurring question of labor competition. In many of these attacks, plans to return were often treated as being responsible for other undesirable characteristics. Sometimes, however, the critics simply unleashed broadsides. Thus Peter Roberts, of the YMCA's industrial department, described the "Sclavs" as "ignorant, clannish, unclean, suspicious of strangers, revengeful and brutal. . . . They have not been taught to think for themselves." The "Sclav," he asserted, "is the child of a lower civilization than ours." In other writing Roberts condemned their drunkenness and said that their patronizing of houses of prostitution reached such an extent on paydays that sometimes lines of male customers stretched outside the buildings as they waited their turn. And the era's social darwinism can be glimpsed through Roberts's admission that it would be difficult to improve the massive numbers of children being born into these conditions: "What to do with this class baffles the wisest reformers," he wrote. "It may mean hardship to apply to it the doctrine of Nietzsche, and yet some means should be used to eliminate this parasitic class from the social body."[4]

Frank Julian Warne titled his 1913 book *The Immigrant Invasion*, and he presented the New Immigrants' arrival very much in terms of an invasion, comparing the modern influx to the coming of the Saxons to Britain or the Huns to Italy. But, unlike those invasions of yore, large numbers of these new invaders planned to plunder the nation's wealth and return home. Warne especially attacked the southern and eastern Europeans' living conditions, which he claimed were a result of their desire to save all they could for their future life back in Europe. These conditions and their acceptance of low wages forced other workers to sink to their levels. However optimistic a person might be regarding the future, Warne said, "if he is intellectually honest," after examining the American industrial scene, "he cannot do other than entertain and express serious forebodings as to the future of a large part of our population—the wage-earning class."[5]

These issues were much debated in the years leading up to the beginning of war in 1914. The longtime leader of the restriction movement,

Sen. Henry Cabot Lodge of Massachusetts, had put the issue bluntly as early as 1891: the tremendous growth in immigration, he stated, "is making its greatest relative increase from races most alien to the body of the American people and from the lowest and most illiterate classes among those races." And as it grew, he warned darkly, this migration was demonstrating "a marked tendency to deteriorate in character."[6]

POLITICAL REACTIONS

Despite such expressions of distaste for the immigrant, other critics were paradoxically directing their blows at the efforts of foreign governments, clergymen, and the foreign-language press to discourage assimilation of these immigrants into American life while luring them back to Europe. Hungary's attempts were vociferously condemned by two Hungarian immigrants: Marcus Braun, of the U.S. Immigration Bureau, and Lajos Steiner, who testified before a U.S. congressional committee in 1919. Braun lashed out at foreign government support of colonies within the United States, such as Hungary's activities in subsidizing schools and churches, distributing books, and sending government and church agents to preach Magyar patriotism; such governments' aim was to prevent the immigrant from becoming an American citizen "and to induce him to consider his life in America only a 'makeshift'—temporary." Steiner attacked "systematic work" by Hungary to prevent the immigrants' Americanization and persuade them to send their savings home. "They are induced to return to their native countries to reengage in agriculture," thereby boosting land values there.[7]

Many others voiced similar complaints, including Commissioner of Immigration Terence V. Powderly, who forced the Italian Bureau of Emigration in New York to close in late 1900 because he thought it was being used to import strikebreakers. Powderly was a former president of the Knights of Labor. Among scholars joining the attack—after 1914 when the issue was heated further by the angers and apprehensions of war—was University of Chicago professor Robert Park. Park complained that foreign-based institutions in the country did more than retard assimilation: their basic approach to the United States was as a region to be colonized by Europeans, each group retaining its own language and culture and using English only as some sort of lingua franca between communities. Others argued that machinations of foreign governments and foreign-controlled organizations were absolutely crucial in these activities. "All that is needed to Americanize the immigrants," one letter writer proclaimed in *Outlook* magazine, "is prevention of organized and foreign subsidized anti-American propaganda."[8]

The sharpest criticisms, however, were leveled by one of the most important American officials dealing with the subject, the new commissioner-general of immigration, F. P. Sargent. Sargent used his 1904 report to deliver a broad, far-ranging attack on the "induced" immigration piling up in the cities. Foreign countries were becoming alarmed at their population losses, he claimed; unable to block departures, they had directed all their political, social, and occasionally religious sources to one end: "to maintain colonies of their own people in this country, instructing them through various channels to maintain their allegiance to the countries of their birth." Such action was crucial to those countries, he charged, "because it insures the return of the emigrant with his accumulated savings."[9]

This opposition to the New Immigrants, and to their tendency to return home, began to work its way into the political system. Part of the controversy centered on the immigrants' avoidance of U.S. citizenship, and new state and local laws required naturalization or declaration of intent before immigrants could be hired for public or sometimes other types of employment. New York, Illinois, and Pennsylvania barred aliens from working on state and municipal public works by the late 1880s, and the latter state also attempted to place a tax on alien laborers. In some western mining districts and states similar acts were passed in response to immigrant participation in strikes. The Supreme Court overturned such laws in the 1890s, however, charging violation of the Fourteenth Amendment. A federal proposal to require all incoming immigrants to immediately declare their intention to obtain citizenship—an idea that found some support early in the era—never acquired sufficient backing to become law.[10]

What began to gain momentum instead was a call for a literacy test, a simple test of the reading abilities of incoming passengers on the immigrant ships. Designed to appear objective and nondiscriminatory, the idea actually was aimed squarely at blocking the influx from southern and eastern Europe. Repeated allegations that the New Immigrants were undesirable, ignorant, and illiterate provided the basis for Senator Lodge's statement that the United States had the right "to exclude illiterate persons from our immigration, and this test, combined with others of a more general character, would in all probability shut out a large part of the undesirable portion of the present immigration."[11]

As the various literacy test concepts began to come together in the 1890s, pushed by the newly formed Immigration Restriction League and championed most ardently by Lodge, another idea was grafted onto the main stem—a requirement that no one be admitted to the United States who still maintained a home in a foreign country. This addition took form in the Corliss amendment, first submitted as a separate bill in 1896 by Republican representative John B. Corliss of Detroit. Debate on the measure, which reemerged as an amendment to the Literacy Test Bill in 1897, revealed that Corliss may have aimed it mainly at Canadian workers crossing to work each day in the Detroit area, in his congressional district, although most other supporters showed their anger at returning immigrants in general. Corliss pointed to a recent recommendation of the U.S. Immigration Bureau that "provision should be made to exclude aliens coming year by year to perform labor in the United States, with no intention to settle therein." Linking the ban on maintaining homes abroad to a literacy test, with an added section barring noncitizens from public works, would seemingly keep out all undesirables. Representative Mahany of New York made it clear just who was to be covered: "Those whom it is the universal sentiment to exclude," he announced, "are the paupers, imbeciles, criminals, and other off scourings of Europe, together with alien-contract laborers, and the 'birds of passage,' who, retaining domicile and citizenship in other lands, fatten on the substance of our own." Major criticisms of the Corliss bill appeared immediately, with most concern shown over its impact on Canadians, Cubans, Mexicans, and others living near American borders. These were the major burdens dragging the amendment down to defeat in 1897, just as the literacy test itself was picking up broader support.[12]

Part of the backing for the literacy test came from organized labor. On the surface, this presents a contradiction: unions heavy with immigrant membership seeking restriction of immigration. But the development is neither illogical nor unpredictable when examined in context. The fundamental concern of American labor unions has always been with the job and job conditions, and when either has been threatened then protection in some form has been sought. Overall, it has been a job-conscious labor movement aimed at protecting members' livelihoods. Immediately after the Civil War, the National Labor Union, a short-lived, largely reformist organization, became concerned over British immigrants flocking to jobs in America. The union's leader, William Sylvis, sought cooperative pacts with British trade unions to hold back their members during times of economic difficulties in the United States. And when U.S. delegate A. C. Cameron spoke at the Basle Congress of the International Workingmen's Association in 1869, he bluntly told the Europeans that the only interest of American workers in the International was to see it function as an immigration control.[13]

The rising anti-Chinese movement in the West borrowed such arguments, and Montana's governor summed up many of them in 1869: "The coolie laborer has no family to support or educate, . . . he has no interest in our society or government, and does not expect to become a citizen, and until he does he cannot be forced to enter our army." Their high return rate to China made them temporary sojourners only, saving their earnings for life in the "Flowery Kingdom."[14]

Laborers were in the forefront of campaigns against the Chinese in San Francisco in the 1870s, and the opposition picked up supporters in the East when a shoe factory in North Adams, Massachusetts, brought in Chinese to break a strike. These activities were part of the buildup to passage of the 1882 Chinese Exclusion Act, and three years later organized labor took the lead again to win enactment of the Foran Act, which banned American firms from contracting employees abroad. Again the link between Chinese and European labor migrants was made explicit: Rep. Martin Foran of Ohio, urging support for his bill, railed at the "degraded, ignorant, brutal Italians and Hungarian laborers," arguing that they knew nothing of American institutions, customs, or habits. "They are brought here precisely in the same manner that the Chinese were brought here."[15]

UNIONS TARGET RETURNERS

The Knights of Labor, which rose to become the country's major labor grouping in the 1870s and 1880s, stressed the linkage of New Immigration, Chinese immigration, and temporary residence in America. It preached labor solidarity, organized semiskilled and unskilled as well as skilled workers, and in the process took in many immigrants, almost all from the Old Immigration. Its leaders remained unenthusiastic about eastern and southern Europeans, noting the newcomers' strikebreaking and the downward pressure they exerted on wages. A former editor of the Knights' newspaper argued that no one should be admitted to the United States who could not speak English and that immigrants should be required to declare their intention to become citizens before entering the country. Although it desperately needed new members in the 1890s, the Knights supported the Lodge-Corliss bill and thereby continued its decline by lining up against the groups growing most rapidly in the labor force.[16]

Other union leaders drawn from the Old Immigration generally followed this line. In part, the reason lay in the fact that the union movement outside the Knights was centered in the crafts, the skilled trades, whereas the New Immigration was heavily unskilled. In 1887 the German Socialist newspaper *New Yorker Volkszeitung* attacked Poles, Slovaks, Italians, and Belgians as having been imported by monopolists and called them a helpless proletariat that could not think of gaining an independent means of livelihood. Intra-European prejudices did not evaporate crossing the Atlantic.[17]

All this positioning pointed to the gulf developing between the New Immigration and the AFL, the alliance of predominantly skilled trade unions which had emerged as the nation's dominant labor grouping by the 1890s. As with earlier controversies over the Chinese, instances of New Immigrants working as strikebreakers received wide publicity and identified them with strikebreakers in the minds of AFL members. Comparisons to the Chinese were emphasized by the AFL's United Mine Workers, which argued that the peasants of southern Europe then flooding into U.S. labor markets stole money from the pocketbooks of American workers and returned home.[18]

Short years later James T. Farrell, the novelist of Chicago's working-class Irish, put this antagonism into a novel:

And they needn't have lost the strike, if only they had all shown unity, courage, heart. But they, the foreigners, Syrian bus boys, fat Dutchmen, foreigners, hadn't been interested in strikes. They wanted Shrifton's crumbs. They wanted their tips. They had come over, not to make America their home, but to milk it as well as they could, and go back. . . . Scabs![19]

With some exceptions, noted in the previous chapter, there were only sporadic instances before 1900 of New Immigrants enthusiastically supporting American trade unions. Moreover, labor agitators and editors within ethnic groups were frequently critical of the American capitalist system. Mutual antipathy therefore developed between the AFL and much of the New Immigration, seen in an editorial in the Chicago Lithuanian newspaper *Lietuva*:

American labor organizations are the greatest enemies of immigrant workers. . . . This hatred shown immigrant workers is mostly propagated by American labor organizations.

Probably, the greatest enemy of immigrant workers in America is

Gompers, president of the American Federation of Labor. He is working hand in hand with American fanatics and chauvinists; he is author
of all kinds of restrictions against immigration.[20]

Various other factors combined in the era to push the AFL further
from extending any all-embracing welcome to the New Immigrants.
Built up by leaders of skilled unions who were zealous in holding on to
control, the federation watched its own restrictive approach to employee organization succeeding while the broader and more inclusive
approach of the Knights was foundering badly. Survival of the fittest
indicated to the AFL that its approach was best. Moreover, the era was
extremely perilous for labor, with the boom-bust economy periodically
jolting union campaigns, while hard blows were delivered almost daily
by the court system and the barons of steel, railroading, mining, and
other industries.[21]

The AFL's reluctance to embrace the New Immigrants has received
considerable examination from scholars. Gwendolyn Mink argues that
the arrival of the New Immigrants at this juncture in America's industrial and political development further fragmented the American labor
force while guiding the AFL to choose the safest proven course of limit-
ing itself to skilled workers. This had been the AFL's tendency since it
was put together as a skilled-worker alternative to the Knights of Labor. Deepening class divisions, which brought the rise of labor political
parties elsewhere, were therefore superseded in America by ethnic divisions, which heightened the anxieties of native-born and Old Immigrant
workers and turned them away from making common cause with unskilled southern and eastern Europeans. French scholar Catherine Collomp argues that the AFL and its English-born leader Samuel Gompers
were trying to become part of the American mainstream, even siding
with the Immigration Restriction League and other groups outside labor's usual embrace. Noisy socialists challenging him from the AFL's
fringes only pushed Gompers closer to such conservatives.[22]

The AFL's debates over the literacy test and the Corliss amendment
revealed an uneasy membership, according to A. T. Lane, a third
scholar to examine the issue. Gompers forced through AFL endorse-
ment of the literacy test bill in 1897 even though most members seemed
to have favored an outright five-year ban on further immigration. From
then until the Dillingham Commission began its investigations in 1907,
the AFL debated the issue frequently, shifting from condemning employers of the New Immigrants to attacking the foreigners themselves.
Immigration restriction thus became firmly linked with the philosophies

of the nation's largest and strongest labor organization, although it must be noted that in some member unions such as the United Mine Workers there were sporadic advances for New Immigrant membership. In 1910 the mine workers' president reported that fully one-third of the nation's 700,000 miners could not speak English; such a glaring statistic cried out for pulling the foreigner into the ranks.[23]

What is missing from these recent examinations of organized labor's nativism is recognition of the significance of the phenomenon of return migration. Because most late nineteenth-century and early twentieth-century immigrants left Europe fully expecting to return, their goals remained back in the village. Would such workers show interest in unions, even if warmly invited to join? Because these were overwhelmingly from the peasantry, holding bottom-level jobs and not agitating to move up, the AFL's high dues and concentration on skilled workers deterred most of them. The New Immigrants' penchant for jumping jobs and their multiplicity of languages also discouraged organizers.[24]

Unions therefore symbolized several things to the New Immigrants beyond the chance to gain higher wages: strikes, dues, required meetings, sacrifices for long-term goals. Unions meant shorter hours, too, but immigrants often wanted longer hours. Longer hours meant more pay, speedier accumulation of savings. Their own short-term plans for America, combined with an American industrial machine that valued unskilled, cheap, easily interchangeable workers, was more at fault in this antagonism than the decisions of a few union leaders.

The structure of American labor organization itself was a major obstacle. In 1913, John R. Commons compared the labor situation in the United States and Europe:

No understanding of the American movement, compared with that especially of England, can be acquired until one perceives the importance of race and language. . . .
. . . the advantage of a common race and a common race feeling, particularly among British and German wage-earners, has made it possible for unions to hold their ground without serious menace from non-unionists. The non-union Englishman is much more opposed to taking the job of the union Englishman than a non-union Italian [in America] to taking the job of a union Irishman.[25]

To early labor economists such as Commons, and to many later historians such as Britain's Charlotte Erickson, the employers' use of the New Immigrants as strikebreakers was at the heart of the issue, overwhelming other factors. Herbert Gutman agreed that some of the era's friction came from the simple fact of a changing ethnic makeup, but he stressed that coal operators often exploited these differences to hurt unions, and, as a result, much of working-class history between 1890 and 1920 was shaped by ethnic antagonism. Surveying this development from an international viewpoint, German labor historian Dirk Hoerder points to the anti-Italian actions by workers in both France and the United States, and to anti-Polish actions by workers in both Germany and the United States, and concludes that, given the extent of migration, it is remarkable that so little direct action by unions against immigrants occurred, especially in view of the employers' use of imported labor to break strikes.[26]

With American organized labor moving into the restriction camp, linking both nativist and reformer groups shocked at the growing urban chaos, the Dillingham Commission had nearly an open field to attack the New Immigration. In its 1911 report the commission endorsed the literacy test but also devoted considerable attention to the evils of return migration, calling for deportation of any aliens who tried to persuade others not to become citizens. The Dillingham investigators further urged that, "as far as possible, the aliens excluded should be those who come to this country with no intention to become American citizens or even to maintain a permanent residence here." These were usually men arriving singly, the commission stated, and it therefore recommended refusing entry to unskilled laborers unaccompanied by wives or families.[27]

WAR AND REMIGRATION

With Sarajevo in 1914, Europe plunged into the maelstrom. Precedents already in place directed remigration now; immigrants from several national groups had rushed in earlier years to defend their countries in times of peril. Germans had gone home to fight in the 1864 Prussian--Danish war, the Prussian–Austrian war of 1866 (the "Seven-Weeks' War"), and especially the Franco–German war of 1870–71. This tradition was in the background as other groups heard the call to arms from the homeland.[28]

Among the New Immigration, the first large return in wartime came during the 1897 Greek–Turkish war. But a larger movement was set off by the Balkan war of 1912, with Bulgaria, Serbia, Greece, and Montenegro opposing their longtime foe, Turkey. In such heavily Balkan communities as Granite City, Illinois, immigrants had been holding marching drills since 1910, and at the outbreak of hostilities they began flocking to New York for transport home. A rally in nearby St. Louis raised $3,000 to be sent home for the Greek-Bulgarian cause, and long lists were compiled of persons pledging to return for military duty. A special $12 steerage rate from New York to Greece was announced by Greek shipowners. Some 500 Bulgarians and Greeks left by train from Granite City at the end of October 1912, preceded by a day of patriotic songs and marching. The local newspaper noted that "men who had come from the 'old country' together five years ago, had worked side by side and had been roommates ever since, were called upon to say good-bye to each other for the first time and perhaps for the last." A local collection raised $4,600 for their transportation east. Out of a total workforce of about 7,000 in the Granite City area, some 1,500 immigrants left in late 1912 and early 1913 to defend their homeland. Local mills suddenly had to scramble for workers, drawing in Armenians, Lithuanians, Austrians, and others. Some 45,000 Greeks had returned home from the United States by early 1913.[29]

Americans looked on benignly: "The minute men of a new epoch are mobilizing among us," observed the social welfare journal *Survey* as returning immigrants converged on New York. But the editors noted that such persons often left behind nothing more substantial "than a wire cot in [the] boarding boss's establishment." For these workers were "foot loose of ties in this country," mainly young men whose wives and children were overseas. "They are the class of men, preeminently, who come to America only to earn and save for the family at home."[30]

The presence in America of thousands of their young, single males was not missed by the warring powers of 1914, who sent out calls for reservists and others to come home. It was estimated in late 1914 that America contained some 1.5 million immigrant men, twenty-one years of age and older, whose homes were in the belligerent countries of Europe. Patriotic appeals to them appeared in profusion in the foreign-language press. And just as had occurred during the Balkan wars shortly before, thousands flocked to consulates across the country to begin the process of return. Italy, Russia, and France even refused to recognize American citizenship as a legal excuse for escaping military duties at home.[31]

Despite such campaigns, wartime remigration was down sharply from earlier totals of civilian returns, undoubtedly because of the increasing attacks on ocean shipping. In prewar 1913, for example, a total of 35,031 Germans had returned home, but the year the war be-

The outbreak of war in Europe in 1914 had reverberations across American immigrant communities, and soon thousands headed back to help their homelands. This group of German reservists gathered at the German consul's office in Chicago on 5 September 1914 to make arrangements for returning. Photograph by Chicago Historical Society, D.N. neg. 63, 292.

gan this number fell to under 12,000. Similarly, the English and Scottish total was 88,382 returning in 1913, plummeting to 15,110 in 1914, and dipping further in 1915. U-boat attacks in the Atlantic and the spread of the war to many areas of the Continent dropped the totals for all immigration from Europe as well as remigration: immigrants from Europe numbered 1,058,391 in 1914 but only 197,919 in 1915. Return migration had been exceeding 300,000 annually but tumbled to 204,074 in 1915, 129,765 in 1916, and 66,277 in 1917. Returns would not again be so few until Depression-torn 1930, after the U.S. restriction laws had sharply reduced immigration itself.[32]

Austria-Hungary's leaders, worried for two decades over the supposed pan-Slavism of their Slovaks, watched with relief as Slovak reservists returned willingly to join the empire's armies. But some Serbian nationalists illegally recruited within the United States for troops to throw off their opponents from Vienna. Also, some 400 young Poles made it home to Poland to fight in Gen. Józef Piłsudski's army. A massive drive in Canada and the United States brought 38,108 applicants to enlist in a Polish army under Gen. Joseph Haller; 20,720 eventually sailed for France but arrived just a month before the armistice. The Czechoslovak Legion, based in France, also recruited among immigrants in the United States.[33]

Northern Italians poured home from across Europe as the outbreak spread, escaping the struggle that Italy would not join until 1915. This early rush homeward gave further evidence of the northern Italians' preference for job-seeking nearby rather than across the ocean: from 1 August to 15 September 1914, 162,361 returned to the northern province of Veneto, 79,440 to Lombardia, and 58,576 to Piemonte. Highways through the Alps were jammed with returners in early August, 20,000 passing through Basel in just three days. The total Italian return by 15 September 1914 was 470,866 males over age fifteen, mainly from the north, but in May 1915, after Italy formally entered the war, large numbers also arrived from across the Atlantic. From July 1914 to December 1915, for every 100 emigrants who left Italian ports, 412 returned.[34]

Within the United States the war years brought major changes to the immigrant colonies. Germans, the most organized and politically active of all immigrant groups, suddenly became the enemy and their ethnic organizational apparatus was left a shambles. In the industrial plants, the shift to war production forced managers to confront unfamiliar problems as the accustomed streams of New Immigrant workers were suddenly cut off, leading to recruitment of southern blacks, Mexicans, and others.

Return migration all but vanished. As David Brody has written of the immigrant steelworkers during wartime, "their very inability to leave the country tended to strengthen the ties to their jobs." Further, the lack of other sources of labor led to new efforts to keep immigrant employees content, including offering them higher wages. Unions were no longer to be brutally suppressed, especially while AFL officials were sitting on Wilson administration defense policy boards. Adopting Wilson's war slogan, "Make the world safe for democracy," the AFL launched vigorous organizational campaigns to bring democracy to the plant floor. The New Immigrants responded in droves. Granite City's Hungary Hollow became Lincoln Place, and so-called immigrant jobs were no longer looked down on. Laborers at the Cuyahoga Works in Cleveland were informed by a government representative, "Your greasy overalls . . . are as much a badge of service and honor in the eyes of your country today as the uniform of the army or navy."[35]

There was soon another side to the wartime transformation of the immigrant issue, however, one that would ultimately affect many immigrants' decisions to return to Europe. This was the rise in demands for total, unconditional support of the United States. "Hyphenation" was out. Marchers in a New York City preparedness parade in 1916 passed beneath a giant electric sign that proclaimed "Absolute and Unqualified Loyalty to Our Country." The concept spread rapidly as America moved from war observer to war participant, from sidelines kibbitzer to occupant of trenches in the Argonne and even wartime casualty. Soon criticism of the nation or its institutions was no longer tolerated. Loyalty pledges proliferated, and in New York City schools these were sent home for immigrant parents to sign. The literacy test—passed but vetoed in 1897, 1913, and 1915—was vetoed again in 1917 but this time was passed over the president's veto.[36]

In addition, Congress in 1918 imposed an income tax for what were termed "non-resident" aliens, twice as great as the tax on citizens and "resident" aliens. As John Higham observes, "the definition of a 'non-resident' alien was never entirely clear, but the act had the effect of driving thousands of foreign workers to declare their intention to become citizens." A law was also passed allowing—in reality, encouraging—indigent immigrants to remigrate by providing government funds to pay for their fares. The only stipulation was that they must have been in the United States less than three years, and they would not be allowed into America again.[37]

A NEW EUROPE AWAITS

Even before the end of the war, discussion began to turn to the question of what the peace would bring for both immigration and return migration. Would both rise suddenly—or were the immigrants now more content and at home with America, especially with the wage gains brought by war production? Rumors began to float that changes might be in store. A Croatian newspaper in Chicago reported in November 1917, "The news is going around that after the war two or three millions of people may leave the United States." The newspaper cited reports of numerous requests for ticket information from steamship companies, a prediction by New York's immigration commissioner that two million would depart for Europe after the close of the war, and similar expectations by the head of the U.S. Chamber of Commerce and other business leaders. A Hungarian newspaper in Chicago, short days after the signing of the formal peace pact with Germany in mid-1919, told of reports that 1.3 million would leave soon, carrying back $4 billion in savings.[38]

Despite such predictions, the docks were not immediately thronged with ticket-waving remigrants, although the numbers began to increase. In the year following the November 1918 armistice the returns hit 123,522 and they continued to rise until 288,315 left during 1920. The influx entering the United States, however, numbered 141,132 in 1919, mushroomed to 430,001 in 1920 and then exploded to 805,228 for 1921. It was apparent that the docks would be overcrowded with eager Europeans—but they would be entering, not leaving, the United States.[39]

Before this fact was grasped, however, anxiety gripped the employment departments of American industries: word went out that the nation was short either 4 million workers (according to a speaker at the First National Immigration Conference, in early 1920) or not less than 5 million (testimony before a House committee at the same time). *The Nation*, nervously surveying the employment scene that year, noted that arrivals at that point were only exceeding departures by small numbers and warned gloomily that the exodus of Poles, Finns, and Bohemians "has been limited only by the ability to obtain passage by sea." According to a writer in *Outlook*, "capitalists are cudgeling their brains for remedies." Two Chicago businessmen proposed to import 5 million Chinese.[40]

Part of this outward flow back to Europe was stimulated by the birth of new states there: Czechoslovakia, Lithuania, Latvia, Estonia, Poland, the Kingdom of the Serbs, Croats, and Slovenes (eventually Yugoslavia). There was also a drive for an independent Ukraine, rumblings of new status for Ireland, and redrawn borders over many areas of the Continent. In the land of the czars, the Bolsheviks had come to power and now called for help building a workers' paradise. An estimated 12,000 rushed to the USSR in the first eighteen months after the armistice, and U.S. statistics put the total for 1921 at 15,229. The Soviet Union also attracted large numbers of radical Finnish immigrants from the United States who had turned against capitalism in the mining and lumber camps. Some 10,000 Finns went to Soviet Karelia from the early 1920s through 1934.[41]

Among the multitudes crossing eastward in steerage during the postwar crush was Constantine Panunzio, an Italian immigrant who had taken American citizenship and was now curious about the increasing remigration. Members of two national groups he talked with "had a distinct idea that they were going to a new world"—Yugoslavia and

Czechoslovakia, created by the peace talks. Stories had reached them of the Czechoslovak government dividing up large estates and selling the land to poorer classes, and it seemed in their eyes that the new world was no longer the United States: "We have a new country now, the kind of country we used to fight for when we were young. We have the chance to make it a republic now. We go back to make just the country we want."[42]

Immigrants in America buzzed with news of the "great changes in Europe." During the war, Croatian nationalists had spread the word among their compatriots about advancing the southern Slav cause. Aware that many immigrants steered clear of political talk and looked forward only to returning to the family farm, the Croatians had their cause argued by a returned immigrant who was dispatched back again to America as a political bird of passage. The government of the new Kingdom of Serbs, Croats, and Slovenes quickly created an emigrants federation to send out literature and undertake other projects aimed both at keeping some control over the immigrants abroad and bringing more of them home. Conversely, the Hungarian regime, beset with chaos as a result of its wartime defeat, sent out word for emigrants to stay put for the present.[43]

Campaigns for Irish independence from Britain had long been a staple of Irish immigrant life in American cities, and events in the war years now held out promise that the break was at hand. But though the Irish had carried, even flaunted, the mournful burden of their "exile," in reality they were one of the premier groups of the Old Immigration and had achieved considerable status in American politics, business, and labor organizations. Newly arriving Irish still tended to be unskilled, taking their places at the bottom of the employment ladder; but as David Doyle has argued, by the turn of the century "Irish America had attained class-structure parity with native stock Protestant white America." As early as the 1890s, Irish-Americans could claim thirty-six members of the House of Representatives, four U.S. senators, members sitting in the Cabinet and on the U.S. Supreme Court, as well as important appointments in the diplomatic service. Although many Irish-Americans were still located in unskilled jobs, where they jostled with the New Immigrants, if they raised their gaze only slightly they could see others of their group among America's manufacturers and millionaires.[44]

Still, events in Ireland were not altogether encouraging to those dreaming of returning to a quiet, safe homeland. The Irish home rule fight had been making headway, and Britain's desires to avoid wartime rioting in its own backyard discouraged oppressive action against protesters. The Irish parliament, Dáil Éireann, was proclaimed in 1919 but banned by the British within months; however, it quickly installed a workable court system over much of the island. When Parliament in London passed the Anglo-Irish treaty in December 1921, giving virtual independence to four-fifths of the island, the Dáil ratified it the following month. Part of the nationalist movement rejected these steps, and a bloody civil war continued until the 8,000 antitreaty republicans surrendered on 24 May 1923. The turmoil did not encourage returns.[45]

Poland was a different case. Chafing under lengthy partition by the neighboring states of Germany, Russia, and Austria-Hungary, Poles called their overseas settlements "Polonia" and considered them a fourth province of Poland. Polonia even developed an emigration legislature. During the war the Polish Central Relief Committee in Chicago created the Return Migration Commission to prepare for the movement homeward once the shooting stopped; a similar group was operating within Poland.[46]

Feuding between different groups in Polonia marred these efforts, although the creation of an independent Poland in November 1918 briefly papered over the splits. Requests for passport and visa information began to pour into Warsaw from Poland's sons and daughters abroad. When the first Polish consul arrived in New York in July 1919, he was immediately beseiged by thousands waiting in front of the consulate to apply for passports home; he had to close the office at times because of the crush of applicants. Advice booklets proliferated, warning would-be remigrants of the need at home for money, skills, and especially organizational know-how. "We will see you in Poland," announced one. "Let's go back!" urged another.[47]

Much attention was focused on the Haller Army and others who had made it to Europe to fight for Poland during the war. Some had even joined Poland's post-1918 battles against its Soviet, Lithuanian, and Czechoslovak neighbors, but large numbers of veterans returned to the United States before deciding to go back to Poland for good. In November 1921, the Polish military minister in Washington sent out word that preparations were being made for uncultivated land in Poland to be distributed free to 500–600 veterans of Haller's Army. Preference would go to outstanding soldiers, invalids, and the most decorated, but they had to be present in Poland in early spring 1922. Records of the Association of Polish Veterans in America indicate that a bureaucratic nightmare quickly developed as veterans in America sought to learn whom among them had been selected. They were finally informed of this only two days before they were due in Poland on 20 March 1922.

Polish scholar Adam Walaszek estimated after going through records of the program that only fifteen Haller veterans eventually claimed their land.[48]

In Polonia, meanwhile, the return fever mounted. Mass meetings were held in Chicago, where pleas to go back were made. Plans were announced for formation of Polish cooperatives in business and agriculture, to be run by remigrants. One observer concluded that it looked like everyone would be returning. And, indeed, the Poles' rush home reached 10,109 for 1919, rose to 19,615 in 1920, and hit 42,572 in 1921 before dipping to 33,581 in 1922 and falling sharply to 5,439 in 1923. The return total never exceeded 3,700 annually from the United States for the remainder of the 1920s.[49]

The fact that remigration began to slow after 1921 reflected the new reality of life in Poland: a country devastated by war, in existence as a modern nation only briefly, torn by internecine feuds, beset by its neighbors in sporadic warfare—such a country was simply in no condition to devote much attention to those returning. In addition, the remigrants were coming from America, a land which not only had escaped the horrors of the Great War but which had enjoyed an economic boom. They were not prepared for what awaited them.[50]

Conditions were disastrous. Inflation hit the returners immediately. The U.S. dollar was worth 9 Polish marks at the end of 1918, but by the close of 1923 one dollar equaled 6,375,000 Polish marks. For some this was a windfall, but many had changed dollars too soon. The returned emigrants quickly organized their own protective groups—the Association of Poles from America, the Alliance of Reemigrants from America, and others—but frustrations began to drive some of them back. And during these difficult months, letters from Poland soon acquainted those in Cleveland, Milwaukee, and elsewhere with the realities of life for the returned emigrants.[51]

Despite the obstacles, many remigrants launched businesses and some managed to buy farms. But the rush back to independent Poland was, overall, a failure. No central planning department provided information for those returning, villagers began to look down on the "Americans" who expected so much, and other residents were given priority on land parcelation. Remigrants found their dreams of a democratic, affluent, peasants' Poland highly misguided: "I was surprised and indignant on seeing that people do not bathe in villages, they do not know what a bath is, whereas most country cottages are joined directly to barns and pigstys," one remigrant complained. Essential goods were scarce or absent, and many felt that the standard of living had fallen since their original emigration. "Nowhere is there more poverty than in Poland." Other Poles who came back grew frustrated with local officials. One man had money saved to buy a small plot of land but was told that his application would take eight months. He then began a small shop and was doing well until the tax collector came, followed by other officials who informed him that since he was a U.S. citizen he would have to close the store. Embittered, he gave up and sold. Emigration to other lands—France, Canada, the United States—began to increase once again, and one scholar maintains that 20,000 remigrants from America had turned and gone back to the United States by 1924. A consulate official in New York admitted that those who came back to the United States "usually become the biggest enemies of Poland."[52]

When the war was drawing to a close in 1918, the cry through the Polish settlements in America had been, "Let us save Poland first of all!" But by the time the emigrants' congress met in Detroit in 1925, disillusionment had set in and the new slogan of Polonia was, "The emigrants for themselves." Soon U.S. citizenship was inserted as a requirement for membership in the Polish National Alliance. Return dreams were fading. The patriotism of returned emigrants, a former Polish vice-consul conceded, "was a flower which grew fast, but also died very fast."[53]

AMERICAN CONCERN OVER THE EXODUS

Europeans going home for the reconstruction of their homeland—Poles, Czechoslovaks, Lithuanians, Irish, Finns, Yugoslavs, Ukrainians—these and other travelers heading east at a time of expected American labor shortages had U.S. business experts worried. The War Labor Policies Board, still functioning after war's end, received a confidential report early in 1919 which argued that to block the return flow would simply give substance to the allegations of European revolutionists. Far better to open wide the channels of communication so that letters would flow back to the United States informing potential remigrants that there would be no "fabulous sums" paid for serving in the Red Army, that land would not be given free to Hungarians, and so on. Truthful accounts would then reach those "who are preparing to return because they have fallen under illusions as a result of being ignorant of the true state of affairs in their respective countries." The later Polish experience demonstrated the accuracy of these predictions.[54]

A more direct attack was launched within the United States by the Inter-Racial Council of Frances Kellor, who had become more of an activist on the assimilation issue. The council took over the American Association of Foreign Language Newspapers, formerly a feature service, and began running advertisements such as this in the foreign-language press in 1919:

ARE YOU GOING BACK TO YOUR OLD HOME?

Here, in America, one has no right idea of the bad condition of business and trade which now reigns in Europe. . . .

And now your new land wants you for an American, in every sense of the word—she wants to share with you the victory which she has won. America victorious will now, together with the Allies, enter a period of prosperity such as she never had before. . . .

The lack of food in the Old World is terrible.

America must feed the world. This means work on beautiful, fruitful farms, for those who long for the country.

Your native country needs that you remain in America to make safe the markets, to help build the world with American surplus materials and money which the world needs.

The employers everywhere recognize that the workingman has come to his consciousness—recognizing the rights and honor of labor.

This means better working conditions, better living conditions, and better wages. . . .

Don't throw away your job to go to Europe, not knowing more about the conditions and whether they want you.[55]

Through such arguments and thinly veiled warnings, the "100 percent Americanism" of the war years entered the postwar era. The spirit of superpatriotism gained momentum just as the predicted labor shortage turned instead into a labor glut, with serious unemployment. Aggressive Americanism found fertile soil in which to thrive in this period of insecurity, and the immigrant who longed to return to Europe was a frequent target. Remembering former president Theodore Roosevelt's wartime pronouncement that "we have room for but one language," the 1919 American Legion convention urged Congress to require all aliens to learn "the American language."[56]

The AFL that year of 1919 recommended a two-year suspension of immigration, after which applicants would be admitted only if they first gave written declaration of their intent to become citizens. One union journal claimed that 80 percent of wartime disloyalty cases had been against aliens, and the head AFL organizer for New York City believed that foreigners should be forced to learn English: no union literature in foreign languages, no organizers hired who spoke foreign languages. A similar approach was followed by the Hotel and Restaurant Workers

Union, which ignored the lower levels of its industry where immigrants were numerous: "If you are an American at heart," an official of the union said, "speak our language. If you don't know it, learn it. If you don't like it, MOVE."[57]

To leave the story of labor's new postwar approach resting on such examples would be incomplete, however, for in September 1919 the Amalgamated Association of Iron, Steel, and Tin Workers launched an all-out strike, with AFL backing, against the steel industry. As historian David Brody has shown, pressure for the strike came "from below"— from the largely immigrant force of unskilled and semiskilled workers, who joined with skilled workers to rebel against reversion to prewar treatment. That treatment included long hours, recriminations against union members, and a deaf ear to wage requests. Workers were disheartened after the gains and favorable treatment of wartime. The strike was bitter, and coming in the aftermath of the Bolshevik revolution in Russia, with threatened communist revolts elsewhere, the confrontation was soon presented as one of "Americanism vs. Alienism," as the New York *Tribune* argued. The fact that large numbers of strikers were immigrants who were not fitting into American life was seized on by company spokesmen, as was the disclosure that strike leader William Z. Foster had formerly been a member of the syndicalist Industrial Workers of the World. Southern blacks were imported by the steel companies in large numbers during the strike, but it was also noted that immigrants expecting to return to Europe stayed on the job; they still had monetary goals to reach. These developments, along with vicious repression by police in the mill towns and a turn of public opinion against the "revolutionary" strikers, broke the back of the union drive and it collapsed early in 1920.[58]

With the strike's end, AFL president Samuel Gompers moved farther along the road toward total opposition to the New Immigration. The newcomers were unassimilable, he argued; they either refused or were unable to become part of American life. He also feared their radicalism. The steel strike's failure may have helped drive him more rapidly in this direction; at any rate, he publicly repudiated Foster in 1923 after the strike leader visited the Soviet Union and praised communism.[59]

RURAL AMERICA'S WORRIES

Other stresses tearing at the nation's earlier wartime unity originated in rural America, long suspicious of both the growing importance and the growing evil of large cities. An aggressive religious fundamentalism swept through many rural districts after the war, riding a crest of anti-evolution sentiment that produced the Scopes "monkey trial" in Tennessee, helped secure passage of the Prohibition amendment, and created an environment within which a new Ku Klux Klan grew spectacularly.

This was a Klan that targeted immigrants, not Negroes; that based its hatred more on religion than race. The Klan's Chicago magazine *Dawn* listed among its basic precepts the standard anti-Catholic rebuke that "no Klansman can hold allegiance to any foreign government, emperor, king, pope or any other foreign political or religious power." Also, the Klan's members favored "prevention of unwarranted strikes by foreign labor agitators"; and "each Klansman believes his rights in this country are superior to those of un-naturalized citizens." Blacks were noticeably absent from lists of Klan enemies, and the organization even held out hope for Protestant immigrants from northern Europe to join its newly created subsidiary, the Royal Riders of the Red Robe. The Klan scorned non-Protestant immigrants and charged that unclean foreign settlements existed because corrupt American politicians ignored hygiene laws. Public schools were forcing native-born pupils to mingle with "children of ignorant or degenerate persons," *Dawn* complained, adding: "The majority of newcomers are ungrateful. They fill their aching stomachs in this country, amass wealth which they never dreamed of before, discard their rags for decent business clothes, surround themselves with comfort and prosperity, and then abuse this country that did not invite them and is not holding them here."[60]

John Higham has traced the development of American nativism through various stages to the 1920s, when race feeling (which classed New Immigrants as members of inferior races), superpatriotism, fear of Bolshevism, and rural anxieties over big-city evils came together to produce the nation's most far-reaching restriction of immigration. After earlier efforts were found wanting, the 1927 National Origins Act attempted to base national limits on the percentages each country occupied within the entire American population. The final act limited immigration to 153,879 yearly, with some 126,000 to come from countries of the Old Immigration: Britain was allotted 65,361, Germany 25,814. Countries of the New Immigration, however, could send just 24,222 yearly, topped by Poland's 6,524 and Italy's 5,802.[61]

Immigrants were targets for a variety of Americanization drives, conducted in schools, within church denominations, and by community watchdogs of purity. A wave of "speak American" demands swept the nation, typified by the Iowa governor's proclamation making English the state's official language. The governor asserted that freedom of speech did not guarantee the right to speak any other language than English, and he barred use of foreign languages in schools, public places, even over the telephone.[62]

IMMIGRANTS RESPOND TO ATTACKS

The nativist campaigns were felt immediately by the immigrants. Social worker Mary McDowell found Czech immigrant women terrified at rumors that they would be forbidden to speak their own language, this after their organization had raised $8 million in Liberty Bonds and $25,000 for the Red Cross during the war. They complained also of the "Raid for Reds," the growing searches for evidence of radicalism in the offices of immigrant groups. Some said it was like Russia; others said it was like Prussia. Polish government officials claimed that even the Roman Catholic clergy were going along with Americanization and blamed this in part for declining remigration. The Ford Company's famous wartime Americanization program shifted its focus in the early 1920s; now it aimed at repressing any signs of union sympathies among its employees.[63]

Immigrants began to voice a variety of new complaints about the country. Many of their objections centered on growing restrictions on freedom in this supposed land of the free, restrictions sometimes directed against immigrant drinking, sometimes against mere expression of opinions. The new Prohibition amendment set off a rash of police searches for bottles in the aliens' railroad baggage, and the harsh oratory of the antialcohol campaign seemed to bear out earlier fears that this movement was directed mainly against foreigners. Interviews on a returning Scandinavian ship showed that, although Prohibition was never the sole cause for leaving America, it was often mentioned as one of the reasons.[64]

Many were also offended by the rising 1920s sabbatarian movement, which sought an end to all Sunday activities (except industrial labor!) not church related. A Catalan returning to Europe complained, "You Americans talk liberty like it was God Almighty; but you can't get a drink of wine without breaking the law. And look at the places where you can't go to the theater or a ball game on Sunday, or drive an auto—some where you can't even buy a package of cigs!" He also criticized treatment of Negroes, another issue often cited by returning immigrants; the Catalan told of being threatened after he helped a Negro girl find a street address, and again when he tried to resist a streetcar conductor who told him to leave a section reserved for "niggahs."[65]

These searches, these warnings, these disdainful scowls and suspicious looks all had an impact on those who had once dreamed of living and working in the Land of Liberty. For many, it showed that America's much-vaunted freedom was slipping away. "It isn't the old America any more," a Norwegian said as he ended seventeen years in the Northwest and headed home. "That was a fine country, a real freedom's land, but not any more." A Swedish woman added: "Used to like America, but it's a different country now." Many others agreed, especially the Finnish socialists heading to Soviet Karelia; one of them wrote facetiously, "America is a 'free country,' we do not need any kind of opinions here." The United States was all right, a Scandinavian dressmaker told an interviewer as she crossed the Atlantic eastward, "if you think the way they want you to think." A Swedish official expressed dismay at the school system for inspiring children with an uncritical love of the United States, and a Norwegian returner said that, though Americans might criticize different aspects of their society, "when that flag goes up, don't you say nothing!" The broad impact of post-World War I nationalism was well illustrated in an Irishman's recollection that returned emigrants "used to say that it was against the law in America to dispraise the country."[66]

Immigrants returned to Europe for many reasons in the years 1880–1930. Many had achieved their financial goals; others went because they had failed. Many were homesick or had specific family issues that drew them back—inheritance, aging parents. If patriotic devotion sometimes pulled the immigrants homeward, patriotism in the United States often repelled them, especially the "100 percent Americanism" of the World War I era and afterward.

A cautionary note, however: there is danger in fitting all those who returned into neat categories. The revolt against American superpatriotism would be only one item in a long list of reasons for return, in which nostalgia and dreams of land purchases mingled with bitterness at the actions of a policeman. The editors of a recent volume of Italian emigrant letters argue that, in much writing of immigration history, "all too frequently the immigrant becomes a helpless victim of large impersonal structural forces such as economic cycles and labor markets. Nowhere do we gain insight into the personal motivations and ambitions of individuals or the impact of the migration experience on them." The immigrants described here, making up their minds to return, represent millions who juggled myriads of home thoughts from abroad with multifarious American realities—and then turned eastward, boarded steamships, and headed across the Atlantic. There were perhaps as many motives as there were individuals.[67]

Turning their backs on the New World, where they were increasingly seen as the "wretched refuse" of Europe rather than "huddled masses yearning to breathe free"—phrases joined in Emma Lazarus's poem on the Statue of Liberty base—the immigrants steamed toward their own shores. Now their American money could be used among their own people, and so could their American experiences. The impact of neither, however, could be predicted as the steamship surged through the foam.

PART THREE

The Remigrant at Home

CHAPTER 6

Peasants Back on the Land

New structures were going up all across Europe as the nineteenth century closed—houses with tile or slate roofs instead of thatch, a large window with a view to the road, walls of brick or plastered white, doorways sporting brass knobs and shiny varnish. Boards replaced logs, tile replaced thatch. Italy's popular statesman Francesco Saverio Nitti surveyed the scene across the Mezzogiorno and reported proudly:

> In tiny villages, the pick-axe strikes down filthy hovels, patrimony of the feudal age, and the new homes of "Americani" began to rise and old dwellings are renovated; a transformation in the building art occurs. Around the urban centers land is divided into lots which "Americani" try to cultivate with their own hands, using their own ready cash and intensive culture and small-holding family farms spring up.[1]

These "American" villages brought together many of the tangible, as well as intangible, results of return migration. The "American houses," which sprang up like mushrooms after a rain, were quickly noticed by visitors. When Carlo Levi was exiled to a tiny southern Italian town by Mussolini in the mid-1930s, his early walks through the poverty-stricken district brought him to some homes that were surprising, different. These had a second floor and balcony, even fancy varnish and doorknobs. They were exceptional among the drab huts of a peasant village. "Such houses belonged to the 'Americans,'" he noted.[2]

The American houses were outward symbols of changes that affected

The "American house" began to appear in many areas of Europe as return migration swelled. Sometimes possessing a slate roof, at other times with tiles, shingles, and painted walls, the house contrasted sharply with others in the village. The Polish community of Lubczy in Pilzno presented this contrast in 1911: on the right is the former home, a thatched hut; on the left, the new house constructed after return of the immigrant who stands proudly at the side of the road. Photograph Collection, from the Historical not only the Continent's physical surfaces but also its inner life, customs, and traditions. For the remigrants were often different people when they returned, and their accomplishments soon reached beyond the Italian saying, "He who crosses the ocean can buy a house." Their determination, as well as the structures they built, could inspire their neighbors. It was said that "the people went wild from envy and desire" when a Pole returned and bought land on which he built two houses in his Galician community. He and his deeds were noted; his capacity for achievements and the source of his funds were obvious. All were explained by the fact of his round-trip journey abroad. Asked about the home he proudly showed, an Italian commented simply, "America bought this house."[3]

This chapter takes up the basic question of what the remigrants did with their money. Also addressed are their impact on innovation in agriculture and the workplace, their encouragement of modern practices, and the ways the surrounding community dealt with these returners, their ways, and their money.

THE LAND QUESTION

Houses were important, but there were other objectives behind the years of labor on factory, coal mine, and railroad crews in America. Land was at the heart of the peasant's desire, the only investment he considered in most cases. Studies in Italy, Hungary, Galicia, Finland, and other centers of European return migration all document the importance of land purchases among those who had ventured across the ocean and come back. Houses were generally second in importance, followed by shops or other businesses, and then personal interests such as education, paying back debts, medical care, or simply a richer lifestyle. As Emily Greene Balch found in her examination of the Slavic emigration, the peasant was most careful that he kept his land: he might have a leaky roof or be in debt for his crop, but he knew that from property flowed the answers to important questions—his children's marriages, pensions of his elderly parents, paying off the inheritance of brothers and sisters. On land rested status; from land came dignity.[4]

Much of the American earnings had arrived home before the remigrant, and funds were also sent by emigrants who would never return. Dispatched through banks in the immigrant communities of New York, Cleveland, Chicago, and other cities, or through postal savings letters, American dollars had immediate impact on the European communities. The "America cheque" was eagerly awaited in Ireland at Christmastime, and a common saying was that American money kept many a small farm alive. Politicians in European parliaments looked with awe at the changes stemming from this massive flow, and a member of the Galician assembly, the Sejm, admitted that his country's population was "entirely dependent upon the economy of another nation." Money sent back to Lucca reached "unexpected proportions," an Italian writer observed; migration "is really the most important industry in this province." Far to the south, the prefect of Cosenza conceded that if the local economy had "not totally collapsed, it is only because migrants keep sending money." A Norwegian district public health report for 1910 agreed that America "has saved farm and home for many a man in this province."[5]

But when the emigrants began returning, they carried even more dollars with them, often in belts or hidden elsewhere in their clothing. A local study in Transylvania found that returning emigrants brought back $400–600 each during the early years of the century. A Galician community was receiving an average of $850 from each emigrant in the years just before World War I, and it was estimated that the entire province of Galicia gained $232 million annually from its emigrants. Reports from various Italian districts claimed remigrants averaged from $250 to $1,000 each in their wallets and hiding places as they arrived home; in 1920, the peak year, the total received from all emigrant sources in Italy was estimated at one billion lire—$200 million in U.S. money. Remigrant savings became the principal source of cash in areas of the Italian south. Small wonder that a U.S. dollar bill was often pinned alongside the sacred pictures on the inside wall of a peasant's cottage.[6]

The villager coming back with money was frequently a target for the unscrupulous, who sought to take advantage of him. But as a new source of funds for borrowing he often drove other moneylenders out of business, for his interest charges could be much lower. Mortgage credit costs in Galicia declined by as much as 20 percent in 1900, as the emigrants began arriving back in numbers. Debts that were previously "worked off" could now be repaid, in coin.[7]

Quickly they turned to the land question. Land purchases, in fact, had usually begun while the emigrants were still abroad, and funds were dispatched home with instructions to buy a small plot here, another there. An Italian told of his five years of construction work in New York, "a backbreaking job." But each day, he recalled, "I dreamed of the land I would one day buy with my savings. Land anywhere else has no value to me." In fact, such emigrants had frequently known of available land before they originally departed; that was what prompted their trip. And so they figured and refigured its cost as the ship steamed westward, and later kept calculating how much more was needed as they toiled in the smoke and din of a mill or construction site.[8]

The story of a family from Zaborów, in Galicia, was fairly typical: the peasant inherited 2.5 morgas (a morga is 1.38 acres), and his bride brought another 2.5 morgas to the union. The husband then emigrated to the United States and Canada for five years, spent most of his time laboring in a Chicago laundry, and sent home enough money for the purchase of five more morgas. When he returned he was able to buy an additional four morgas, for a total of 14—more than 19 acres—as well as purchase some machinery and improve buildings. An Italian case had an unusual twist: Antonio Mangano told of remigration to the district of Isernia in the Abruzzi, where for years "almost the entire population rented and tilled the soil of a single landlord." Several crop failures drove the peasants abroad in large numbers, but before long many began to return, purchasing and dividing among themselves "the same lands which some time ago they abandoned, paying fabulous prices for them, too."[9]

This was what was new about traveling to the New World: the grand opportunity to make a mammoth economic leap upward. Earlier sojourns in nearby areas of Europe had meant family survival, but crossing the Atlantic now signified a chance to actually improve and enlarge property and to thereby assure well-being for years to come. This is what drove much of the increasing flow to the west and sent the birds of passage flitting back and forth, always trying to get enough for that additional plot, to pay off previous purchases, or to remove the load of debt from their backs. A Port of New York inspector quizzed fifteen entering Italians who said they had previously been to the United States: "When I asked them what they did with the money they carried over, I think about two-thirds told me they had bought a little place in Italy, a little house and a plot of ground; that they had paid a certain sum; that there was a mortgage on it; that they were returning to this country for the purpose of making enough money to pay that mortgage off." Most of those who returned to the village of Szamosszeg, Hungary, bought land, one investigation showed, and many thereby raised their status immediately to that of a "wealthy peasant."[10]

Such information helps explain a major fact of return migration: those returning generally went back to rural areas. Dino Cinel has documented that Italians emigrated heavily from districts that had abundant land for sale; when it was not available, however, they often turned to militant organizations instead. A mayor in a Sicilian town noted the emigration from his community but admitted that, "when they came back and realized that they could not buy land because it was not for sale, they left forever." Few others followed them, he added, "since there is no hope of buying land upon return." Some could buy houses, but not land.[11]

This generalization proved true in many other regions of Europe. Even overpopulated areas often experienced little emigration if there was no hope of purchasing land on return. When large landowners refused to break up their holdings, the door was closed to new peasant farms. A Pole in Detroit indicated the importance of available land when he wrote home to his brother: "I have nothing to return there for [,] either[,] because we lost the property, and if I am to be a *parobek* there, then I prefer it here." Examining data for east-central Europe, Ewa Morawska surmised that it was more than small farmers or tenant farmers who ventured abroad in hopes of building up funds for future purchases: members of farmers' households also had hopes of acquiring land and a house, and even the children of poor cotters came back with such dreams. But those with no such prospects remained at home or, if they emigrated, did not come back. There was nothing for them there.[12]

Remigration tilted heavily toward land-hungry farmers. It was very rare in Finland that groups other than farmers or tenant farmers returned permanently, according to one investigation, and children of these two groups ranked next in percentages of remigration, indicating that they too were interested in seeking land. In fact, only 11.3 percent of those classed as workers returned, the study found, compared to 57.8 percent of the farmers and 47.1 percent of the tenant farmers. Swedish investigations confirmed that the flow of remigrants was stronger to agricultural districts. It all affirmed what had become a basic truth: land was a major goal of return migration.[13]

Another Swedish study sought to determine what had been done with the money carried back to Långasjö parish by remigrants in the early years of the century. Of twenty-three individuals traced, sixteen had purchased a farm or farmland, four had saved the money in a bank, and others used some of their funds to buy a home, start a business, or construct farm buildings. Some accomplished more than one of these goals with their American money.[14]

Many of the plots sold to returners came from nearby small owners or from large operators hard pressed for cash. In 1880 the resident agent for a large Irish estate in county Wexford testified that "returned

Yanks" had purchased many of the farms sold from the estate; only they possessed the required money. A similar story was told in the Italian province of Cosenza, where 450 of the 500 acres offered for sale during one month went to *Americani*—farmers who either held no land previously or had emigrated to make possible the enlargement of their holdings.[15]

In Galicia many large landowners cut up their estates and sold off portions when they found themselves in difficult financial straits. They were often suffering, in fact, because heavy emigration brought labor shortages that pushed up wages for their farm workers; at the same time, competition from North and South America sent grain prices plummeting. Their own large estates were often wretchedly run. Parcelation—breaking up large holdings—was the answer, with up to 90,000 acres in Galicia sold through this system annually at the beginning of the century; the total for 1902–12 from parceling out Galician large estates was put at 607,000 acres. Balch encountered an estate of 700 acres for sale in Hungary, quickly grabbed up by a hundred Ruthenian peasants who raised the required $40,000 themselves. When a lawyer offered to supply the $64,000 needed for another land purchase, he was turned down: the peasants announced that they would send to America for the money. In Russian Poland, more than 2.5 million morgas—3.45 million acres—were acquired by parcelation from 1873 to 1914, paid for almost exclusively with money earned abroad. America was becoming peasant Europe's bank.[16]

The importance of parcelation has been debated by historians. Julianna Puskás, for example, contends that local studies in Hungary show that other peasants provided most of the land purchased by "Americans." In other areas, however, large landowners often moved into the business of subdividing their own properties, either to reverse their own declining financial status or simply to provide extra funds for new projects. The practice was so widespread in one Polish district that fifty-eight people made their livings as agents parceling and selling land. In Italy, the dominant form in many areas was that of land sales to remigrants by other peasants, although in northern Friuli and interior Sicily there was some splitting of large estates. On the whole, parcelation of estates was not widespread over Italy, Robert Foerster concluded, and it was conspicuously rare in Calabria, which nevertheless recorded extensive purchases by the *Americani*.[17]

One result of the rush by remigrants to buy plots was a sharp rise in the commercialization of farmland across vast areas of Europe, areas that had seldom known the business of buying and selling land. Generations of land transfers by inheritance, with only an occasional sale, now gave way to the business of haggling and selling and purchasing plots for cash. But this occurred only after thousands of small farmers, tenants, renters, and others dependent on the soil had heard tales of high wages in America, made the crossing, and labored in American industry long enough to save the required amounts. Then they came home with their bounty.[18]

The results were momentous. Twenty-five percent of the real estate in a village in Sweden's Småland was purchased by U.S. dollars brought back by returners in the period from 1897 to 1941. Even poor land, overpriced land, vineyards devastated by phylloxera sold, much to the surprise of Italian officials. Peasant ownership of land in some districts of Hungary was reported to have increased 418 percent from 1899 to 1903, while in both Austria-Hungary and Congress Poland districts of heavy Slavic emigration showed an increase estimated at 173 percent. Later, after World War I had brought border changes, returning emigrants to the new Poland bought almost half of the property being vacated by Germans in the western districts.[19]

Important social changes lay within these purchases. Small landowners were buying more land, but those without land were buying their first plots, sometimes only tiny holdings, often purchased from hereditary owners. The most dramatic changes were in Italy, where the number of landowners increased by 280,000 from 1901 to 1911, then continued to shoot up in the next decade, nearly doubling for the nation as a whole. American money was widely credited as the motor behind these changes. Sicily, for example, by 1921 had three times the number of landowners it had recorded in 1911; accordingly, the numbers of renters and daily farm laborers declined sharply. This meant that the percentages of households headed by men who were both farmers *and* landowners rose sharply in areas of heavy emigration. It was true in Palermo Circondario, whose households went from 25 percent headed by farmer-landowners in 1881 to 40 percent in 1921; or Chiavari, rising from 38 percent in 1881 to 60 percent in 1921. The broad impact of these changes can be seen in a 1909 statement by an Italian senator: land purchases by returning emigrants, he asserted, constituted "almost an economic revolution. . . . The land thus passes rapidly into the hands of the cultivators," replacing the idle rich who previously lived off their rents. One of the Italian parliamentary investigators claimed it had brought "a grandiose change" to the Abruzzi.[20]

European parliaments buzzed with talk of somehow channeling this land rush, protecting the purchasers, reducing or removing obstacles, and from these acts benefiting the nation at large. Finland's Migration Committee attempted to assure that remigrants could farm their own land, since this was what they were returning for. Italy heard repeated proposals for organizations to be formed such as a "Public Institute for the Acquisition of Small Property in Favor of Returnees from Emigration," or state-run projects to break up the *latifundia*. Nothing emerged from these proposals, however. In fact, the government urged remigrants to put their dollars into bonds of the Italian Savings Association, and when it failed most of its 400,000 creditors were returned emigrants. A similar fate befell Greek returnees who loaned money to their government only to see it default.[21]

Other countries debated various plans. Members of the Galician Sejm heard pleas to drop the penalties on illegal emigrants in an effort to encourage their return; these proposals came to nothing. Ukrainians charged that officials were aiding the settlement of Poles in Ukrainian-dominated eastern Galicia by closing credit facilities of the Parcelation Bank to their group. After World War I, Polish returned emigrants received help from their new government's Remigration Bureau, mainly to locate land for sale. Similarly, Sweden's National Organization against Emigration sought to act as the remigrants' agent in seeking land.[22]

Not all governments wanted everyone returning to buy land, however. Early in the century Germany, mainly Prussia, worried over increased land purchases by Poles in the East Mark (Prussian Poland) and sought to prohibit these. The leader of the Östmarkenverein was blunt in describing his organization's aims: "The objects of this association are: To make every school thoroughly German, every public meeting German, and every government official German; to print the German text before the Polish in every Polish newspaper, and—may God grant it!—to preach only German from the pulpit some day." A German critic noted, however, that during 1904 in Posen and West Prussia twenty-nine German estates were "lost" to Poles, and Poles continued to buy land in the East Mark even at high prices.[23]

These estate transfers pointed to another result of remigration in most areas: land prices shot up rapidly, often advancing three times or more as potential buyers bargained for plots near their homes. Prices in Cosenza were reported to be 200 percent above the land's true value, and a report to Italy's minister of foreign affairs stated that "able speculators, foreseeing the return of the emigrants, acquire large amounts of land at a low price, and after cutting it up into convenient units, they resell the land at a very high price to the repatriates." The same was reported in other areas: land prices in parts of Hungary rose 50 percent above 1875 levels by 1900, then zoomed to "unreachable heights" by 1913. Balch found Croatian districts where arable land that previously sold for $60–80 per yoke (a yoke was the amount of land needed to feed one person) increased to $400. A tomolata (0.69 acres) of land at Bisanti in Italy's Molise, previously sold for $80–90, went for $200–300 after repatriates arrived in numbers; land near Chieti that sold for $60 per acre a decade earlier was bought by a remigrant in 1907 for $500–600 per acre. A strip of land along a frequently overflowing river in Calabria, valued at $200, was purchased by a returned emigrant for $920.[24]

That such inflated prices did not reduce sales was testimony to the persistence with which returned emigrants pursued their goals. One historian of Polish emigration has argued that the sales were possible because the "conservative peasant" was "imbued with the idea of the sanctity of the soil" and lacked other outlets for his savings. Unfortunately, if the peasant was then forced to hire workers, he found that farm wages had also gone up—doubling in Hungary from 1901 to 1910, doubling and tripling in parts of southern Italy. It was ominous for the futures of those who had gone abroad to earn enough to become substantial farmers at home.[25]

ALTERNATIVE INVESTMENTS

Not all remigrants wanted land. Many directed their savings instead toward starting or buying businesses, ranging from small shops like the Barbiere Americano that Antonio Mangano discovered in an Apulian village to large enterprises such as the steelworks built by Polish returnees in Wyszków. Many simply sought to live off the interest of their savings. It was noted that money flowing in from America created by itself greater demands for goods, stimulating the birth of new businesses even without the additional direct investment by those coming back.[26]

Many preferred to put their funds into small shops. As late as 1955 in Ireland the claim was made that every pub in Killarney was run by a "Yank," and one observer ventured that "there is scarcely a town or village in Mayo but has a few shopkeepers who started life in America," accumulated some money, and returned home. Italy too had remigrant barbers, watch makers, and harness makers whose presence was noted by visitors, their shop walls invariably featuring pictures from American magazines; more attention was probably drawn, however, to the Sicilian saloon that flew the Stars and Stripes. Large travel agencies were established by remigrants in Sweden and Greece, and several savings banks were founded in Romania by a successful emigrant who came home after six years in America. In the early 1950s in Greece, Theodore Saloutos encountered a department store, the country's largest modern dairy establishment, the first modern Greek hotel, and a string of tenement houses, all built years earlier by returning emigrants.[27]

With vast amounts of American money arriving, the possibilities existed for even larger enterprises. A Russian Jew from Bialystok came back with $20,000 and launched a factory, and Finland gained several industries founded by repatriates: Jaakko Vassi's machine shop at Ylihärmä, which began making harrows and enlarged to become an exporter of agricultural machinery; the Wickström motor plant in Vaasa, started by a repatriate from Chicago who produced engines for boats and threshing machines; and the Mieto Brickworks of Kurikka, whose founder had worked in a similar enterprise in the United States. Finland also gained mining and construction companies with the remigrants.[28]

Poles in America were the major targets of patriotic efforts to convince those who had emigrated to come back and assist the nation—in this case, to help with Polish reconstruction after World War I. Business skills were high on the list of desired attributes. "Our profit and dividend will be a rich and happy People's Poland," proclaimed the Polish Mechanics' Association, the major firm created by Poles abroad and transferred to Polish soil.[29]

Launched in Toledo, Ohio, in 1919, after the new state of Poland had been created, the Polish Mechanics' Association had strong ties to political groups both within Poland and in Polonia. It developed a membership of small investors totaling 18,343 by 1921 and reported capital of $3 million that year when it transferred its activities to Poland. Soon the association owned a bank in Warsaw, a tool, lathe, and machine casting plant, and two brickworks. It also published a journal and launched other businesses connected with machine tool manufacture. The Polish Mechanics' Association remained the most successful of the large enterprises set up in Poland by remigrants, although it eventually needed government help; several of its ventures still exist.

Some two hundred cooperatives and corporations were launched by other Poles coming back from abroad, from movie production firms to shoe factories to transportation companies. Many failed in the chaos of the 1920s, however.

AGRICULTURAL INNOVATION

A fundamental question ran through the experiences of these remigrants who bought land and launched businesses, and it has remained to perplex modern scholars: Was this remigrant an innovator in
his homeland? Was he, in Francesco Paolo Cerase's phrase, "a crucial
carrier of social change"? The issue was present in 1910 when the Italian Parliament probed the pitiful conditions of Sicily and the Mezzogiorno and concluded hopefully that "mass emigration and return
migration have become the most powerful source of social change in
Italy." The debate continues today as modern scholars examine the impact of homegoing guest-workers from western Europe. Some of today's scholars have looked back to the era of mass emigration to study
whether innovation might be expected from a vast return flow. Cerase
and Cinel investigated the historical situation of Italy, with Cinel label-
ing the remigrants "conservative adventurers"—that is, basically unin-
terested in innovation on return. Cerase offered two major categories of
remigration: the "return of conservatism," in which returners from
abroad used their earnings to rise in traditional activities, and the "return of innovation," through which needs and aspirations developed
abroad were pushed ahead at home with new means and abilities.[30]
    To venture into the subject of innovation is to enter an area where
precise measurement is impossible. Land sale statistics are no measure
of the innovative use of a farm; in fact, in this terrain quantification
could mislead. As Virginia Yans-McLaughlin found in her investigation
of Italian immigrant families in Buffalo, New York, the varieties of
human relationships "underscore the shortcomings of historical explanations and conclusions based solely or primarily on quantification."
Relying on statistics, she argued, narrows the historian's vision by re-
stricting what can be investigated, revealing only "a one-dimensional
view." As a modern student of Croatian emigration put it, "the influence of the repatriate has not been measured statistically, nor can it be."
With these warnings in mind, one can still examine the impact of the
remigrants in various contexts, drawing on reports by contemporary
observers as much as possible. But it must be realized that economic
and social conditions of the homeland frequently set restrictive ground
rules for innovation, and this fact was often more important than the
ideas carried by the homegoing emigrant. The surrounding culture
could welcome change; it could also restrict it or even snuff it out.[31]
    Remigrants began arriving back home in numbers at a critical junc-
ture for European agriculture. The old order of agricultural society,

bowed under centuries of tradition, was giving way to the pressures and opportunities of an era driven by new markets, transportation systems, capitalistic approaches, even different crops. Countries that had relied on farming populations for capital now found these sources inadequate, unable to meet national needs. Again European eyes turned overseas: reports told of American farmers using new machinery, with abundant harvests that were already being exported to Europe. America, source of increasing amounts of money sent or carried home by emigrants, might now become the starting point for a revolution in European peasant agriculture.[32]

Changes envisioned by those who considered U.S. influence crucial were presented optimistically by the Norwegian Immigration Commission:

> The returned Americans put their stamp upon it all; the rural districts are scarcely recognizable. The farmers are not so burdened with debt as before; people live better, eat better, clothe themselves better—thus the population itself improves. All those who come from America begin to till their soil better than it was tilled before. . . . Crop rotation is introduced, machinery is acquired, the buildings of the farm, dwellings as well as others, are improved, more rational dairy methods are practiced, and gardens are laid out.

Returned Americans had a "very considerable part" in the changes in the Sörlandet district, "in some places even the largest part," the commission added. Remigrants' influence went so far in Ireland that it was sometimes exaggerated: in parts of Ulster the term "Yankee" came to be applied to any farm implement brought in from the outside—even English wheel plows.[33]

Seeds carried back in remigrant packs produced plants that were new and impressive to neighbors. A Polish diplomat noted in 1924 that those returning were growing previously unknown vegetables and flowers in their village plots, and this desire to reproduce things discovered in America was common. And so tobacco plants thrived in Norwegian soil, tomatoes in Finland, and lettuce in Ireland, while those coming home to the Mezzogiorno helped shift a primarily cereal culture in certain areas to such items as almonds, cherries, and grapes. Some Calabrians who worked in vineyards under improvement contracts even went to America to earn the funds needed to replace vines destroyed by phylloxera.[34]

America is credited as the source for flax seed brought to northern

Ireland, and in Finland it was returners who first used turnips for cattle feed. Also, mink farming began in Finland's Ostrobothnia region in 1928, started by emigrants returning from America, and in southern Italy it was noted that livestock raising—particularly swine, goats, sheep, and oxen—increased sharply as the remigrants began showing up in numbers. A Finnish analyst concluded that the development of local agriculture in the Malax district would have been impossible without the influx of "Americans."[35]

If farms produced new crops and took on new appearances, and people in isolated Polish communities could be heard shouting "arajt" (all right), then something more than land transfer was taking place. Not all grew directly out of the remigrant experience, however: the increased use of iron plows, reapers, threshers, mowers, and harrows in Italy during the early years of this century came mainly through large land-owners because of the high cost of labor. Parliamentary investigators there noted, however, that returned emigrants often turned to new plows and fertilizer that others rejected. With government advisory committees' encouragement, "the so-called *americani* . . . became good farm cultivators," according to a 1910 document. In Yugoslavia and Hungary contemporary reports told of the returned emigrants' willingness, even eagerness, to acquire better farm equipment with their savings.[36]

In Finland, especially, American farm implements such as harrows were quickly adapted to Finnish conditions, and a Turku machine shop produced copies of American combines in the early 1900s. Equipment also was imported from Sweden and England, it should be noted; still, Finnish scholar Reino Kero concludes, the spread of American farm machinery was probably facilitated by the large return migration of Finns from the United States. Those coming back to Norway were regarded as being ahead of nonemigrants in buying farm machinery.[37]

Often it was an idea, a method, a new approach to doing things. County Galway folk told of a Cahergowan remigrant who introduced a new way of binding wheat sheaves using the wheat itself to form a sort of belt—called, inevitably, the "American Belt." On the other side of the island, in Ulster's Mourne Mountains, a massive dry stone wall still stands, a field boundary known for generations as the "Yankee Wall" after the emigrant who came home from California and built it. A priest at Rabice, in Galicia, was cheered not only by the fact that almost all the parish's 200 persons who had emigrated to America had come back but also because they then made major improvements in the water drainage in their fields. Similarly, a repatriate in Norland, in northern

Norway, successfully farmed swampy land that local people had not believed could be cultivated.[38]

One of Finland's most noted remigrants was Kustaa Kaltiala, born in 1879 and a veteran of at least two trips to America. Kaltiala came back bursting with ideas: hay was now dried on wooden racks rather than allowed to lie low; trees were thinned from his forest to increase growth; new animal shelters were built; cattle breeding was improved and more intensive methods of cultivation adopted. Kaltiala also began the practice of feeding turnips to cattle. Elsewhere in Finland remigrants inaugurated large-scale chicken raising and constructed American-style barns that allowed better air circulation and made the collection of cow manure easier. Houses made of boards rather than logs appeared in some rural districts as the "Americans" came home. And on the Norwegian coast a new net for catching herring was introduced by returnees.[39]

Latvia's agriculture was prodded into the modern era partly through the efforts of one determined remigrant, Kārlis Ulmanis, who lived in the United States from 1907 to 1913. Ulmanis, who later became Latvia's prime minister, was a dairy worker in Nebraska before enrolling in the University of Nebraska's School of Agriculture, from which he graduated in 1909. He wrote for dairy and cheesemaking trade journals and ran a dairy in Texas before heading home again. Back in Latvia, Ulmanis helped form Mazpulks, a youth group based on the American 4-H movement, encouraged the spread of agricultural fairs, and all the while pushed to modernize Latvian farming through use of fertilizers, crop rotation, and improved food processing and sanitation. His campaign has been called the "Americanizing" of Latvia.[40]

Countries that still relied heavily on agriculture for capital cheered as investment increased in the agricultural sectors, thanks to those returning. Often such investment was aided by rural organizations. This was especially true in southern Italy, a region marked by the enthusiasm of remigrants to join agrarian leagues, mutual aid organizations, and cooperatives. At Paolo the peasant league's secretary reported that two-thirds of the membership consisted of those who had returned from America, and the claim was made that most of Sicily's peasant league members were remigrants. A remigrant organized a cooperative at Matera, in Basilicata, with members aiding each other for planting and harvesting, their leader supervising the sale of produce. The several hundred members realized a profit of up to 75 percent of their investment in raising goats one year.[41]

But it was something more than specific innovations that were seized on by many of those extolling the impact of remigrants on agriculture. A Norwegian questionnaire in 1913 found most respondents agreeing that, although the returned emigrants were not pioneers, they deserved praise for their work habits, their dedication to the task at hand, their open-mindedness concerning new approaches. The Norwegian Immigration Commission stated that "they have a will to take hold, and have in America learned a rate of work, which is different from what people are accustomed to here at home." A Swedish doctor agreed that, although many had never worked on American farms, "they have learned to work more intensively out there."[42]

Ireland abounded with tales of their returnees' work habits: rising in the morning before anyone else, throwing themselves into their jobs with a vengeance, and in the process sometimes managing to look a bit silly to their neighbors. "I'm telling you they were hard workers," an Irishman recalled; "they would have a day's work done before the men of their townland would get out of bed." At Balinskelligs they told of "Tom the Dog," who had learned early rising in America: on summer mornings he would get up at 4 A.M. and head to the seashore for fertilizer, but on arriving back at the farm at 6 o'clock and discovering his brother and family still asleep, he would shout: "Get up you pack of devils, or what do you think! There is nothing in this devil of a country but sleep and beds!"[43]

Sleep and beds might well be targeted for change, but peasant agriculture had many other areas in need of improvement. In any case, the general conclusion of recent scholars, as well as many turn-of-the-century observers, is that the overall modernization of European agriculture did not result from the contributions of remigrants. The primary basis of such conclusions is that few repatriates had worked on American farms and therefore could not pass on ideas from America's fast-changing agriculture. The Italian parliamentarian Pasquale Villari noted of the Italian remigrant, "in America he was a navvy, he worked in the mines or on the railroad; he will certainly not have improved his notions of farming. Isolated as he is, he will still stick to primitive methods. He will certainly live more comfortably but he will contribute little to the general prosperity, to agricultural progress which is essential." This point was reaffirmed when an Italian critic talked with an *Americano* and discovered that he knew only one thing about farming in the United States: cornfields there appeared in "perfect rows." That, of course, was what he witnessed from his passing railroad car.[44]

An investigation in 1938 of what emigration over the years had meant to a village in southern Poland concluded flatly that remigrants had no impact on farming practices—because they only knew Polish agriculture, not having worked on U.S. farms. Another Polish study found that some of the efforts to introduce new crops failed, and also that those returning did not buy better tools or equipment. Only those coming back from Germany, to Polish areas near the German border, introduced new farming methods, for they had worked on large German farms. What one Irish expert discovered while interviewing more recent returners was probably true for earlier periods: differences in the American scale of farming, as well as in many of the crops grown, made it a separate system of agriculture from that followed in peasant areas of Europe.[45]

In truth, the factors that lured thousands overseas with plans to return home quickly also directed them straight to American industry, not to American farms. Agricultural labor in the United States promised only long-term rewards at best, through eventual land ownership and the luck of abundant harvests in tandem with good crop prices. In that turn-of-the-century period other regions of the globe held out better prospects for pioneer cultivators of the soil, and those wishing to launch a new life in agriculture increasingly headed instead to Canada, the Argentine, or Brazil.

But travelers passing westward through Ellis Island often had their sights set to the east, on land back in the home village, and this fact limited them to jobs in America that promised regular paydays while leaving them free to quit at any time. Savings could then be accumulated week by week while living costs were reduced penny by penny. Beyond this, their reluctance to invest time and money for learning English, and fears of leaving their own group's enclaves, further limited the options. The result for most was minimal contact with American farming. "None of the people I knew worked on the land in America and the only farming they were familiar with was the Irish," a county Galway widow recalled. The same thought applied to many in the years of mass emigration.[46]

For an unfortunate number of remigrants, their return not only brought no improvement for their region's agriculture but also failed to raise their own living standards. Zeal contributed at times to their downfall: many paid too much for the plots they had coveted for so long, then discovered too late that they had acquired the landlord's poorest soil. Knowing nothing of modern fertilizers, they were unable to enrich their holdings; further, their new hectares or morgas were still too limited to justify purchase of machinery, which they could not afford at any rate. "I came back to buy land," one remigrant told Italy's parliamentary investigators. "But the land is not enough and I have to hire myself out, as in the old days." This was a frequent step. Robert Foerster concluded that "not many emigrants certainly can live quite without working after their return, particularly not many in Basilicata." Those buying land seldom got enough for "independence," he observed. Predictably, large numbers were eventually forced to sell, then recross the ocean to again build up their savings.[47]

In a return movement of such scale there were examples to the contrary, of course. The Irishman who introduced the "American Belt" to Cahergowan demonstrated by his intimate knowledge of American grain harvesting that he had spent time on farms overseas. An investigation of returning Finns found that a portion of the remigrants had worked on American farms. Similarly, Norwegians who attempted extensive clearing projects, drained and farmed northern swamps, and (according to local public health authorities) were more daring in attempting new agricultural methods—these gave evidence of their experience across the Atlantic, probably on midwestern farms. As fantastic as their stories may have seemed to listeners at home, these tales nevertheless revealed a close acquaintance with American agriculture, as shown in the recollections of comments made by a returned Norwegian: "He told me, when he was plowing [in America], he had to take a sight on some landmark in the distance to keep the furrow straight. He plowed with one or two teams of horses. And he only plowed one round, back and forth each day. His fields were that big."[48]

These experiences pointed to a major difference between the earlier and later migrations to America, in some ways to the broad contrasts between Old Immigrants and New Immigrants (although, as has been noted, by the end of the nineteenth century the Old Immigration also had shifted heavily toward young males who sought industrial jobs). America's Midwest and Great Plains farm belts are also German-Scandinavian belts, filled with communities in which Norwegian, Swedish, Danish, and German names are still common. Finnish names are also frequent in certain "cutover" farming districts of northern Michigan, Wisconsin, and Minnesota. There is no comparable broad farming region of extensive Italian, Polish, or other Slavic influence, although there exist individual rural communities of these nationalities dotted over the map of the United States. This difference suggests that Scandinavians and Germans may have been better prepared than many others to introduce innovations in farming when they returned home. In the final analysis, however, it was the situation in the native land—not just the new ideas from abroad—that were crucial. In some areas, agriculture was already shaking out of the cocoon of tradition; this was especially true in Germany and England, where agricultural revolutions were well under way and any remigrants with American farm experience might have had an impact. Although most emigrants who returned to Europe had worked in major industries in the large cities of the United States, Scandinavians and Germans would have had more opportunities to visit relatives or friends on farms, perhaps working there during factory layoffs.

And when they returned to Europe, they went back to farming in large numbers: almost 6,700 remigrants in 1920 (out of 50,000 living in Norway) were concentrated in Rogaland, one of Norway's major agricultural areas; another rural district of southern Norway, Vest-Agder, counted 4,500 adult male remigrants out of a total adult male population of 19,000. Ingrid Semmingsen notes that, accordingly, almost every farm there would have averaged at least one returned emigrant. These men and women were then in a prime position to introduce American ways. Comparable conditions in Sweden can be glimpsed in a report from the Jösse region of Värmland, discussed during the Swedish Royal Emigration Commission investigation of 1908–13:

> When you later have the chance to hear old farmers in a reading room or cafe in Arvika conversing in English, you understand how it all fits together and find it hardly surprising. Many have been in America and have returned—you notice that, when you go along the roads, in the clothes and Panama hats on some of the men working out in their fields as if they were on the farm in Minnesota.[49]

But in many other peasant agricultural districts, the goals of the remigrants themselves combined with the community's attitudes to reduce chances for innovations. Cinel called those returning to southern Italy "conservative adventurers," because they were initially daring in heading to a strange and distant land for work but then returned "determined to preserve as much as possible of their social and personal past." This, Cinel concluded, made their migration a conservative phenomenon. Cerase went farther to label the remigrants' rush for land in the Mezzogiorno "an anachronistic reaction" against the revolution that was sweeping over agriculture elsewhere. The old order had failed;

but those going back to southern Italy, seeking to have their own small holdings, "tended to reproduce an agrarian structure which had already proved itself not viable." The high hopes for remigrants and their money, Cinel added, "provided an escape from unpleasant social and economic realities, which demanded radical reforms in the South." Expecting great changes to come automatically, the remigrants could and did postone the difficult task of uprooting traditional usages. In northern Italy, on the other hand, changes were already under way, and the returners' new ideas apparently helped accelerate the process.[50]

Southern Italian conditions were duplicated in many other areas, especially in central Europe, where the small holding held sway. For many the plot of land became like a savings account, to be used for bringing in rental money. The community in such districts then directed both the funds and ideas coming from abroad into traditional methods and activities.[51]

Because of such developments, historians have judged that the remigrants' impact on rural Ireland was negligible, and J. M. Synge's encounter was probably not at all unusual: touring the Aran Islands in 1898 to gather material for *Playboy of the Western World* and other works, Synge fell in with a returned twenty-year veteran of the United States who had lost his health overseas and now had even forgotten his English. "He seemed hopeless, dirty, and asthmatic," Synge reported.[52]

Similar results could be found elsewhere. The return to postwar Poland was described as generally conservative, with funds usually spent in the traditional manner. During the years between the wars in Hungary, it was mainly large estates, not small farms such as those operated by remigrants, that introduced new equipment and varieties of wheat. Despite early expectations, the Italian parliamentary investigation of the south concluded that new farming methods had generally not been introduced by those returning. And in 1924 the Finnish Migration Committee asserted that most of the returning emigrants had failed; they had seemingly learned nothing during their years abroad.[53]

As long as they went back to their old villages, settled again among their own people, and took up their former occupations, the odds were enormous that the remigrants would not lead an agricultural revolution. An Irish tale made the point bluntly: a woman who returned from America wanted to put a second floor on the cottage she shared with her two older brothers who had remained on the farm. "By God," she was lectured by one of them, "You're not going to make New York of Ballyfad!"[54]

TECHNOLOGY AND GADGETS

Among the vast numbers emigrating into American cities were some who would carry home the memory of America as a cornucopia of gadgets, new machines, and technical know-how. The peasantry could remain untouched by these, but away from agriculture changes were under way among those prepared to welcome new ideas from overseas. All this was part of the long-term Americanization of Europe, going on for years and continuing today as American inventions are carried abroad by businesspeople seeking markets while European inventions are modified in the United States and sent back.

Contributions of remigrants in this interchange were extensive. These ranged from bringing back American phonographs, Singer sewing machines, bicycles, hatchets and doubled-bitted axes, among smaller items, to developing iron rolling mills. New logging procedures were introduced in Finland and new fishing methods in Yugoslavian coastal waters, and in the Apennines of northern Italy the first regular rural bus service in Lucca was launched by a remigrant. Not far away in Fornaci di Barga, aging brick and cement kilns were transformed by a group of returners into an industrial establishment that subsequently attracted large paper and textile mills and a munitions factory.[55]

Similarly, Finland owes some of its industrial growth to remigrants, especially in the critical wood-processing industry. The wood pulp thermal-mechanical process is believed to have been introduced by Georg Holm, who had worked in Massachusetts pulp and paper mills before returning in the 1890s. He was technical director in at least two Finnish paper mills that began using the new process by 1897, with American equipment. Holm also helped introduce American paper-making machines. The manufacture and adaptation of American-style harrows in Finland has been mentioned above, as has the machine manufacture by Jaakko Vassi, who worked for a Chicago motor manufacturer.[56]

Others brought changes to stores and shops. Irish pubs now sported padded seats. Theodore Saloutos encountered a beauty parlor in Greece run by a former resident of the United States who had trouble keeping his help; as soon as he taught them American hairdressing methods, they were hired away by other shops. His parlor became "probably the most modern beauty shop in Athens." In Hungary's Nyitra district a remigrant opened the Amerikansky Schtore, which sold a wide variety of items never gathered before under the roof of a single business, including bathtubs and building materials. But the major difference from other local shops was that it had only one price for each item: bargaining was not allowed. This idea began to appear elsewhere as the emigrants returned from America.[57]

In communities with a large number of remigrants, American influences could reach deep into the minutia of daily life. Carlo Levi found people in the village of his Mezzogiorno exile using a vast array of American-made goods, including scythes and scissors, and they even spoke of pounds and inches instead of kilograms and centimeters. "Life at Gagliano was entirely American" regarding these devices and measuring systems, he said. Significantly, they did not give up ancient customs; they merely used modern instruments to carry them out.[58]

SKILLS AND KNOW-HOW

To many, the impact of the returned emigrants was less in carrying back scissors and pulp-making machines than in knowing how to tackle projects, big projects. One man coming back to Poland built a new house for his parents, after finally locating the materials for a shingled roof, wood floors, brick walls. All the while he attracted onlookers who soon began helping just to learn how it was done in America. Those returning to Greece saw the need for better roads in rural areas and led campaigns to build them just as they fought for better sanitation within towns and homes.[59]

The remigrants' reach in business extended far beyond the Amerikansky Schtore. Alfred Vagts has documented the extensive flow back to Germany of emigrants who acquired business skills, as well as making important contacts, in the United States. This *Rückwanderer* frequently brought back capital as well as know-how, for some who emigrated for an apprenticeship worked their way up into the directorates of cotton firms, banks, and other businesses during America's nineteenth-century economic boom. Many were Jews from southwest Germany such as Friedrich Kapp, who kept his connections with financier Jay Cooke when he returned and became one of the founders of the Deutsche Bank. The bank, in fact, relied heavily on returning emigrants for leadership, and it based much of its growth on good relations with American firms. Charles L. Hallgarten, born in Mainz in 1838, was representative of this group: he followed his father to America and became involved in banking, then returned to Frankfurt where his energies went both into finance and into introducing such American activities as adult education libraries and the Community Chest. Siegmund Bergmann became an assistant to Thomas Edison, and eventually a partner, before going back to open his own electric works in Berlin in 1891. Similarly Philip Rosenthal fled his Westfalian home at age seventeen and went to America, where he became director of porcelain sales in different regions for a Detroit firm. Sent back to Germany in 1879 on business, he founded his own porcelain factory in Selb which grew to 5,000 employees by the time he was driven out by the Nazis in 1934.[60]

Surveying these activities, another German writer argued that the remigrants' contribution was a broader view of the world, affecting their own thinking and stimulating the spread of outside ideas in societies that were cramped by tradition. Combined with their determination to work hard, this meant that returned emigrants could do much in a society that welcomed as well as needed them.[61]

THE COMMUNITY'S RESPONSE

Would local people be receptive to their returning countrymen? That was the key. Saloutos reported on a remigrant who was shocked by the backwardness of sanitation in his native village in Crete, so he built an outhouse. He hoped to influence others to acquire the habit of using a toilet, but villagers were suspicious and shunned it, preferring to eliminate bodily wastes along the roadways and in the brush near their huts.[62]

Since most of those returning went back to farms rather than into the business world, direct transfer of extensive American commercial and industrial knowledge was problematic. In addition, those accustomed to the availability of building materials, electricity, natural gas, even abundant hot water, ran into problems as they realized these were still rare luxuries in the village. A county Galway commentator said that American ways were generally not introduced because "it couldn't be done here. . . . American ways are so different from those at home." In business, he added, an Irish proprietor would succeed because he was very close and tight, not "too keen on making profits," but in America an open-handed approach was necessary to succeed.[63]

It all seemed to come down in the end to a proper match, a proper fit between remigrant and homeland, whether in agriculture or business or industry. It required remigrants to introduce things that would work, not like the Greek who later brought back an X-ray machine to a village without electricity. Returned emigrants had to adjust their thinking, but this was often hard to do. And just as the family and village had often guided their activities overseas, they could restrict their range of options at home. Cerase found that the most bitter comments came not from interviewees who had returned to farming tiny plots in the Mezzogiorno, or who came home to live off their savings, but from those who attempted to launch new businesses, new approaches to gaining a livelihood. They were angered and frustrated by the community's reactions. The truth was that, in the end, the man or woman coming home from America was often part of a minority too small to dent tradition. Their contributions often lay instead in awakening a general spirit of modernism, a curiosity about the outside world.[64]

The American house in a Polish, Italian, or Irish village was tangible evidence that remigrants could do things differently: they were in some ways agents of change. The change, however, often did not extend beyond their own property. In Julianna Puskás's telling phrase, "the money showed on the village but not in the village." It changed the outward appearance but not the way people lived. Having dreamed of owning more property at home while laboring in the bowels of America's industrial colossus, remigrants were not ready to give up their traditional dreams when they came back, and one result was the further multiplication of dwarf holdings, often too small for independent living. They followed their parents' occupations. Still, they brought back stories of another life, and some new vegetable plants; they might even be aware of some different farming methods, and the timber industry in northern countries benefited from the remigrants' days in the northwoods. It may not have been a frequent development, but the proper match between innovative remigrant and receptive culture did occur occasionally.[65]

Things had to mesh. Countries such as Germany which were accelerating industrially could use repatriated business skills more readily, and workers with experience in U.S. banks and machine shops returned to take advantage of the opportunities. The Amerikansky Schtore was forerunner to an array of changes. In such districts the community's limits on innovation were more elastic. This would also be a crucial point for those on a round-trip ticket whose baggage from America consisted not only of money, or tools, or seeds but also of ideals of democracy, labor's rights, and individual worth. These, too, would challenge traditional ways in Europe.

CHAPTER 7

Workers' Ideas Carried Back

A merica was more than the land of the dollar to the outside world; it was also a country whose people had chased out aristocratic rulers, separated church from state, elected men of humble origins to leadership, and opened fertile ground for the growth of new philosophies. This America too crossed the Atlantic eastward with the returning emigrants. Though forming a baggage that was intangible, these ideas and images attracted attention and often angry opposition at home, frequently simply because they were new. "There came with him something of a fresh breeze from the land to the West," a contemporary observed of a repatriated Swedish pastor. The thought occurred in different ways to many who watched as the returning army of travelers arrived back in the villages.[1]

This chapter examines the ideological aspects of remigration, including the returned emigrants' roles in labor movements, political campaigns, and nationalist drives and the rising opposition from government and religious authorities.

EXPECTATIONS IN THE HOMELAND

For some who returned, America was viewed as opening a new route to their own nationalistic goals at home. As early as the American Civil War, immigrant Thomas Francis Meagher recruited his Irish countrymen for the Union Army by proclaiming, "If only one in ten of us come back when this war is over, the military experience gained by that one will be of more service in a fight for Ireland's freedom than would that of the entire ten as they are now."[2]

Measuring the impact of ideas is notoriously difficult. Further, American concepts and currents had other ways of reaching Europe than in the minds of remigrants—as witness the tremendous popularity across the Continent of such late nineteenth-century reform books as Henry George's *Progress and Poverty* and Edward Bellamy's *Looking Backward*. Both were translated into European langages immediately, and George's single-tax plan was adopted in several German, English, Danish, and Norwegian cities; Bellamy's popular futuristic novel gave impulse to the restructuring of the European socialist movement. Such books represented one threat to the established order from America. Returned emigrants, however, were another threat and often a more real one: persons coming back could make speeches, even to illiterates; they could travel to the meanest hovels, conspire, change plans to fit new circumstances. And their frequent participation in local societies and church groups often prepared them to move into governmental affairs. Having once lived in America they were uninformed, uninvolved peasants no more.[3]

One of the Continent's most successful challengers to the status quo was Guiseppe Garibaldi, whose military leadership was crucial in unifying the Italian states in 1861. And this same Garibaldi had once lived on Staten Island and made candles in a Bleecker Street shop. Few remigrants had such dramatic impact. But, though their names may not appear today in national histories, the consequences of their return were often great, especially when added cumulatively to ideas spreading through other sources. This can be glimpsed in the case of a Slovenian remigrant encountered by the young Louis Adamic: the repatriate claimed that while working in Pittsburgh he had once shaken the hand of President Theodore Roosevelt himself. What is more, the former steelworker even referred to the American president as Tedi and claimed that everyone in the United States did so. Few Americans would have doubted such a report; few Europeans would have accepted it unquestioningly.[4]

Such tales brought both hope and fear to those at home. Sharp divisions over the potential benefits of repatriation were grounded, of course, on different expectations of what those returning might do. Hungarian officials, for example, considered blocking Slovaks from returning because of threats to the regime's unity. Conversely, Poles who agitated among their countrymen to go home after World War I determinedly sought the transfer homeward of ideals of democratic self-government.

One such Polish agitator took inspiration from what he had observed some years earlier in a Finnish village while escaping czarist rule. He met there a Swedish Finn just back from three years' work as a miner in the United States. What impressed the Pole was not the money brought back by Nils Peterson but his library—cheap popular editions of Marx, Eugene V. Debs's speeches, Jack London's writings, socialist pamphlets, magazines, newspapers. Armed with ideas from these books and his American experiences, Peterson gave lectures to the villagers, and that first evening the Pole sat entranced as the remigrant explained self-government to the local citizenry. Much of what Peterson knew, the visitor realized, had been learned in America. To this Polish agitator, the example from a Finnish village spoke directly to the potential of the return movement for Poland: "I beg you," he pleaded with his returning countrymen, "don't go back only with money."[5]

A Europe torn by dissension between old and new, traditional and revolutionary, and by hundreds of ethnic, political, religious, and economic rivalries could look with either apprehension or enthusiasm on the returning numbers. Were they tainted? Were they loyal to the old ways, the old religion, the old leaders? Would they accept again the system under which they had once lived? The whirl of such questions meant that the welcome given to remigrant dollars often barely concealed the underlying fear, or hope, that this returned citizen might challenge the existing order.

LABOR ORGANIZERS

Because most labored for wages in America and knew American industry firsthand, remigrants were assumed to be ready to become labor movement activists. Social Democrats in Hungary cheered their return, for they looked to this group as a source of new skills for labor organizing, political action, and other struggles for human rights. A Hungarian editor in 1908 considered them "especially valuable" because "these are the hardened masses, who have learned their own strength in the fight with an industrial great power." After resettling, he predicted, they would not accept Hungarian restrictions on organizing and political expression: "The new, modern Hungary expects the returned emigrants to demand great social reforms."[6]

And in fact many had participated in American labor movements that challenged the capitalist order. When the Italian Workers' Party met for its 1892 congress in Genoa—the meeting that gave birth to the Italian Socialist party—one of the anarchist leaders present was Luigi Galleani, returned from his years in America which included founding the *Cronaca Sovversiva* (subversive chronicle) in Paterson, New Jersey. And just as British Chartists had recrossed the Atlantic earlier, such German radical leaders as Wilhelm Weitling and Friedrich A. Sorge came back to Germany after attempting to establish socialism within American labor groups. The same was true of Zygmunt Piotrowski and Michal Sokolowski, who promoted socialism among Polish immigrant workers in the United States and then returned to leadership positions in post–World War I Poland; Piotrowski became head of the TUR, the Workers' University Association.[7]

But it was clear that most emigrants who labored in American industry in the turn-of-the-century years were employed in bottom-level jobs, on railroad crews, as assemblyline helpers, or elsewhere in the great maw of the industrial machine. Union organization was seldom present, or strong, among them. Most had little experience to offer labor unions back home.[8]

An exception appeared, however, among those who came in contact with one of the few American labor organizations of the era that deliberately sought out immigrants, aiming its message at the drifters and itinerant workers passed over by the craft-based AFL. This was the Industrial Workers of the World (IWW), formed in 1905 under the principal leadership of western metal miners, a group whose ranks had always shown an extensive immigrant presence. The earliest center of western lode (underground) mining was Virginia City on Nevada's Comstock Lode, which reported in the 1870 census that 63.5 percent of its inhabitants were foreign-born, almost all Europeans. Unionism there was already well established. This pattern was generally followed as the mining frontier spread across the West in succeeding years.

Quite typical were the ethnic divisions present in the Bunker Hill and Sullivan Mine in northern Idaho in 1894: 84 native-born Americans, 76 Irish, 27 Germans, 24 Italians, 23 Swedes, 19 English, 14 Scots, 14 Welsh, 12 Finns, 11 Austrians, 8 Norwegians, 7 French, 5 Danes, 2 Swiss, and one each from Spain, Portugal, and Iceland. A Western Federation of Miners leader told the 1909 convention that fully one-half of their membership was foreign-born.[9]

This background was important in creating the new IWW's underlying ethos and approach to organization. The western miners' William D. ("Big Bill") Haywood called the IWW's "Continental Congress of the Working Class" to order in 1905 with the declaration, "I do not care a snap of my fingers whether or not the skilled workers join the industrial movement at this time. We are going down into the gutter to get at the mass of workers and bring them up to a decent plane of living." Soon the IWW spread, through the mining districts, among the harvest hands, along the railroads where hoboes showed their red IWW cards like tickets for riding "side-car Pullmans." It was an organization that unabashedly sought out those rejected by society and by other unions.[10]

The same was true of the Socialist movement headed by Eugene V. Debs, who ran for president five times and appealed for the support of those being ground by the capitalist colossus. While touring Michigan's Upper Peninsula in 1916, Debs encountered massive crowds of enthusiastic immigrants, their support all the more impressive to him because they had to "bear the brunt" of corporation control in tiny mining communities. He wrote to a friend after a massive parade and rally at Negaunee: "They were mostly Finns and other foreigners and all hell and the arctic regions could not have dampened their ardor or quenched their revolutionary fire. . . . I never saw a sturdier, cleaner, finer proletarian parade and I was prouder than a prince to have a place in it."[11]

These and similar other radical movements made impressions on many immigrant workers while also providing additional fuel for those who were already radicals before they stepped onto U.S. soil. Several returning Norwegians had learned their unionism and radical activism through the IWW, Socialists, or similar groups in the West and the Great Lakes region. Norwegian-American historian Odd Lovoll has observed, "It is revealing of trans-Atlantic connections that leading Norwegian politicians on the left directly experienced political dissent in America before engaging in reform efforts at home." Foremost among these was Martin Trammael, an IWW member who left the United States to become "the stormy petrel of Norwegian labor for twenty years" and editor of Oslo's Socialist daily. Several other Norwegian labor activists also began in the IWW in the United States, including Chicago accountant Erling Falk. After returning to Norway, Falk became editor of the radical labor paper *Mot Dag* ("Toward Daybreak"), which played a key role in 1920s infighting between the Communist and Labor parties. It was said of Falk that "he aroused extraordinary devotion in many able students, who later became prominent in Norwegian public life."[12]

Similar statements could be made of Olav Kringen, another Norwegian emigrant who returned home after working in leftist labor politics in America, including service in Minnesota as an editor of the Norwegian-language newspaper *Gaa Paa* ("Press Forward"). Kringen went back to Norway in 1897 and, from his position as a contributing correspondent, aligned *Gaa Paa* with the Norwegian Labor party's moderate reform wing. And Norway's feminist movement was bolstered by the return from America of Aasta Hansteen, a writer and painter who had emigrated in 1880. After nine years in the United States, she came home to become a leader in Norway's campaign for women's rights. Such two-way journeys provided further evidence of the exchange of philosophies and ideas accentuated by return migration.[13]

Finns, ubiquitous in the lumber and mining camps of the Pacific Northwest and Great Lakes regions, also sent activists home to launch political and union careers. Many had been connected with the Work People's College, a syndicalist school in Duluth, Minnesota, when the IWW was at its peak before World War I. Though some, such as Yrjö Sirola, were radicals before coming to America, most opted for radicalism in the process of raw struggles with the large corporations controlling Mesabi Range iron ore mining and similar industries. Sirola would later comment that his years in America provided the stimuli that pushed him into revolutionary socialism.[14]

A parallel route was taken by Niilo Wälläri, who arrived in 1916 at age thirteen by jumping ship. Wälläri worked in the mines, joined the IWW, and studied at the Work People's College. Deported to Finland in 1920 during the postwar American "Red Scare," he began a career in Finnish labor unions that eventually led to the presidency of the Suomen-Merimies-Unioni (Finnish Seaman's Union). The rolls of Finnish union leadership include many others who were active earlier in the United States, such as Kaapo Murros, A. B. Mäkelä, and Väinö Rüppa, all editors of Finnish-American labor newspapers before their return to Finland. Similarly, Oskari Tokoi—who would later reach the top echelons of Finnish government life—learned his socialism while working in American mines and after returning rose to become head of the Finnish Federation of Labor Unions.[15]

Sweden did not receive a major impulse of radical unionism from remigrants, according to one study, but it nevertheless gained several activists who had also taken the IWW route. Several were convicted in the wartime IWW trials, then deported to Sweden in the early 1920s. Edward Mattson, however, fled to Canada before returning to Sweden and launching a career as leader of the iron miners' union. Sigfrid Stenberg, a Swedish IWW activist who was arrested, imprisoned, and deported, later wrote from Sweden that he had lost none of his beliefs about the correctness of the IWW's vision. In a 1925 letter to IWW leader Ralph Chaplin back in the United States, during a time of mounting IWW factionalism, Stenberg asserted, "As far as the I.W.W. is concerned, I believe, that, in spite of all disruption within and all attacks from without, it will survive. It is after all the idea that cannot be downed." Swedish workers were reluctant to join an IWW-sponsored boycott of American goods because their own country was so small, he reported, adding: "But the question of the importance of a country should not be considered when there is a principle of international solidarity involved. However, I pound along in spite of all, because I consider it my duty to do so." Stenberg stated that fellow IWW deportee Ragnar Johnson was continuously giving speaking tours in Norway. And so the returned labor activists proselytized, pursuing dreams that had first taken form in isolated mining towns, lumber camps, and meeting halls far across the Atlantic.[16]

In addition to these remigrants who had learned their radicalism in North America, many others had already been leaders in European socialist or anarchist movements and traveled for short periods to the United States to spread ideas among their compatriots. Since they later worked with returning emigrant radicals at home, their activities merit mention here. Bernardino Verro, a socialist leader from Sicily, lived in Buffalo, New York, during his 1897–99 American stay, and Sebastiano Bonfiglio arrived in the United States in 1906 and was active in the Italian Socialist Federation before returning in 1911 to the Sicilian socialist activism he had known earlier. Socialist leader Nicolò Barbato was "probably the most popular class leader in Sicily" before his 1904 journey to the United States; he remained five years. Perhaps these European radicals were further influenced by observing firsthand the lives of their friends in America; however, as one historian concedes, "too little is known of the American experiences of these people" to do more than recite the facts of their travels.[17]

The record of returned emigrant labor activists is therefore a mixed one. It is clear that the mass of remigrants had not participated in unions in the United States and had little contact with the radicalism of turn-of-the-century American labor circles. But their numbers did include many who went back to industrializing European economies and tried to put into practice organizing skills and ideas from overseas. Sometimes the citizenry served to restrict, at other times to encourage, radical behavior. Measuring the remigrants' impact is difficult, but in general the evidence supports the conclusion that the optimism of European labor leaders over the impact of remigrants proved to be excessive.

Too few were experienced, as Julianna Puskás writes of Hungary, "and they were insufficient in numbers to become the moving force" behind post–World War I democratic upheavals. Should they therefore be ignored in measuring the broad impact of the return movement? Scarcely, for their new spirit and ideas "gave more life and momentum" to the growing union campaigns, as a historian of Italian labor has noted. And in specific activities they were important: "It is not by chance," Puskás observes, "that research into local history reveals that the 'Americans,' that is, the returned emigrants, are always to be found among the local activists during the revolutionary times of 1918–1919" in Hungary.[18]

AN IMPULSE TO POLITICS

Conclusions about remigrant influence are mixed when the focus shifts to political activities, although individual accomplishments were numerous and success stories dramatic. Whereas American and European industry had much in common, the contrasts were sharp between European government systems and America's free-wheeling political democracy. Many of those returning reacted in disbelief when encountering the restrictions still in force at home. Marcus Thrane, an immigrant socialist, was upset when he went back to give speeches in his native Norway in 1882: the Christiana Labor Society decided he was still too radical to use their hall for his talk.[19]

Others overcame their shock and began to agitate for local improvements. An observer in Cosenza, in the Italian Mezzogiorno, reported that, thanks to the remigrants, peasant societies had been organized in all communities of the province, often as mutual aid groups first. They were always based on the underlying philosophy that such organizations were economic necessities. Many of these evolved into political organizations. Elsewhere in Italy it was reported that remigrants were interested in local schools and public services and pursued these causes vigorously: "Social progress of the people, extremely slow so far, begins to make headway, thanks to the *Americani*." Emigration, it seemed, turned men's minds in the direction of "social ills and shadows," one historian of Norwegian emigration has concluded, and they began to work for improvement in their home communities.[20]

One of the social ills frequently tackled was illiteracy and the lack of schools. Scattered reports tell of the remigrants' desire for their children to go to school, their new feelings of shame over their illiteracy, their support for anything connected with learning. And so they brought back books and printed materials, set up circulating libraries, and flocked into the new village adult evening schools. The movement received a boost when the United States began to debate the use of a literacy test to screen out the masses of illiterate immigrants. Starting with a plan that was narrowly blocked in 1897, the U.S. Congress returned to the issue every few years until the literacy requirement became law in 1917. By then each American threat had stimulated new efforts by Italian politicians to build schools and increase school aid; the Italian Emigration Council supported a plan in 1903 to establish adult schools in centers of major emigration. The crush was so great to enter these schools by the early 1920s, as reports told of new American moves to restrict immigration, that police had to be used to control eager crowds of students.[21]

To others the time spent abroad led to an increased sense of national identity that motivated many to undertake other improvement campaigns at home. Remigrants in the southern Polish village of Babica supported construction of a local People's House instead of the new chapel that was sought by the local clergy and traditional leaders. Across Europe, elections, libraries, societies to help the poor, and community sanitation took on new interest for many returners. The expanding political rights of Irishmen sparked a wave of remigrant electoral participation that sent P. J. Smyth to Parliament from West Meath some fifteen years after his return from America. Some Irishmen would later argue that individual American doctrines were not implanted by such persons, but in fact many Irish emigrants had drunk deeply at the well of American democracy. This was especially true of the early Fenian leaders in America who launched their drive to liberate Ireland at a Philadelphia convention by adopting a constitution that was almost an exact replica of that of the United States.[22]

The record of returned emigrants in Europe is filled with numerous instances of public officeholding and other activism in local, provincial, and national affairs, including much work in forming voluntary associations. In a 1918 survey in Finland, respondents noted that remigrants "usually got elected" to local offices. "I suppose it was only the most adventurous and active people who went off and emigrated in the first place," one Finn observed. Another explained the preponderance of returned emigrants elected to school district offices by noting that they were more ready to express their opinions freely. A Greek labor leader reported that remigrants from America were often named to local committees "to help explain how things are done in the United States."[23]

And so the remigrant shows up over and over in lists of elected officials across Europe. These include Skulsk, Poland, where the mayor was a returned emigrant who came back after World War I. At least four remigrants sat in the Polish Diet in postwar years. "Yanks" were present in large numbers on Irish local councils, and at least two remigrants became mayors in Greece, one serving twenty-five years.[24]

Similarly, Anna-Leena Toivonen's survey of Finnish government records and personal memoirs found that many who rose to positions of responsibility had become "self-made men" through their American experiences. Fifteen remigrants sat in the Finnish Eduskunta (parliament) from 1917 to 1933, eight belonging to parties on the left, seven on the right. The total included one of the first women in that body, Eveliina Ala-Kulju. One scholar asserts that Eduskunta members Iisakki Penttala and Jaakko Mäki had become acquainted with social democratic ideas in the United States and carried these along with other concepts of government back to Finland. Another Finnish political leader was Otto Andersson, a Swedish-speaking Finn who returned from America and with other remigrants launched the Social Democratic Association in Munsala in 1911; eight years later he too was elected to the Eduskunta. In Dalmatia, meanwhile, returned emigrant Ivan Lupis-Vikić, a Croatian, served as a deputy in the Diet, while outside the meeting halls he was secretary of the Association of Returned Emigrants in Split.[25]

Beyond these, America sent back to Europe three men who would later become their countries' top leaders: Johan Nygaardsvold, a construction worker in the United States, rose to become prime minister of Norway; Oskari Tokoi, who labored in American mines for a decade before coming home to Finland in 1900, was elected to Parliament as a Social Democrat in 1907, became speaker in 1913, and then was named prime minister of newly independent Finland in the chaotic days of 1917; and Kārlis Ulmanis, who returned to Latvia in 1913 after eight years in the United States, became the new country's first prime minister in 1918 and its president of state in 1936. Ulmanis's activities on behalf of Latvia extended outside government work into the realms of modernizing agriculture and encouraging support for education. Throwing himself into the struggles that carried Latvia into independent statehood during World War I, Ulmanis eventually served as prime minister seven times. He was taken away by the Soviets and died in 1942. It is significant that Finland and Latvia gave the reins of leadership to men experienced in America's political life as they began their existence as independent nations, and that Norway and Latvia also had remigrant leaders as World War II came on.[26]

Others served just below the position of prime minister. Yrjö Sirola, previously noted as a labor agitator, was foreign minister of the Red Guard provisional government when Finnish Communists captured Helsinki during the Russian Revolution of 1917–18. More widely known to Americans is the tragic Czech leader Jan Masaryk, who committed suicide or was pushed to his death in Prague in 1948 as the Iron Curtain descended over Czechoslovakia. Masaryk had gone to the United States in 1906 when he was twenty-one, apparently with plans to become a violinist; economic reality soon dictated that he try something else. Employed by the Crane Valve Company of Bridgeport, Connecticut, he returned home in 1913 for a visit but was called to military service when battles in the Balkans spread in 1914. Masaryk fought in an Austrian regiment during the Great War, served the new Czechoslovak diplomatic service in the interwar years, and eventually became minister of foreign affairs and deputy prime minister in the exile government of the 1940s. He was working to balance an independent Czech regime between East and West at the time of his death.[27]

These electoral victories, along with the remigrants' involvement with school boards and other groups, should not obscure the fact that to many Europeans the mere thought of these emigrants coming back was distasteful. The critics paid attention not to news of the returnees improved skills and bulging coinbags but to reports that they had acquired dangerous ideas. Some immigrant radicals even encouraged this dislike, filling their newspapers with warnings for the landowners and churchmen at home: "When the sound principles of Washington, Lincoln, Roosevelt and Taft bear fruit," a Greek-American editor in New York proclaimed in 1908, the homeland will be happier, for "the holy and sacred soil of Greece and of the enslaved provinces is fertile, ready to be cultivated with the new fruit bearing seed." He was not referring to agronomy.[28]

From these and other bits of evidence, traditional elites feared that the very underpinnings of society would be overturned—if not by skeptical and irreverent peasants coming back, then by radicals who would lunge at the throats of the ruling class. To such conservatives, America became not the bright and shining beacon in the west but instead the land of the 1877 Great Strike, where mobs chased soldiers away while they laid waste to Pittsburgh. It was the site of the Haymarket Riot where (it was said) anarchism had run riot in Chicago. Had not Gaetano Bresci, who assassinated Italy's King Umberto in 1900, once been a silk weaver in Paterson, New Jersey?[29]

IRISH OPPOSITION

Ireland presented the contrast between reception and rejection in dramatic form. Skepticism or fear of remigrants was present there from the close of the famine in the 1850s through the Easter Rising of 1916, and even beyond to the eventual creation of the Irish Free State in 1922. These fears had to compete, of course, with the general enthusiasm with which the populace greeted the returning "Yanks."

America had always stood as a challenge to British control of the island, for the American example of 1776 was cheered there and Irish rebels often found refuge in the United States. Wolfe Tone, one of the heroes of the Irish revolutionary past, fled to the United States for protection in 1794. Young Irelanders also wound up in the United States after the failure of their 1848 rebellion, by which time a substantial number of their compatriots were already there, forming a congenial environment for revolutionary plotting. An early arrival was rebel John Mitchel, who announced in 1853, "I mean to make use of the freedom guaranteed to me as a citizen . . . of America to help and stimulate the movement of European Democracy and especially of Irish independence." Many others made their initial discovery of Irish nationalism in their new land of residence. Indeed, it was only beyond the island's shores that a substantial Irish liberation movement could be openly organized, encouraged, and financed. The United States offered the best locale, for it possessed numerous districts with heavy Irish settlement, and Irish-American politicians were scattered through all levels of government. Britain's home secretary admitted at one point that there was "an Irish nation in the United States," hostile, rich, untouchable—and only ten days' sail away.[30]

And so the official spokesmen, the Irish landed gentry, and those who functioned comfortably within British-controlled society looked with concern and often alarm at events unfolding in the United States. Liberation talk was not aimed so much at regenerating Ireland, the Dublin *Review* charged, as at making the island "a *corpus vile* on which to try the experiment of American communism." Henry George's *Progress and Poverty* also came under attack, for it reasserted the land question, crucial in the Irish debate. The charge was leveled that his single tax on the unearned increment in land values was morally wrong as well as unworkable. A Cork Unionist flayed the entire independence movement in 1892, proclaiming that Unionists would not give up their "glorious heritage" and liberties under the British Constitution "for a degrading and enslaving mess of Irish-American pottage."[31]

Clergy also questioned what was coming from America, particularly when those returning shipped back blasting powder as well as revolutionary ideas. The Fenian movement, launched in the United States before the Civil War but spurred to greater activity by the postwar influx of veterans as members, initially came under the Catholic church's censure because it was a secret society. Its counterpart in Ireland during the drive for independence, the Irish Republican Brotherhood, was also secret. Paul Cullen, archbishop of Dublin from 1852 to 1878 and Ireland's first cardinal, was already attacking the movement's newspaper in 1869 as "most wicked and insolent . . . more Protestant than Catholic," supported by money from America. These fears grew as the Fenians, now up to 50,000 members, invaded Canada at Niagara in 1866, attempted an uprising in Ireland the following year, and then began filling British prisons through the successes of Her Majesty's informers. Fenian bombing of a British prison in 1867 increased the church hierarchy's attacks on the movement, and in 1870 the pope condemned Fenianism.[32]

The American connection was frequently part of Cullen's attacks. He sought to make Ireland as Catholic as possible, and he saw in the Fenians and related groups a threat to impose American-style religious toleration, which would "abridge the liberties of the Catholic Church in Ireland." When the British prime minister sought his support in 1870 for a new Land Act, Cullen expressed his unhappiness that the British tolerated returns of "a great number of adventurers from America who have plenty of money at their disposal." And why, he asked, did the government allow publication in Dublin of Fenian and other newspapers—"an infidel and revolutionary press subsidized and maintained to a great extent by foreign gold." He also feared that returned emigrants in general were contaminating the church's Irish flocks with "infidelity" and ideas of "excessive liberty" learned in America. It has been argued in Cullen's defense, however, that his attacks on the Fenians were not made to support the British, for the cardinal repeatedly criticized British land policies that were forcing evictions and emigration. His main concern was with revolution, which he feared would be self-destructive for Ireland.[33]

Cullen died in 1878 and was succeeded by Archbishop Edward McCabe. McCabe also condemned the Fenians and their offshoots, and Irish bishops under his leadership called on clergy "to guard their flocks against all secret agencies of violence and intimidation, which can only come from the enemies of the people"; the laity were urged to back the priests "in the suppression of all anti-social and anti-Catholic abuses."[34]

This hierarchical change came in a turbulent period whose controversies must be summarized here to make understandable the debate over returns from America. The Fenian–Brotherhood movement gave way to the Land League, fueled by two successive crop failures in the latter 1870s. Led by Michael Davitt, just back from the United States, the Land League spread rapidly across Ireland, demanding that land ownership be given to the farmers who were working it as tenants and that land be taken away from the few thousand aristocratic families who owned it under British control. Land League membership soared to 200,000 within a year, and law enforcement across much of the island became largely ineffective because of it. Again an American connection was established, and by late 1881 there were also 1,500 branches of the Land League in the United States, collecting half a million dollars for the cause by the fall of 1882. Its arguments owed much to George's *Progress and Poverty*, a book that exercised a major influence on Michael Davitt. British officials contended with some truth, therefore, that the unrest during the ensuing land war was stirred largely by remigrants influenced by U.S. democracy.[35]

The Irish Roman Catholic hierarchy increasingly showed divisions over the land issue. Alarmed conservatives wrote to Archbishop McCabe of the pro-League activities of some local priests, and one correspondent quoted a sermon given by the Reverend Father Coughlan on the subject:

> "I hear the people of this parish are Land Leaguers and Nationalists, I am a Land Leaguer for the principles of the Land League are both moral & religious. . . . In a remote part of Donegal in the North of Ireland the Bishop[,] long before the Land League began[,] as a rule excommunicated any person who took a farm from which another had been evicted. I intend to pursue the same rule. . . . The govt. of England has given us two Coercion Acts, but they might as well try to imprison the Autumn breezes as to crush the principles of the Land League."

He added that if the police stopped him he would "let them see what an Irish priest can do." The large crowd cheered the priest as he left, the letter writer admitted. Others wrote to warn the archbishop that British officials were infiltrating their congregations to gather information.[36]

Then came the Irish National League, which gained further church support from both clergy and hierarchy. In 1885 Archbishop McCabe died, succeeded by Rev. William Joseph Walsh, who had been a staunch defender of the Land League. The nationalist movement, relying on continued support in dollars and recruits from across the Atlantic, had finally accomplished the enormous but essential leap toward identification of its own cause with that of Ireland, its people, and its church.[37]

The years leading to the Easter Rising of 1916 repeatedly gave evidence of the importance of the American connection. The wave of dynamitings in England in 1883–85—at Victoria Station, Scotland Yard, London Bridge, even the House of Commons—was financed from the American Irish community, and the dynamiters were largely trained in America through the Clan-na-Gael, another successor to the Fenians and the Land League. By then the movement had broadened under the leadership of Charles Stewart Parnell to link land reform and home rule through parliamentary action. Roman Catholic leaders in the United States, however, were split over the movement, just as their counterparts in Ireland had been; a geographic division even appeared between Clan-na-Gael supporters in the western and midwestern states and opponents along the east coast. "Chicago was completely Clan-na-Gael territory," one historian has concluded. The organization raised funds and also sought to block the U.S. government from embracing British colonial policies.[38]

Those arriving from America found little welcome from British officialdom as they returned to Ireland. Coming back after 1900 to join the final two decades of the drive for independence were two key participants in the evolving drama: James Connolly, an Edinburgh Irishman who had worked in Ireland for seven years spreading socialism before emigrating to the United States, and Tom Clarke, who went to America after his release from fifteen years in a British prison for his role in the dynamite campaign. Clarke returned to Ireland in 1907, Connolly in 1913. Events during the Easter Rising in 1916 made the American connection clear, and Patrick Pearse proclaimed before the Dublin General Post Office that Ireland was seizing the moment, "and, supported by her exiled children in America and by gallant allies in Europe, but relying in the first on her own strength, she strikes in full confidence of victory." Remigrants Connolly and Clarke were among the fifteen leaders executed for their part in the Rising. Final success would not be recorded until January 1922, with the end of a brief civil war and ratification of the Anglo-Irish Treaty by the *Dáil Éireann*.[39]

To deny the importance of return migration in this saga of Irish independence would be to deny that the string of returning radicals played any role in the course of events. It would also be to deny the cumulative impact over decades of vast numbers of Irish emigrants who "returned to their country impressed with democratic ideas," as British officials complained. These Irish men and women had, after all, seen a society where farmers owned the soil they tilled, where citizens selected their leaders, and where hundreds of their compatriots—certainly several thousand by 1920—occupied positions of importance from city precincts up to the U.S. Congress. It may be true, as historian Kerby Miller contends, that much of the immigrant leaders' oratory in the United States on behalf of Irish independence was simply required of any performance before an Irish-American audience. But the overall record leaves no doubt that America was prominent in the drive for Ireland's independence, and return migration was one of the crucial ingredients.[40]

ATTACKS IN POLAND AND
AUSTRIA-HUNGARY

The Irish example was not lost on other European religious and governmental leaders. Pro-German and pro-Russian newspapers in divided Poland raised the alarm of a "Polish Fennianist movement" that allegedly could provide 40,000 soldiers from America to battle kaiser and czar for Poland's independence.[41]

Although the Roman Catholic church in Poland had been linked with Polish independence for generations, many priests nevertheless feared remigrants for their alleged radicalism, sometimes linked to religious skepticism. Remigrants could influence villagers and upset the existing social structure; in fact, many began questioning the peasants' dependence on local clergy and officials. Priests were soon retaliating through sermons, in which they warned parishioners "not to trust the migrants and shun their company as that of unbelievers and corrupt people."[42]

Many Polish remigrants quickly entered political life, agitating for village changes; sometimes they shared leadership with businessmen, other times they participated "zealously" in activities of the Polish People's party. Several post–World War I Polish returned emigrants eventually made their way to seats in the new nation's parliament.[43]

Leaders of the powderkeg that was Austria-Hungary also had growing concern over emigrants coming home from America, that faraway land where members of the empire's polygot groups could freely listen to speeches on national identity uncensured by Budapest or Vienna. As early as 1854 the U.S. minister noted paranoia among Austrian police over an alleged organization among emigrants in the United States "which looks to revolution in the Austrian Empire." Those returning home faced problems because of this, he warned. Various incidents in ensuing years buttressed these fears, such as a 1913 assassination attempt against the commissary for Croatia, Baron Skrlec. The would-be assassin, Stjepan Doicic, had joined Croatian patriotic societies in the United States and read deeply in Croatian nationalist newspapers there. He was, according to the Chicago Croatian journal *Znanje*, "a patriot in the fullest sense of the word. What other dollar patriots were just talking about he was ready to put into action, in that unlucky land of Croatia."[44]

Visitors to the dual monarchy noted that those returning had a sharpened hunger for political liberties and saw Austria-Hungary's rule over their homelands in a new light. Emily Greene Balch found that the returned Slav "chafes. . . . It is hard to be sufficiently submissive to the pettiest official of the town after an experience of American free-and-easiness." Nationalist politicians warned of discontent among those coming home, and a Croatian cautioned the Austrian parliament in 1910 that remigrants "inevitably create a permanent discontent with present conditions." In Croatia many joined the Croatian People's party. Restlessness was spreading among the southern Slavs, and as World War I drew to a close a Serbian nationalist asserted that the returners' dissatisfaction over the lack of democracy "engendered a spirit of brooding revolt." The postwar creation of Yugoslavia was aimed at satisfying such nationalist drives.[45]

To the north, efforts to maintain Magyar control over Hungary also faced challenges from many of those returning. Balch noted that Slavs, who made up fully a tenth of Hungary's population, had only one representative among the 453 members of its parliament. Reports circulated that Slovaks in Pittsburgh were against everything Hungarian, prompting Budapest authorities to send a questionnaire to their consulates in America: were their emigrants pan-Slavist? Grand Slovak? Did they spread their ideas when they got home? These and other questions revealed government fears over the large-scale return from America. By 1903 some officials in Upper Hungary were calling for a prohibition on the return of some 90 percent of the Slovak emigrants. Four years later Hungary's president declared that only those who spoke Hungarian should be allowed back, for there should be no Slovak elements disturbing Hungary's inner peace.[46]

Within Slovakian districts in Hungary there was evidence to support the Magyar fears. As early as 1893 local reports stated that "Slovaks returning from America are playing the role of nation-builders"; thanks to America they became "true Slovaks." The way to educate a son in

Slovak nationalism, one enthusiast claimed, was "to send him to America." Slovak newspapers from the United States were popular among the former emigrants. The government banned two such newspapers in 1894; they could not be sent through the mails or even carried into Hungary. Historian M. Mark Stolarik concludes that such prohibitions were largely ineffective. One Slovak community was described by officials as a "nest of Slovak nationalism" because so many residents had lived in the United States and continued to receive American newspapers. A Magyar pastor came under sharp attack in another community when he criticized a remigrant for reading such journals; however, in two other towns the pro-Slovak religious leaders, a Catholic priest and a Lutheran pastor, were protected by villagers from removal. Harsh means were sometimes used: in 1907 a remigrant was jailed for seven months after he was caught agitating for Slovak national rights.[47]

There was, then, much evidence behind the lament of a Hungarian subprefect in Heves County:

> The international ideals of the New World corrupt the moral purity of decent Hungarians, reshape their typical character, destroy their sober common sense, their respect for others and their self-control. Familiarity with the more efficient and highly developed government of America, greater individual rights, more efficient bureaucracy, and smaller tax burdens make them dissatisfied with what they find here on their return, and it is to be feared that if they come back for good they will become the incendiaries of passions and disaffections, enemies of law and order.

It is no surprise that, when revolution finally arrived in Hungary in 1918, returned emigrants were notable for their participation.[48]

Troubles in Hungary, Ireland, Poland, Italy, and elsewhere revealed a continent in upheaval. And within the challenges to the status quo was evidence to support both the hopes of reformers and fears of conservatives over the impact of the returned emigrants.

CHAPTER 8

Churches, Traditions, and the Remigrant

The churches of Europe watched nervously as the trickle homeward from America became a torrent. Virtually every region had a dominant church, government-supported in most cases (though not in Ireland) and frequently linked to the upper classes. Part of the clergy's concern centered on fears for the faith of those caught in the religious maelstrom overseas. And American Protestant pamphleteers, hovering over the new arrivals at Castle Garden and later at Ellis Island, were soon casting eyes on Europe itself as a promising field for missionary activity.

This marked a reversal. An eastward flow of religious influence overturned tradition, the centuries-old pattern of missionaries sent out from Europe to "plant" churches among heathens and emigrant colonies, saving both groups from disbelief and the clutches of other denominations. That older pattern from Europe to America continued to operate; now, however, Baptists, Mormons, Methodists, and others were coming back from the United States and openly touring the Continent seeking followers. Worse, in the view of European clergy, they were often escorted by remigrant converts returning to work among their own people. Thus some established churches faced growing national minority opposition and American missionary invasions, all at the same time. Fear of the remigrants, then, appeared not only because they had been exposed to strange doctrines but also because they often insisted on spreading them, establishing branches of new churches in their home communities.[1]

These trends and the resulting controversies, including major up-heavals in Polish and Swedish churches, are examined in this chapter, as well as cultural changes inspired by the return migration.

CONVERTS FROM ABROAD

There had been harbingers of the European religious controversies within American cities, where immigrant clergymen were sometimes challenged by parishioners caught up in other causes. Hungary's struggle with pan-Slavist agitators within its urban colonies abroad has been noted; Hungarian Roman Catholic priests received aid from Budapest and were rotated home to keep the national connection strong. Still, many priests were unhappy with the suffering they experienced in America at the hands of nationalistic Slovaks and other groups.[2]

A representative case is that of Wojciech Stasiński, a Pole who became active in the Polish National Alliance and the Polish Socialist party while in America and was soon embroiled in conflicts with immigrant priests. When he refused to donate for construction of a new church in Ohio, the priest ordered other parishioners to block him from his boardinghouse. When he organized a meeting to commemorate a Polish uprising, he was suddenly arrested and freed only after his fellow miners backed him and a Czech dentist put up his bail. Stasiński blamed the priest for his string of troubles. Returning to Poland in 1920, he threw himself into various political movements, argued with local clergy, and soon found newspapers reporting that he had lost his Catholic faith in America. He persevered, however, and began moving up in the political movement led by Jósef Piłsudski.[3]

America was a disaster for the faith, many European religious leaders decided. Emigration therefore had to be opposed. The idea that moral dangers lay in wait across the ocean was a traditional European fear, but the strength of this view increased as the twentieth century opened and the numbers returning reached into the millions. Polish priests responding to a 1913 church questionnaire were divided over the issue. Some saw no special problems befalling those going to North America, especially when compared to the moral disasters of the migration to next-door Prussia. But others had serious reservations about America: "They are coming back degenerated, so they do a lot of wrong to the parish," the priest at Krzeczów in Galicia complained. Others noted sexual misdeeds and excessive drinking. "They want to earn money, so they don't have time to get demoralized," the Wilkowice priest commented, though he added: "But we don't know what they are doing in America, what influences they are meeting." It was still a religious terra incognita.[4]

Other leaders felt more certain about American influence. A Swedish pastor warned that those who failed in America should not be allowed to return, because they would help overturn Swedish Christendom and the country's existing social order. In Ireland especially, religious leaders expressed doubts over the spiritual wisdom of the emigration, fearing moral dangers in what Cardinal Cullen called the "swamps of America." Another worried Irish churchman argued that to become Americanized for an immigrant was to be "dechristianized," and he contended that Irish were the most easily Americanized of all immigrants because of their knowledge of English. Other emigrants kept their native tongues in the United States, Father M. F. Shinnors asserted, "and their ignorance of the language of the country is a protection for their faith." Based on his missionary tour, he considered the Irish as "rushing to their own spiritual destruction" and relayed the estimate of American Catholic leaders that up to 10 million Catholics had been lost to the faith there. He also passed on the Americans' plea: "Stop the tide of emigration. Save your flocks from the American wolf. . . . For your people, America is the road to hell!"[5]

As religious influences coming back from America became more controversial, traditional leadership in European communities began to react and respond. This occurred in Europe's antialcohol movement, a campaign of long standing, which in the 1830s and 1840s began to feel reverberations from the new drive for total abstinence then shaking U. S. temperance activities. As with many other ideas spreading from America, these came with remigrants but also arrived in publications, letters, and through visitors. New temperance organizations were multiplying across Europe by mid-century, with Ireland producing one of the major leaders, Father Theobald Mathew. Father Mathew traveled to the United States and led parades for total abstinence in Irish communities there.[6]

But the returned emigrant also goaded this new movement. It was noted that even in Sweden, where a national temperance society had been launched in 1837, the new movement combining religious revivalism with reform in drinking habits began with a remigrant who established the first Swedish lodge of the International Order of Good Templars in 1879. In Dalarna province in north-central Sweden, emigrants coming back from Minnesota started a new local temperance movement in the same period. Similarly, Emily Balch found that returning Slavs took a new look at the drinking in their homeland and criticized the fact that drunks were not arrested as they were in America, especially rich drunks. Some Roman Catholics remigrating at the turn of the century, however, warned that the exploding temperance crusade in the United States was heading toward a ban on the use of wine in celebrating the mass; the charge was quickly denied by a visiting leader of the American prohibition movement.[7]

One visible result of the immigrants' immersion in the American environment was that remigrants seemed independent. This spirit was already visible crossing the ocean, in the returning steamships' steerage sections, where it was noted that crews acted in a more civil manner toward those who had lived in America. Arriving back in the village, the returners would encounter a former employer who soon complained that they were less deferential, that they did not greet him as respectfully as before. Antonio Mangano talked with a communal secretary in Pulsano on the Gulf of Taranto who protested that over the years he had always been good to these people: "Then they were very humble and always came into my office with great fear, hat in hand, hardly daring to lift their eyes from the floor. When they return, they come in here and look on me as no better than themselves. They do not even take off their hats." And Edward Steiner met a lady who complained that she could no longer find a decent servant among the girls returning: "What kind of country is that anyway, that America? These servant girls come back with gold teeth in their mouths, and with long dresses which sweep the streets, and with unbearable manners. They do not kiss our hands when they meet us, and when they speak of their mistress in America they speak of her as if they were equals." This new independence was praised by some Italian leaders, however, who hoped for massive improvements in the moribund Mezzogiorno. But among many others the response was not so positive. When those returning to Hungary were less servile, clashes with local authorities resulted.[8]

Some noted a decline in the status of village leaders, especially religious leaders. Remigrants tended not to pay so much attention to the priest, and their dollars donated for a new church bell meant that this was no longer the gift of just a few rich benefactors, nobles, large landowners, or others of the elite. The peasant who had traveled to America now had a part in the project. Local priests and pastors were not treated as deferentially as before; in the final analysis, then, the remigrants were disputing the clergy's monopoly on the truth. It was people returning from abroad to the Apennine village of Montefegatesi who formed a major part of the group that openly refused to participate in the church's ceremonial and sacramental activities. From this group, moreover, came construction of a local theater, organization of a marching band, and a 1902 monument to Giuseppe Garibaldi, this last promoted by two men who, like Garibaldi, had formerly worked in New York. All those in the community who labored on a monument to Dante had worked overseas also.[9]

Remigrants frequently read books, subscribed to American newspapers, took part in campaigns to start libraries and schools. Their example spurred others to become literate. All this challenged the priest and village elders in Midezyrzec, Poland, who—one onlooker charged—did not want books to circulate because they did not want the peasant to "learn that he also is a man." And so the ignorance of Midezyrzec's peasants continued, he complained: "More than once I have asked some older peasant what are these stars which shine on a beautiful night. 'Well, these bright ones are souls of bishops, those smaller ones, souls of priests,' he said. 'And where are the peasant-souls of our forefathers?' I asked him. He answered: 'In the fire, in hell.'"[10]

This rebellion rested on the fact that state churches in many European areas had become cold and formalistic; the sermons contained little that was relevant to those who had seen large cities and giant factories abroad, who had known the excitement of political debate and challenges to long-accepted ideas. The Swedish State Lutheran Church in the nineteenth century was described as a "magnificent ice palace" where no free prayer occurred and where some followed the *Psalmbok* more closely than the Bible. Among its pastorate, it was claimed, were clergymen noted for drunkenness, blasphemy, and lewd behavior.[11]

Other shortcomings were evident. Villagers in a town in Italy's Abruzzi Mountains heard their priest explain why the grain crop had failed: there was a Protestant heretic in their midst. They then tried to kill the Protestant. Such examples of clerical omnipotence could grate against travelers coming home from countries such as America where, according to a Polish priest's report, the immigrants considered the priest as something of a clerk.[12]

Scholars examining issues in European villages have reported that the social distance between parishioners and priests did not seem as great as it had been earlier. Though secularizing influences were spreading throughout the western world, then, reports of remigrants showing a coolness or opposition to established religion are numerous and should be included in any weighing of influences. As one Italian who returned to his native Mezzogiorno found, peasants who came back were "as a rule, opposed to the clericals, if not to the church itself, because of the

Protestant or socialistic influences" that had surrounded them in America.[13]

COMPETING DENOMINATIONS

The main challenge to the traditional church sometimes came in the form of another church. It appeared suddenly in the village and soon not only competed for members but also weakened the clergy's monopoly. Southern Italy became aware of this invasion around 1900 as trickles within the returning flood brought back different ideas on religion. Northern Italy had long known the Protestant Waldensian movement. But now immigrants were becoming converted overseas, and Antonio Mangano advanced the claim that in America there were more Italian Protestant churches than Italian Catholic churches. It is doubtful that this was true; the membership, at least, of Italian Catholic churches would have outstripped that of Protestant congregations. But years later, when Francesco Cerase was conducting interviews in the Mezzogiorno, he frequently came on Protestant enclaves: the striking fact, he said, was that these communities had often been founded by migrants returned from the United States.[14]

Baptists arrived first in the Italian south, followed closely by Methodists. Mangano told of a peasant from Calitri who was converted at a Baptist mission in Hartford, Connecticut, then returned to his hometown and started a church. Soon it had fifty members, and it grew to several hundred before long. Another case cited by Mangano was of an Abruzzi emigrant who was converted in Astoria on Long Island, at a Methodist mission. Back in his village of Sale, he launched a church with Waldensian help. From the multiplication of such instances, as well as the arrivals of U.S. missionaries, the Italian Protestant total jumped from 65,595 in the 1901 census, the majority Waldensians in the north, to 123,253 in 1911.[15]

Cerase notes that remigrants who joined Protestant groups had often learned to read, another challenge to the authority of the priest. Sunday schools were started, creating an institution that Cerase called "in many ways the most important activity of the Church and the channel through which the Protestant community won the esteem of both the peasants and the most educated among the local population." Intellectuals and some Catholics ended up sending their children to Sunday schools in some communities.[16]

Retaliation by local Catholic clergy was immediate. One Italian Prot-

Although immigrants might not switch their national allegiance in America, many did change their religious loyalty. Typical of the new immigrant churches was this Italian Methodist Episcopal Church in Youngstown, Ohio. Many of the Italians in this 1918 photograph would likely have been Roman Catholics before coming to the United States, and when they returned home and launched new denominations they disrupted their home communities. Photograph by General Board of Global Ministries, The United Methodist Church.

estant recalled that the local priest "truly persecuted us with a combination of ridicule, boycotts, mockery, and calumny." Protestant youngsters were called "children of Satan." Elsewhere, shouting crowds formed when ministers arrived, and stones were thrown at the house where an evangelical minister stayed. Cerase learned of one case in which a popular Catholic preacher spent a month in a village to try to overcome the new church: "He tried to incite the population and even organized about 50 children to hurl stones against the Protestants but finally departed, having accomplished little."[17]

Early Protestant groups were soon meeting new competition as well, for Pentecostals began arriving, also from the United States. The call therefore went out to prepare more missionaries in America, and soon the U.S. East Coast was dotted with Protestant seminaries and mission schools training Italians. Members continued to emigrate, return to Italy, and often go again to the United States. These new congregations held close ties for years with denominational leaders across the Atlantic. One Italian Protestant leader told Mangano: "Our work here is largely dependent upon what you do in America. . . . Tell your people in America that the best way for them to convert Italy is for them to convert the Italians in America." Much of the Protestant surge, therefore, rested on return migration.[18]

A POLISH SCHISM

Poland's Roman Catholic church faced an additional threat from abroad: the Polish National Catholic church (PNCC), created from various Roman Catholic dissident movements in Scranton, Chicago, Baltimore, Cleveland, and other districts of Polonia. At the focus of the new group's anger was America's Roman Catholic hierarchy, occasionally its parish leadership but more often the higher levels where Irish and German dominance was nearly total.

Polish immigrant groups who sacrificed to construct their new churches in American cities sought to control these buildings the way they saw Protestant congregations doing. They also tried to choose their own local committees and their own priests rather than submit to the control of the Irish-German hierarchy. Frequently the hierarchy's decisions left Polish parishes without a Polish priest. A typical response came from a PNCC group at Nanticoke, Pennsylvania, which vowed, "We, therefore, resolutely refuse to recognize the pretensions of the Irish in America to any superior rights and their treatment of us Poles as if we were slaves of the church of Rome or of its politics." From the first high mass celebrated in 1897 by Rev. Francis Hodur in Scranton until 1919, some fifty formerly Catholic churches joined the PNCC movement in the United States and Canada.[19]

Launching the new church back in Poland itself was probably never far from the founders' minds, and by 1911 the PNCC imposed a free-will tax to support missionary work there. The end of World War I presented a dramatic opportunity, and soon PNCC emissaries were heading eastward. Bishop Hodur visited the newly created Polish state in 1920 and said that the trip confirmed his belief that "sooner or later the Polish National Catholic Church will rise in our native land beyond the sea." An organization was promptly launched in Poland with Kraków as the episcopal seat of the new bishop, and a theological seminary opened.[20]

Poland's village priests, already facing challenges from skeptical remigrants, now had to contend with the PNCC. Although the new post-war government's attempt at a census of each returning religious group reported only tiny numbers of PNCC repatriates—less than one percent of those remigrants in 1920–23, for example—it is probable that this represents reluctance to tell the truth to the government. By 1939 there were a hundred PNCC churches in Poland claiming some 400,000 members.[21]

The PNCC threat was considered so dangerous that Poland's official Jesuit publication urged that return migration be stopped. In a 1920 article titled "The Danger Coming from the United States," Father Romuald Moskala warned that enthusiasm over the return movement had its dark side, particularly the migrants' moral and religious deviation. Already, he noted, the PNCC's newspaper *Straż* was sending large numbers of copies into the country, attacking both the Catholic church and capitalists (some in the PNCC had links with Poland's Socialist party).[22]

In Polish villages the Catholic church launched a counteroffensive. Copies of PNCC publications and other independent newspapers were seized and burned or were delivered in shreds with offending articles cut out. Clergy gave sermons against the movement; one remigrant was forbidden to read *Ameryka Echo*, a liberal weekly from the United States, because "it was an infernal paper." Another reader of the newspaper reported that, when the priest learned that parishioners were reading *Ameryka Echo*, "he clearly admonished people from the pulpit ... saying that they do not know what punishment awaits them for this after death." In another case the returned migrants, all veterans of Haller's Army, were lectured: "You left for America. You made money there but you have lost your faith, the mother of Poland. . . . you should have been hit by the first bullet, you scoundrels." Professed PNCC members said that they were attacked for demanding "the same freedom to profess their religion as in America."[23]

The postwar government finally gave its permission for the church's existence in the mid-1920s, although the PNCC continued to clash with police in several Polish cities when new congregations were formed. One such case occurred at Jastkowice, a village in southeastern Poland on the San River. A Roman Catholic church was erected there, but the people were unable to obtain a priest since they retained title to the building. Remigrants successfully urged them to invite a PNCC priest instead. Police were summoned, blocked the visitor from saying mass, and arrested four members of the local committee, but finally they gave in and allowed the PNCC priest to say mass in Polish. The church building was eventually turned over to the new group. At Grudziadz, the PNCC church opened in 1924 and claimed 5,887 members by 1927. Aiding the PNCC's spread were gifts of food and clothing sent from America, distributed by an activist remigrant priest named Father Bronisław Krupski. Krupski, however, was forced back to the United States after some fourteen months. Even today the PNCC's nickname in Poland is *Kosciol amerykanski*, the "American church."[24]

Protestant denominations, the so-called free churches such as the Baptists, Methodists, and Congregationalists, appeared in such other Catholic countries as Hungary. Seventh-Day Adventists came later. Germany already had a multiplicity of Protestant denominations as well as a strong Catholic church, and so new religious groups did not stand out there as in single-religion countries. No PNCC challenged Germany's Catholic hierarchy. Mennonites returned from Kansas to the newly unified Reich after 1871; more noticeable were the Mormons, who came in large numbers, including remigrants, to convert Germans to their cause. Baptists, the Salvation Army, and eventually Jehovah's Witnesses also sent missionaries to Germany; these probably included remigrants but information is scant.[25]

UPHEAVAL IN SWEDEN

Sweden was different. The role of remigrants there deserves examination because of their intricate involvement in, and encouragement of, the breakup of state church controls. The last half of the nineteenth century brought upheavals to Sweden in religion, politics, and industry as the country was wrenched out of the past. In 1882, at a time when religious revivals were sweeping the landscape and challenging the State Lutheran Church, Swedish emigration reached its all-time peak. Crop failures combined with these developments to turn Småland into "the province of the 'preaching sickness.'" Everywhere people began to question tradition, and read, and listen to proselytizers. The government had passed a law in 1858 that forbade any preaching that would bring schism or provoke disrespect for public worship, and many of the "free church" members were attacked by mobs, singled out for newspaper criticism, even banished from Sweden. Baptists were forced to conduct their immersions secretly in the dead of night.[26]

Baptists, in fact, had been first to gain a foothold through emigrants coming home. A Swedish sea captain was converted in 1845 at a mariners' temple in New York, and when he later returned to Sweden he met F. O. Nilsson, also converted abroad. Nilsson was brutally beaten by a mob in 1850 and banished in 1853, but he returned to preach with a pardon from the king in 1860. The Baptist movement began to expand, and remigrants opened one of Sweden's first Sunday schools in Stockholm in 1855. This was the same year that organized pamphleteering began when Anders Wiberg came back from the United States to direct colporteur work. By 1857, when another converted emigrant, Gustaf Palmquist, returned to begin preaching, the nation counted eight Baptist congregations with more than 200 members. Those figures rose to ninety-five churches with 4,311 members by 1859, and to nearly 6,000 faithful in 1863. A seminary was launched in 1866. By 1930 the Swedish Baptist total was 31,000.[27]

Baptists were active in other Scandinavian countries as well: by 1920 the Norwegian Baptists claimed 4,038 members in forty-six churches, and the Finnish Baptist Union had 712 members in seventeen groups. George Stephenson argues that the Swedish Baptist movement is especially revealing of the influence of America—from leaders converted in the United States who returned, other members trained in America, and U.S. dollars used to establish and maintain Swedish Baptist institutions. But above all, he adds, "the example of free America was an inspiration and a moral influence that gave sustenance in the hours of discouragement."[28]

The Swedish Lutheran church soon had other competition besides the Baptists. The Mission Friends movement grew out of pietist criticism within Sweden. From abroad came the Methodists, who launched their first Swedish congregation in 1868, when 57 persons organized a congregation after Albert Ericson and Victor Witting had come back from

America. They had been converted by Olof Gustaf Hedström, a sailor who was pastor of the Methodists' Bethel Ship in New York Harbor.[29]

Nine months after the Stockholm congregation had been organized, the Methodists had seven congregations in Sweden with fifteen other "preaching places," totaling 424 members; they also ran five Sunday schools. It was not to be a peaceful evangelization drive, however; meetings continued to be interrupted by government officials, and one preacher received an eleven-day prison term.

Mormons had a foreign missions department operating by 1850 when their proselytizing began in Denmark; the Swedish opening came shortly thereafter and early leaders included a former Swedish sailor and a Dane. The Mormons claimed 110 in Sweden by 1851, a total that grew to only 2,183 by 1900; however, many converts had moved to Utah. The Pentecostal movement arrived in 1881 with a visiting emigrant, Fredrik Franson, who preached to large crowds for two years, avoiding jail only because the king overruled local officials. Other Pentecostals returned over the years, with Franson paying another visit in 1907 and again attracting enormous crowds. By then Pentecostals were being converted in Sweden itself, then traveling to the United States for training.

Desire for independence from the Swedish Lutheran church began to spread to Swedish communities in the United States, where the Mission Covenant church soon established a competing presence. The Augustana synod was formed by Swedish Lutheran immigrants in 1860 and, although critics charged that it was indistinguishable from the state church back home, in fact the Augustana group included many who had been dissenters in Sweden. In America they were influenced by the free churches, supporting the religious currents within the Anti-Saloon League, for example. Such moves strained relations between the synod in the United States and the state church in Sweden, which complained of Methodist influences in the American group.

In an interesting sidelight to the transatlantic movement of religions, the Vatican in 1889 inquired of Archbishop John Ireland in Minnesota whether there were prospects for converting Swedish immigrants to Catholicism and then sending them back to Europe to "be a good leaven to their countrymen." No success in this endeavour was reported, however. The incident has been cited as continuing evidence of the Europocentric nature of the Roman Catholic church, at a time when the American hierarchy wanted emphasis put on spreading the faith in the United States.[30]

Not all was a loss to the state church, however. Several dozen em-

igrants returned home to preach after having been ordained as Augustana synod pastors in America. Some met criticism that they were
"American hustling," "not so little Americanized," or had been
"stamped with American naivity." Of one it was said that he had
"something wide-embracing American in him and in his discourse. . . .
he often became bombastic." Most were accepted without major adjust-
ments, however. One Augustana pastor who returned after preaching in
Salt Lake City was authorized by the government in 1911 to try to
counteract the Mormons' efforts within Sweden. Thus did the return
movement contribute to religious turmoil in the homeland.[31]

Such events raised critical questions for the State Lutheran church in
Sweden. Pastors began to encounter disrespect: refusing to remove his
hat when meeting a pastor was something for which a returned emigrant became known—the act proclaimed his American identification.
The church had been criticized for decades for its worldliness, and now
Swedes coming back from America contrasted the state church's impact
on the population with the higher morality they said was possible in a
free-church environment. But flexibility had already begun to creep into
the Swedish religious environment, and remigrants would goad this farther. In 1858 a law had been passed permitting Lutherans to gather
without a pastor, and in 1860 non-Lutherans received the right to peti-
tion the king to organize congregations. This legislation was in the face
of enormous pressures from traditionalists to block non-Lutheran activity. Other chinks appeared over the years in the state church's armor,
until finally civil marriages were legalized in 1908 and dissenters were
no longer forced to pay taxes to support the established church. The
Augustana synod in America was also brought into a closer relation
with the Swedish church when in 1922 the king decreed that it was to
be placed on as high standing as any Swedish synod. American marriages would now receive full Swedish church approval. After 1926, free
church pastors could finally perform burial rites.[32]

In Finland, too, the spread of free churches (such as the Methodists,
present there since 1882) helped bring legislation guaranteeing freedom
of religion. The official Finnish Lutheran church had been critical of
emigration because of the subsequent growth of free churches from
seeds planted by returning emigrants.[33]

As the era of mass emigration and remigration drew to a close in the
1920s, it was evident that converts returning home had been a significant force in shaking the dominant state churches of Europe and dem-
ocratizing religious practice. Often this was carried out in tandem with
missionaries sent from the United States. The Mormons became active

in these endeavours: they had begun their activities in the British Isles in 1837, when an Englishman and six others sailed from New York to Liverpool and soon established in Britain what the official church history calls "the most prolific mission of the Church." Because of Britain's long-standing religious diversity, the Mormons were one of the few cases there of a remigrant-launched religious movement.

Similarly, it was a German convert who returned in 1843 to begin Mormon endeavors in the German states—a rocky road for years, given government restrictions in both Catholic and Lutheran areas. Soon many non-German missionaries followed and helped spread the movement. Remigrants accompanied missionaries from Utah journeying to European countries in later decades; this in turn stimulated a large westward movement of converts heading to Utah to live: 89,000 left England alone for America from 1840 to 1868.[34]

Even in the case of the Mormons, however, it was the remigrants who provided a secure foothold. Their presence was crucial. New denominations in Europe depended on people rather than governments for support. Through them, state churches protected by law and custom were successfully challenged by the free churches, denominations already tested in the rough-and-tumble frontiers of the American religious environment. To a people frozen into life's course by a state church, these converted returners were revolutionaries. Their informal gatherings and their belief in free will replaced the stiff formality and stress on duty that smothered life in the state churches. Their tunes were joyful, their singing lively and often boisterous, their sermons emotional. As their music spread over the landscape, religious liberties expanded.

Ripples from the religious remigration soon touched economics, government, and other spheres. A historian familiar with later developments concluded that the free church groups across Scandinavia supplied surprisingly many political leaders of modern Sweden and Norway. As with the labor activists who recrossed the Atlantic, America was having a delayed but far-reaching impact on political developments in European homelands.[35]

NEW CUSTOMS

Along with their ideas about religion, politics, and labor's rights, returned emigrants brought different clothes, words, foods, and customs. Often these were copied and their use spread, as with the Christmas tree, which folk tradition in Zemplén County, Hungary, says was introduced there by emigrants coming back from America. Since the Christmas tree custom is generally believed to have been spread to America by northern European immigrants, its appearance in central Europe represents a retransfer of traditions via returners.[36]

Clothing styles apparently did not take such a circuitous route. Women came back from America dressed like "peacocks," taking on upper-class airs, a Swedish doctor complained. An Italian writer agreed that the remigrant's "exterior appearance" had changed: previously covered with rags and careless about his personal cleanliness, now he "dressed well, sometimes stylishly," often with "a new suit, a gold chain, a ring, and other ornaments." An Italian government report asserted that in the Mezzogiorno, above all, the remigrant from America was distinguished by the greater cleanliness of house and person—in contrast to those returning from Brazil. It was a rarity to see Poles wearing old-fashioned costumes in the Glinik area by 1900 because of the popularity of American garb introduced by those returning.[37]

Theodore Saloutos found that remigrants in Greece were easy to spot, with their American-style attire rather gaudy compared to the somber clothes of the nonemigrants. A dentist told him of a remigrant who had filled his mouth with gold crowns on his teeth to show that he was wealthy. In a Polish village, similarly, a returned emigrant proudly pulled out his false teeth and displayed them to the wondering throng; no one who had stayed at home had ever seen such a thing. Travelers in the Balkans reported that long after the emigrants' return they still wore American hats as identification. And although some accounts tell of them quickly slipping back into their former styles of dress, more typical was this Irish recollection:

> The clothing of the returned emigrant was always very much admired by the people at home: "It must be a wonderful country and the fine dacent [*sic*] clothes that comes from it," was a remark often heard about it, but the habits or styles of dress were never copied—they were considered "too loud" by the people at home, and were often the subject of sarcastic comment. Every returned "Yank" had a watch and chain, usually a gold one, which was worn in the waistcoat pocket, with the chain extending across the stomach.[38]

Similar memories came from elderly Finns who told Marsha Penti of what their fathers wore when they returned from America:

> It was so that they had very tight pants and such, and shiny, and these matches that they raised to their pipes and fire [came] from them. . . . Well they had these three, four chains on their watches and then they had that "railway" picture on them, that engine picture . . . and a

knalli hat [hat with rounded crown]. . . . Then there were patent leather shoes. Here there weren't things like that.[39]

Remigrant speech was different, too. American words such as *bodi* (buddy) slipped into Hungarian mining; Poles said *arajt* (all right). American words were soon modified into new Italian words, turning "shop" into *scioppa*, "store" into *storu*, and "job" into *giobba*. Finnish returners spoke "Finglish," a combination of key English words adapted to Finnish: *Good Morningis, donitsia* (doughnuts), *paita ja keekiä* (pie and cake). A recent Finnish compiler found returned emigrant words widely in use, including *haussi* for "house," *huntata* for "to hunt" (for a job), *loijari* for "lawyer," *kaara* for "car" (auto), and *sompoti* for "somebody." Even in English-speaking countries many new words were brought back, new phrases introduced: what the Irish called paraffin oil was kerosene to the "Yanks," whose sayings were quickly picked up by others:

"Waal! I guess, as the Yank says."
"Waal! I calculate, as the Yank says."
"It sure will, as the Yank says."
"Two weeks from now, as the Yank says."
"The 'goddam' thing, as the Yank says."

The identification of such phrases with remigrants was nearly complete when a railroad porter in the west of Ireland greeted a group of newly returned "Yanks" by exclaiming, "Here comes a bunch of 'I-guessers'!"[40]

Hungarian folklorist Béla Gunda found that repatriates would often argue among themselves in English, blocking nonemigrants from understanding. She also discovered a children's game, known throughout Hungary, which required guessing an American occupation: the two who were "it" would approach their encircled companions and shout, "We come from America and the name of our trade is 'L____H.'" If someone guessed "locksmith," he or she picked one of the two questioners as a partner, then those two would come up with another American occupation for the players to guess. Gunda also found many old Hungarian songs containing American phrases: "There are old peasants who still recall how during the long sea voyage, the emigrants would gather on deck during the day to look at the ocean; at night they sang the old familiar songs, into which some of their companions 'mixed America.'" These songs remained popular for years in Hungary. She learned of others that had been composed overseas and carried home:

Don't wonder if I'm feeling down.
I've been a grinder for nine years.

Ten years I'll have spent in the factory,
Grinding iron for farmers.[41]

And there were dances, demonstrated in village squares and homes—anywhere people gathered to question their returned friends and family about the New World. At Montefegatesi in the Italian Apennines, one remigrant taught waltzes, polkas, and mazurkas as he paraded around the village holding a new hand-crank American phonograph atop his head. The villagers' traditional dances—the *manifredina*, the *trescone*, the *veneziana*—gave way to new steps from across the water.[42]

American puddings, pies, cakes, and such new garden items as tomatoes began appearing in Europe as the remigrants took up their lives at home once more. These dishes apparently were saved for special occasions and, since emigrant women had often worked as maids and cooks in America, they enjoyed unusual opportunities to learn recipes. One elderly Finn interviewed by Penti relished memories of his late wife's cooking, especially the delicacies she learned while cooking for a family in Milton, Massachusetts:

"PIE, PIE! BLUEBERRY and, and apple and I really liked that APPLE PIE. I liked it incredibly well. And then all those, all those vegetables. . . . And then we had ICE CREAM. She cranked it out this way. She was good at making all these. And then we got some bananas, those, and broke them up in there then when there were guests. Well, they were really amazed that we had such a thing. And, and then I don't remember exactly what it was. It was called MINCEMEAT, something where there was meat.[43]

And the foods were served on separate plates, not eaten out of a common bowl as was still the custom across much of peasant Europe. Pasteurization of milk in Greece was urged most vigorously by repatriates returning from America, who finally won its acceptance over a reluctant public. While Italian health officials complained of diseases transported back from the United States, they also noted that those returning took baths during the crossing, in contrast to the outbound trip when few indulged in such activities. Norwegian remigrants even became know for their clean houses, a characteristic extended to their care of farm animals; similarly, Norwegian returners complained of a lack of cleanliness in food preparation by those who had stayed at home. And in Italy the "American houses," according to a 1917 visitor, were less picturesque but more hygienic than others.[44]

As America became known as a cornucopia of new clothes, dance styles, phrases, and foods, those who arrived bearing these gifts were soon set apart. This distinction was independent of the money they carried, although the two strands were obviously intertwined. "A man who'd come back from America was a very desirable godfather," a Finn remarked, and the new status quickly spilled over into a person's place in the village and even to the question of proper marriage. A father in Castrovillari, Italy, refused to give the hand of his daughter to a young man unless the suitor first made a trip to America. In Ireland stories were told of girls returning with enough for a dowry, enabling them to secure a husband. Krystyna Duda-Dziewierz's examination of the southern Poland village of Babica, however, indicates that often when remigrants sought to raise themselves to the status of landlords or former nobles such efforts worked against village traditions and met resistance.[45]

The New World and the Old never enjoyed a relationship that was all mutual admiration or dislike but instead dealt with each other along both sides of the avenues of attraction and distrust, with clouds of envy and enmity frequently hindering the view. Many Americans feared alien ideas coming from Europe; some European religious and political leaders saw the very bases of society contaminated by what was being carried back across the Atlantic. For ideas also came with the remigrants, and no customs officials could screen them out. From new religious doctrines to new recipes, from labor union concepts to children's games, the return from America held out both challenge and stimulation to the peoples of Europe.

PART FOUR

A Round-Trip
Journey Concluded

CHAPTER 9

The America Trunk Comes Home

The emigrant who once boarded a ship for America was returning, and with him came the "America trunk" that had been loaded so carefully for the outgoing voyage. In Finland, this *American arkku* was filled when it came home with everything from glass dishes to locks from a baby's first haircut to such prized American objects as a phonograph player or double-bitted axe. Its contents were the talk of the neighborhood, valued for decades as mementos.

The America trunk is an apt symbol of both emigration and remigration, of immigrants coming to America and returning to their homelands. The symbol persists, for the trunk occupies hallowed positions today in homes of third-generation Americans who cling to an image of their ancestral saga; in many European homes, similarly, the chest that came back is still revered as a remnant, a piece of that dream which once drew an emigrant across the seas.[1]

But there was more, much more, symbolized in the America trunk. Within its recesses were tools or clothes that carried memories of hard struggles abroad. It provided a continuing connection with America, and because the United States increasingly played a leading role in international affairs, remigrants would be called on to interpret that role. They became *americani* and "Yanks"; America's importance raised their importance. And the items they valued enough to carry back in trunks would provide clues to what America's impact would be: was it tools the returners brought? or books on political theory, nationalist aspirations, labor organization, new churches? Or were the contents of

Both entries and departures began to increase as the new century began. These Norwegians were leaving Chicago for home in the 1902–3 period, and many would serve as progressive elements in Norwegian society while stimulating further emigration. Photograph by Chicago Historical Society, ICH 21308.

the America trunk to be used to impress neighbors, perhaps to be sold to help purchase a shop or an extra piece of land? Modern students of immigration who seek answers to such questions are no different than Charles Dickens, who gazed at the emigrants returning home to Europe on his ship in 1842 and admitted that he was "curious to know their histories, and with what expectations they had gone out to America, and on what errands they were going home, and what their circumstances were."[2]

All these questions—examined in the course of this book and readdressed in summary form in this chapter—were contained symbolically in the crude trunks unloaded from trains or wagons as the emigrants stepped back into the streets of their villages.

THE UBIQUITOUS REMIGRANT

The trunks were but one small part, like the tip of an iceberg, of the enormity of the movement of people, objects, and ideas back to Europe. Percentage rates of return ranged from 30 to 40 percent for such groups as the Italians, down to 10 percent among the Irish. Using these as a rough guide, it is possible to estimate that the total return to Europe may have been as high as four million repatriated emigrants during the 1880–1930 era of mass immigration into North America.[3]

Examined within individual countries, these massive totals mean that one in twenty residents of Italy was a returned emigrant at the time of World War I, and shortly thereafter in a Norwegian county of heavy emigration it was found that one-fourth of all males over age fifteen had lived at least two years in America. Such high numbers signify that for the next sixty years visitors to European villages would encounter former residents of Scranton or Cleveland or Detroit, happy to describe their American experiences, wanting to know how the baseball pennant race was shaping up.[4]

Such encounters were notably the case in wartime, and American soldiers moving up the Italian boot in the closing phases of World War II were greeted warmly in every village by welcomers holding snapshots and other mementos of the United States: "Hello, I'm glad you come. I used to live in the States. My family, she's in Peetsborgh now." Reporter John Lardner, traveling with troops in those final weeks, met Tony Cuda, mayor of Futani, Italy, who had lived from 1906 to 1922 in Philadelphia and Williamsport, mainly working on the railroad. Cuda and other remigrants in the Italian town could not understand the

English used by British soldiers and had to have American troops trans-late. Historian George Gilkey traveled through Italy in the 1950s and reported that one could still find an *Americano* in almost every town.[5]

Cases like these were not limited to the Mediterranean basin. A gen-eration later an Illinois woman visiting in northern Sweden was taken to see a returned emigrant in Bondersbyn who wanted to talk to an American. The eighty-three-year-old farmer told of going twice to the United States; returning to Sweden with a good sum of money after his first trip, he lost his savings when a bank failed, then emigrated once more. He earned enough on that second trip to America to enable him to come home to Sweden for good in 1928. At the end of the visit, he asked if they could sing something he remembered from those times long ago across the ocean: "We'll build a little nest, / Somewhere in the West, / And let the rest of the world go by." His eyes rimmed with tears.[6]

A MORE-REACHABLE AMERICA

The years 1880–1930 stand out in the immigrant experience. Euro-peans crossed to North America in ever-increasing numbers as major improvements appeared in transportation. For generations before, how-ever, an extensive pattern of short-term, work-seeking migration had existed in most areas of Europe, from Macedonians heading out to jobs around the Mediterranean to Irishmen and women crossing to England and Scotland for farm work. These nearby treks continued into the era of mass transatlantic emigration, as was evident in Polish totals: at the peak of Polish emigration to the United States in 1912–13, 130,000 left for America—compared to 800,000 heading for seasonal work else-where in Europe. It is true that development of the oceangoing steam-ship, coupled with an increasing flow of news and publicity about American jobs, helped shift the destinations of many short-term mi-grants to the West, across the Atlantic. North and South America were becoming more closely fitted into the Atlantic economy and, if this meant that midwestern pork could now be packed for consumers in Germany, it also signified that Germans from those same consuming areas, and Poles, Italians, and Finns, could easily travel to find employ-ment in those same U.S. packing plants.

These developments welded mass migration closely to the variations, booms, and busts of American industry. To these immigrants, America became basically the site of factory employment, gang labor on a railroad section, a job underground following a coal seam. One Italian could talk of his American experiences only in terms of trains, rails, and crossties, "as if all of America was nothing but a braid of tracks," a countryman reported.[7]

As the trio of concerns of *journey, job hunt,* and *employment* became more predictable, less dangerous, the trip to America could then be viewed as something other than a lifetime change. Like short-term labor migration within Europe, it became a means to improve life at home, through earning enough to achieve a higher status or more solid position in the village. It was not so much the start of a new life as another step in the process of social mobility. These factors in turn dictated that life in the American "workshop" would be temporary for many.[8]

This study has focused on the United States, but it should be noted that comparable trends existed in Canada and the Hispanic countries. In all, it is impossible to know what percentage of immigrants planned to return home, but it is not reaching far beyond the evidence to estimate that a majority in the 1880–1930 period initially expected to turn their backs on life and labor overseas once they had accumulated some wealth. Various things caused most to change their minds: in the United States these included realizing that opportunities in America outstripped those at home, gaining a better job, becoming accustomed to a higher standard of living, the arrival of news from abroad that removed the necessity for return, or gradual Americanization through learning the language, acquiring American friends, falling in love with a local girl.

Sometimes the shifts in expectations could be traced through a progression of names, as in the case of a Lithuanian immigrant couple who lived in coal towns in Pennsylvania and Illinois, always planning to return to Lithuania until they moved on to Oklahoma and decided to settle down. Their first two children were born in 1896 and 1900, when they still expected to go back to Europe, and were accordingly named Gediminas and Juozas. The third arrived in 1912, when they had become Americans. They named him Edwin.[9]

But until that decision was made, until the carefully plotted return plans were finally abandoned, then every act, every expenditure had to be undertaken with an eye toward repatriation. This fact dawned gradually on an American in 1903 as he traveled about Italy and found that returned emigrants were much different, better persons at home; they had lived in brutal conditions in the United States because of "a feeling among them that they were merely temporizing . . .; that they had come to America to make a few hundred dollars to send or take back to Italy; and that it did not make much difference what they ate, wore or did, just so long as they got the money and got back." Their day-to-day existence in the United States would not improve until they were "drawn into the real American life" and changed their minds about going back to Europe.[10]

Dreams of the village were especially strong among such persons; their thoughts were directed eastward toward home, even while they lived and worked in the West. This longing made assimilation difficult, and ethnic identities were further maintained by life in immigrant enclaves, blocking or discouraging connections with American institutions. Such isolation drew the fire of many Americans and settled members of the Old Immigration. Angered at the spectacle of U.S. dollars being carried overseas, they were also appalled by living conditions among those expecting to return. Labor unions suffered from the influx of these low-wage immigrants who often rejected invitations to join their fight for better wages and conditions. For years the unions approached the newcomers from two directions, often at the same time: seeking to organize the aliens while attacking them as strikebreakers and cheap competition. And the continued exodus of remigrants added to the pressure on union leaders to side with the restrictionist movement.

The United Mine Workers reflected these contradictions: as an industrial union that covered all those working in and around coal mines, it signed up thousands of immigrants even while erupting sporadically against them. Frequently the union found itself pitted against employers who used immigrants as strikebreakers. These greenhorns were generally the most desperate for work and least informed, and were often those planning a quick return home. The mineworkers' weekly newspaper placed its finger on the special problem of the returning immigrant in 1907:

> If a peasant of southern Europe or coolie from China or Japan comes here for the purpose of getting a little money to go back and buy a small piece of land, such immigrants do not come here to become a part of our political and industrial system. They come here to live in colonies, to speak their own language, to trade with their own merchants, to preserve their own nationality, and to return to their own country.
>
> Immigrants who come here for the sole purpose of getting money to take back home are likely to subordinate everything else to that one objective, and to attain it will work cheap and live in squalor, which tends to lower the American standard of living and wages, and consequently reduces the opportunity for the profitable employment of capital.[11]

As these immigrants held back from identifying with their new country of residence, many became part of a subculture within their own immigrant culture; that is, the temporary immigrant did even less than other immigrants to learn English, adapt to American ways, join American organizations. This reluctance further stimulated nativist attacks, which reached a climax with the restriction legislation of the postwar 1920s. Remigrants were not the only cause of the nativist surge, but their lifestyles in America helped fuel the restrictionist drive and they became one of the nativists' easiest targets.

PRAISE AND SCORN AT HOME

As they returned to Europe the remigrants found a mixed welcome. Constructing new-style houses of brick rather than wood, many wore fancy clothes and endeavored to climb the social ladder. But villagers often looked askance at these people who seemed all too often to be putting on airs. One critic was the father of later emigrant Stoyan Christowe, who observed the well-dressed remigrants parading around their Bulgarian village and spat out, "An ox is an ox even if you put golden horns on him."[12]

Their stories were often too fantastic, too farfetched. Norwegians began referring to them as *Amerikaskrøner*—"tall tales from America." One man recalled his uncle's return to Norway in 1929 and his strange revelations about the things he had seen: "He told us about the Christmas trees that went round and round, he talked about streetcars, he talked of electric lights, he told of huge buildings, skyscrapers, he told us how they built them, he talked about the communications, railroads that went to every corner in the land, he told us about an industrial society which was so different from what we knew that it was like a completely different world." Was it all believable? Perhaps not. More recently, a returned emigrant showed his Norwegian grade school pupils a U.S. postcard with a photograph of a giant Pacific Northwest log on a logging truck, the driver standing proudly on top. When he translated the postcard's legend, "Oregon Toothpick," one child retorted, "I've always heard that Americans have big mouths."[13]

Their money was a reality that could not be denied, however. The cash carried home, together with the vast sums mailed back by those still toiling across the ocean, helped stabilize the economies of Europe and served as a stimulus for local booms. Business experience and connections became the most obvious gains from remigration in many districts, especially in Germany. Land, apartment houses, taverns, shops, and other firms were purchased by those coming home with "golden horns." For a time in Bydgoszcz, a Polish city in Pomerania, seventy agencies worked primarily to help remigrants obtain or sell properties. Two generations later the flow of retirees back from America would stimulate similar activities through their Social Security checks and factory pensions.[14]

Most who returned in the 1880–1930 era went into agriculture, and this activity was at the center of much of the debate over their impact. Certainly agriculture was extremely backward in many areas; one estimate by returning Norwegians was that farming in Norway was fifty years behind that in the United States. But would returned emigrants be the ones to launch the required changes? Remigrants rushed to buy farmland, and large-scale commercialization of land became one of the most noted results of the vast emigration and return. But early evidence indicated that remigrants then continued or even expanded traditional and backward farming practices.[15]

In contrast, areas such as Prussia and the English Midlands, where farm progress was extensive in the late nineteenth century, featured either the growth of larger land units with major investments of capital or the contrary development of smaller but more specialized farms that used the latest in farm technology and benefited from growing consumer demand. A student of the transformation of British agriculture notes increased farming complexity through use of artificial manures and new seeds and livestock breeds and adds that this "no doubt . . . also required flexibility of mind." But flexibility of mind regarding agricultural improvements may have been missing among many remigrants coming back to traditional farming in such areas as southern Italy or Poland. Few had worked on American farms, and this fact alone predicted that their impact on the Continent's agriculture would be minimal. Sporadic improvements and changes were widely publicized, but these were unusual, like the tomatoes planted by some Finns or the new flowers appearing in Polish gardens. Only in certain areas, such as parts of Scandinavia, could it be said that the remigrants were a definite mainstay of drives to modernize agriculture.[16]

But in other occupations and situations, where emigrants had been able to learn American methods, improvements were obvious. To begin with, more vigorous work habits were widely noted. Also, many carried home sewing machines, which led to improvements in clothing, and holiday garb began to be worn more regularly. Homemaking benefited: when Irish women returned, they refused to continue traditional hearth cooking because it only permitted meat to be boiled; soon they installed grates or bought ranges. Personal hygiene improved, and a Hungarian report indicated that remigrants even kept their windows open at night, rejecting the traditional belief that night air held evils.[17]

Many threw themselves into various campaigns for government change: Irish Home Rulers sought to throw off British control, Slovaks and Croatians pushed for separate nations, some Finns who had attended the Duluth Work People's College wanted to destroy capitalism. Others agitated for the development of public schools, and the remigrants' presence helped spread English through Gaelic-speaking areas of Ireland and in many other districts across Europe. Returned emigrants began to appear as members of village councils, school boards, even national legislatures; three of them became prime ministers, of Norway, Latvia, and Finland.[18]

A PEOPLE APART

The ironic growth of ethnic identities across the Atlantic, within foreign colonies in American cities, caused the return movement to be feared by some in Europe. Remigrants meant the threat of ethnic group upheavals to Austria-Hungary's rulers, and elsewhere church officials as well as government agents warned of troubles from those coming back. At times, in fact, it appeared that migrating peoples were under attack everywhere: in America they were called the anarchistic off-scourings of Europe, while on the Continent their return was dreaded because of the radicalism they supposedly had picked up abroad.[19]

Repatriates often stayed together after returning to Europe, meeting to exchange news and reminiscences. They soon discovered that, whereas in America they had been regarded as Poles (or Italians, or Magyars, or Irish), back home they were considered Americans. This irony figured in reports from the 1920s, and it remained true in the 1970s when Marsha Penti encountered Finnish remigrants who said that they still were immediately spotted by townspeople as being American.[20]

Organizations followed, perhaps inevitably. Danish newspapers as early as 1876 reported formation of a "United States Club" to unite "all Danes returned from the United States," and similar groups are mentioned in later accounts from across Europe—in Sweden, in Greece (where American Legion posts were started in five cities in the 1920s, formed by returners who had fought for the United States in World War I), in Split and Zagreb in Yugoslavia, in Finland and elsewhere. Stanisław Osada encountered an Alliance of Poles from America when he reached Torun, Poland, in 1922, and he helped form similar clubs elsewhere as well as launching a national organization; eventually these groups created the Patronate of Poles from America, aimed at helping remigrants.[21]

Years later travelers encountered these organizations at almost every stop as they toured the Continent. Oscar Handlin found a "George Washington Greek-American Association" high in the mountains at Tropaia, Greece, in the 1950s; in Oslo there was the Norwegian-American Club and the American Club; Helsinki had the *lännenkävijät kerho* ("western wayfarers club"), and returned emigrant organizations were reported in Mola di Bari and Molfetta, Italy, in addition to that country's numerous American Legion posts. Informal groups were scattered across the Continent. Many continue today, still using English in their meetings; some have branched into sponsoring tours and style shows. What unites members today is probably the same thing that prompted remigrants at the beginning of the century to come together: "We're different," as a returned Finn observed.[22]

What was "different"? Was it mainly attitudes? Opinions on this point are varied. Norwegian public health workers who investigated the impact of remigrants in the 1880s and 1890s concluded that returners had "acquired a wider outlook" and were not restricted by "the narrow and meagre conditions at home." A Finnish *Amerikan-Kävijöitä* looked back on his years abroad and asserted that, even if you did not become rich from the trip, you got wiser; other Finns agreed that they had developed a broader view of the world, seeing beyond their Ostrobothnian marshes.[23]

This expanded outlook could persist along with other return types, such as those in Francesco Cerase's typology: returns of failure, conservatism, innovation, retirement. Dino Cinel, like Cerase a student of Italian return migration, found that many were at least more amenable to change: "It was emigration which opened them to modernity." While some argued that there was no lasting impact, because most soon lapsed back into traditional lifestyles, overall it could still be said that those returning were more open to change and especially to democratic change. Two historians of Polish emigration concluded that the remigrants' influence was largely confined to economic issues and "perhaps a slight democratization of social relations." Theodore Saloutos came to similar conclusions after his investigations of Greek returned emigrants (although he admitted that many had soon reverted to old ways):

They had come into contact with a different language, with different customs and attitudes. They could hardly have failed to acquire new skills and techniques; their tempo of life had quickened; they had seen people worship in different churches; for better or for worse, they were exposed to the American press, periodicals, and literature; they had seen women treated differently; and they had sensed the pulsating effects of living in a strong and wealthy country.

Their ideas filtered through rural Greece and, though they were not proclaimed as heroes by Athens, "their contributions were nevertheless genuine."[24]

GOVERNMENT CONCERN

Athens—and Vienna, Stockholm, Rome, and other capitals—could scarcely sit by while emigrants embarked on an overseas exodus beyond anything known before in history. The reactions of European governments often showed fear, sometimes anger, but always a certain degree of amazement that so many of their citizens preferred to head abroad. That many returned did not entirely assuage these feelings. Investigations were accordingly instituted by most European governments.[25]

There was slight attention paid to return migration in these official studies, beyond urging reduced shipping fares for those coming back. Germany, for example, launched a major thrust of social welfare and labor legislation after 1878 at least partly to dissuade workers from leaving; concern for remigrants was largely absent or unvoiced, even though a large return flow would have reduced many of the government's concerns.[26]

Italy recognized the importance of the return wave very early, although as in most countries the initial emphasis was on stemming the outward flow. Soon, however, remigration was being cheered and given official encouragement. By 1910 an Italian senator was quoted in the Commissariato's *Bolletino* to the effect that the current of remigration "represents an economic force of the first order for us. It will be an enormous benefit for us if we can increase this flow of force in and out of our country." The government started requiring shipping lines to bring remigrants back from North and South America at a third of the normal price in 1907. Six years later Parliament permitted those coming home to regain their citizenship simply by living two years in their homeland; their children were considered Italian citizens even if born elsewhere.[27]

But the beginning of the Mussolini era and passage of restriction laws in the United States suddenly changed this Italian tradition of encouragement and protection. Italy under fascism, as with Hitler's Germany, wanted manpower for its foreign adventures, and new policies were put into effect to prevent further outflow, to lure back those overseas, and to strengthen the loyalty of emigrants abroad. Under Mussolini's 1927 law, workers could go overseas only if they promised to return within three years; families could not accompany them. Now remigration was to be forced; the round-trip ticket was the only one allowed. In the future the government's dreamers saw territorial conquests that would ultimately be populated by emigrants, using their labor to benefit the Italian nation. As George Gilkey concluded after surveying this transformation, "in emigration were many of the seeds of ultranationalism and imperialism."[28]

The other country whose investigations moved toward major concern over remigration and broader societal issues was Sweden. Swedish efforts initially followed trends sweeping the Continent, but the Royal Commission took a different tack that would eventually determine, in Ann-Sofie Kälvemark's words, that "the Swedish reaction appears as one of the strongest in Europe" because it was boosting neither colonies nor a national steamship company. There was early recognition in the investigations that Sweden had to be changed so that fewer people would need to emigrate, and that the country would benefit greatly if those abroad returned. Debates in the Riksdag showed a desire to make Swedish industry follow American patterns, and the eventual Royal Commission report (1907–12) even contained an appendix titled "Industrial Methods in the United States." One Riksdag member, later founder of the Liberal party, argued for easier property owning and the encouragement of small savings and contended, "Let us by such means as these 'move America over to Sweden' in the best sense of the term."[29]

Interest in drawing Swedes home from overseas was always close to the surface in both parliamentary discussions and commission investigations. Indeed, one proposal advanced in the 1904 Riksdag debate was to send a ship to American ports several times a year to carry Swedes back free of charge. But other proposals were included in the commission's twenty-volume report that would, it was hoped, increase remigration by removing obstacles to the return movement. These ranged from cutting military service requirements for remigrants older than twenty-six—a major concern of those who had fled to America without fulfilling their military obligation—to extending legal recognition to marriages conducted in the Augustana synod in the United States. Regaining Swedish citizenship was also made easier.[30]

One important aspect of Sweden's attempt to come to terms with its enormous exodus was the realization that the well-being of the population could no longer rest so heavily on money sent or brought back from America. Society itself had to change. Accordingly, the commission called for redistribution of farmland, stimulation of industry, encouragement of home ownership, extension of compulsory education, and broadened suffrage. The rise of the Swedish labor movement and Social Democratic party (which by 1914 was the largest group in the second chamber of the Riksdag) was part of this parallel transformation. Returned emigrants were prominent in those groups, too.[31]

AMERICA'S DUAL IMPACT

In 1947 an Italian political party used the Statue of Liberty as its ballot symbol in a local election. And in villages of east-central Europe the term *Amerikanci* still carries the meaning of opulence and well-being.[32]

In the swirl of American influences around the globe, such reports prompt a query: how much of the American image in Europe is derived in some way from return migration? And, though it must be admitted that each nation gains images on its course through history and fulfills several different roles to its own people and to others, another question follows: what U.S. roles had a lasting impression on those coming back—America the workshop, the producer, the shelter, the safety valve, the home of exiles, the banker, the exploiter, the imperial power, the superpatriot, the incubator of ethnic identification?

Two distinct images of America dominated the records of remigration: the materialistic view of the land of wealth, and the idealistic view of the land of equal rights and democracy. The image of the New World as a cornucopia of treasure ready to spill into the arms of every newly arrived adventurer has existed since Columbus. But, although equal rights permitted many an immigrant to rise economically to grab for this wealth, it was also true that the world of the rich—the Rockefellers, the Goulds, even the immigrant Carnegie—often overwhelmed the rights of those laboring twelve hours for a dollar in their factories. America's much-proclaimed political equality had little meaning to these workers. Steamships heading back across the Atlantic carried men and women familiar with both extremes. On one such trip Edward Steiner argued with a wealthy American, traveling in a first-class cabin, that it was not the opulence of his country but its ideals that would be more important to the Continent's masses: the steerage, Steiner reminded him, "carries into Europe more saving ideas than the cabin."[33]

But, though negative experiences were abundant, travelers in Europe over the years encountered what seemed to be almost a single view among remigrants, a chorus that overwhelmed dissonant voices. This was a sentiment extolling the United States, an attitude that seemed surprising in view of the conditions they had known. It was surprising because most returners had seen firsthand the contradictions in American life; they could show missing fingers and arms and talk knowingly of the United States as "a challenging giant, both fair and unfair, ugly and beautiful." They accepted the view that life was cruel in America and that the nation's coarse citizenry did not appreciate beauty; as the Italian saying put it bluntly, "Had the peasant known all this, he wouldn't have gone to America." Critics at home feasted on such tales.[34]

Still, despite their difficulties abroad, massive numbers of remigrants carried home attitudes toward America that were overwhelmingly positive. Some of this can be put down to the human tendency to remember happy times and submerge the difficult times. These contrasts did not survive in a simple relationship among remigrants, however: favorable memories involving the United States seem to have coexisted as an intricate part of some very bad experiences. Like a patent medicine that irritates the skin to produce a warm feeling, struggles in America's industrial cauldron were passed through the filter of memory and emerged as recollections of the proud role remigrants had played in creating the American industrial colossus. Their labors were essential. However small their part on the section gang or meatpacking line, they had helped build America.

When Carlo Levi was ordered to exile in the southern Italian town of Lucania, he heard of the toil and suffering many residents had known in America, all to save a few dollars to carry back. But, Levi added, "at the same time, and with no contradiction in terms," they saw America as "an earthly paradise and the promised land." Similarly, a remigrant told the Italian parliamentary investigators, "Eh! signor, better I die in America than live in Italy!"[35]

And these were not rare occurrences: a generation later when he conducted extensive interviews in the Mezzogiorno, Francesco Cerase found overwhelming support among remigrants—many of whom had returned decades earlier—for the view of America as a generous, friendly, egalitarian land; "they seemed highly convinced of the truth of these images." Betty Boyd Caroli came away with similar conclusions from her interviews in the early 1970s, also in Italy, and accounts from across the Continent are generally in accord with these findings. Recollecting the returned "Yanks," an Irishman in county Meath asserted that "they never lost the American appearance not even the American accent and always stated that America was a great country and they were much inclined for American ways." This from people who had toiled in the bowels of American society.[36]

Wars, hot and cold, brought new tests for America's hold on the returning immigrants. Nevertheless, as he traveled through Greece in the early 1950s, Theodore Saloutos not only discovered the overwhelming praise for the United States that other scholars were encountering in Italy and Finland but also learned that remigrants were active in the resistance against Nazis and Italians during World War II. Further, in the post–World War II years the remigrants were known for their eagerness to "resent and fight anti-Americanism," and another visitor pictured them as a barrier to the spread of Greek communism.[37]

Support for things American was based on much more than the sentiments of remigrants, of course. As explained by a Norwegian scholar, himself a returned emigrant, "since 1840, Norway has been 'bombarded' with Americana." The same could be said of all Europe. Further, it was the Americans who came out winners in two world wars, defended Europe through a tense cold war against communism, while its industries unloosed a glittering torrent of consumer wonders: American magazines, movies, music, and later television shows crossed all boundaries. Still, these were able to build on a solid base of support that included the positive attitude toward America held by returned emigrants. Their contribution was to reinforce a more general cultural influence; a German historian speculated that remigrants became "perhaps the most important mediators" between America and Germany. Many maintained this position for years through continuing contacts with the United States—by letters, visits, and close following of American media.[38]

Remigrants thus played a dual role, as citizens of their native lands who nevertheless identified with the United States. They stood in both the Old World and the New. During a century dominated by international conflict, this dual identity was more important than generally realized in forming a solid base of foreign support for America's rise to world leadership.

CONCLUSIONS

This study of the returned immigrants has been a sort of journey in itself, traveling within Europe and North America and on ships passing between the two, poking into peasant villages and U.S. factories, examining migrations into neighboring towns as well as intercontinental expeditions. The aim has been to present an accurate and honest picture of the phenomenon of return migration while admitting the inadequacy of much statistical and other data. Historians have an open field ahead as further probing uncovers relevant documents in Europe and North America and extends the scope to other continents. For this story, long ignored, deserves telling. "Expatriation and repatriation represent nothing new in the history of this country," Theodore Saloutos once explained; "it is new only to those who are unfamiliar with its history."[39]

In an examination of the remigrant from 1880 to 1930, before leaving Europe, at work in America, and after the return home, nine broad conclusions emerge:

1. The temporary immigrant was in truth far different from the immigrant who planned to stay. The expectations of any immigrant were all-important in directing his or her job-seeking, assimilation, and adjustment to American life, and the immigrant who stepped onto American soil planning permanent residence saw these goals differently than did the short-term industrial migrant. The latter was basically a *sojourner*, defined by sociologists as a deviant form of the stranger, who remains psychologically in his homeland while living somewhere else, culturally isolated, tied physically but not mentally to a job. He may have changed his mind eventually, but until that point he lived the life of one who saw his future back in Europe.[40]

Employment became the critical part of the remigrant's American existence. Like a New England girl arriving to work briefly in the Lowell mills in the 1830s, or a Turkish *Gastarbeiter* in Germany today, the temporary industrial migrant in the 1880–1930 period saw the world through different eyes than did (or does) the worker planning to remain. To ignore this fact and its implications is to miss a major facet of immigration's impact and an important explanation of immigrants' failure to assimilate despite lengthy residence abroad. Failing to take it into account would also make it difficult to understand why so many who returned home took up farming rather than the industrial occupations they had known overseas. If one task of the historian is to see the past from different angles, then following the contrary path of the temporary immigrant can provide an important new perspective.

2. The American immigration story becomes less unified, more diverse, when remigrants are considered within the broad picture of the peopling of a continent. There was little in common between the Bohemian family settling the Nebraska prairies in the 1890s and Bohemian men arriving for a year's work in a Chicago stockyard. Assimilation

was soon forced on those farming in Nebraska; it was not even a re-
mote goal of most of those lining up for their wages each fortnight in
Chicago. One immigrant is not always equal to another—an obvious
fact, but one made both more apparent and more significant when the
remigrant experience is considered. Similarly, the story of other aspects
of American history—especially American labor history—is shown to
be incomplete, inadequate, without including the temporary industrial
migrant.

3. There were many Americas contained within the broad vision of
the United States by the 1880s, but America as the symbol of economic
opportunity increasingly became uppermost for immigrants, especially
those planning a temporary stay. Democracy was of little importance
to a sojourner dreaming of adding to his piece of earth in the Mezzogiorno. When economic opportunity and democracy were seen as two
branches of the same trunk, however, one could buttress the other in
forming an image of the nation. But a remigrant who had witnessed few
examples of democracy in his twelve-hour days in a steel mill would
consider America in a different light than would another new resident
escaping from religious unrest and finding herself in the competitive
free-for-all of U.S. church denominations. Economic opportunity became the representative American symbol to millions.

4. The basis of American nativism was not opposition to return migration, but it gained several major arguments in the course of reacting
to temporary immigrants. Nativists began to erupt in anger as thousands and thousands of short-term residents avoided assimilation and
escaped abroad with their American earnings. The exodus goaded many
Americans into ever stronger condemnations of immigration in general,
and the identification of European remigrants with Chinese sojourners
became complete. This provided an opening for earlier, permanent immigrants to condemn later arrivals and to become in effect immigrant
nativists. Antiforeign sentiment among U.S. labor groups leaned especially hard on the temporary immigrant.

5. The striving for status—to hold onto a vanishing position, or even
to climb higher—emerges as one of the main forces behind remigration
as well as emigration. Remigrants often left Europe to seek a higher
status at home; they did not seek a permanent existence and better status in America. The New World may have represented a horn of plenty,
but its wealth would be more useful back in Europe. Basic subsistence
could be met, and after that the possibility of becoming landowners of
importance in the village. Immigrants knew enough about life in the
United States to understand the saying, "America for the oxen, Europe

for the peasant." It was in Europe, not America, that the opportunity to reach a new level of existence waited.[41]

6. The remigrant's importance in stimulating further immigration may have eclipsed even that of the much-maligned steamship agent. A large-scale exodus developed mainly from European areas where there had been an earlier emigration, which had produced a return flow of successes with money to purchase land and to construct "American houses." These acts promoted America with more impact than did handbills posted on village walls. There is also evidence of what might be called "emigration families," providing members from each generation who spent time in the United States and then returned, their tales handed down to stimulate others to try America later. The process was then repeated, generation after generation, and the remigrant ancestors became long-term role models. Their example competed with the emigrant letter as the chief propagandist of emigration. And the picture of America as a horn of plenty became indelibly fastened on a people who grew up hearing American stories around the winter hearth.[42]

7. The return flow must be counted as a major reason that Europe's enormous exodus to America did not result in a net loss for the home society. Some form of general decline might have been expected for a continent that lost 36 million of its most active and future-oriented citizens to the United States from 1820 to 1975. The same could have been predicted for other regions that sent their people to America; one might even apply it to Mexico and the Caribbean nations today. But instead of causing a deterioration, the era of mass emigration proved overall to be one of general advance and progress for the people of many nations. This pattern continues. Certainly many things, tangible and intangible, have contributed to this result, but one is the extensive return flow of people, money, and ideas. As a Polish priest concluded from his study of the emigration from Miejsce parish in 1883, the returns from America meant that the exodus was "not a loss but a gain for this province." It could be said for most of Europe.[43]

The Continent benefited as well from the return of organizational and political skills, as men and women of all ideologies and aspirations came back to launch labor unions and community organizations and to become involved in political affairs. Churches were challenged and new philosophies began to circulate. When Finland and Latvia achieved independence amid scenes of enormous chaos, leadership in each new country fell to those already experienced in labor and political struggles in America. Norway also chose a remigrant as its prime minister to lead the country through the dark days of depression and World War II.

Many others coming back occupied government posts in municipalities as well as in national regimes.

The remigrants brought change in many forms. New words were carried home: modern Finnish has been enriched by many remigrant words and phrases, according to recent studies. Beyond this, many of those returning to Europe displayed an openness, an attitude that shook off the old and helped transform the peasant world. And remigration contributed further to a mingling of cultures which encouraged change as well as helping bring a gradual integration of the cultures of Europe and America.[44]

The United States is more than just people transferred from Europe; Europe is guided by more than influences from America. But the two-way exchange was one crucial factor in the historical development of both, and the remigrant helped in both directions, a continuing link between two cultures.[45]

8. American "exceptionalism," the view that the American experience has been unique and that developments in the United States were basically different from those elsewhere, is dealt a further blow by the remigration story. The United States was not a land where every immigrant came to stay; it was a country seen by many foreigners as a means rather than an end. As such, the American immigration pageant contained many scenes known elsewhere, for temporary stays as well as permanent moves have long been part of human migrations.

Parallels are numerous. Just as was often the case in the United States, temporary migrants were unpopular in the Ruhr, where German unions fought Poles, employers put aliens in the dirtiest jobs, and officials sought their removal. Swiss workers assaulted Italians in 1896, the government meanwhile blocked their naturalization, and welfare groups refused to give aid. This was nativism run wild. Riots erupted against Italian workers in France from the 1880s on; in 1893, fifty Italians were killed and 150 wounded during an attack by French miners at the Aigues-Mortes saltworks. There was physical violence in the United States, but as in Europe the opposition to those planning to return usually took other forms: unions sought their dismissal, politicians argued for bans on their employment, and editorial writers aimed darts at those who carried off national wealth.[46]

Recent developments show the repetition of the remigration theme as well as its continuing importance as a world phenomenon. Temporary migrants spread over Europe during the nineteenth century as they had done in earlier epochs, and the phenomenon continues: by 1971 there were some 9 million temporary foreign workers in Europe, two-thirds of them in what was then West Germany. Italy, which once sent thousands of industrial migrants abroad, now had itself become the destination for many Third World workers who have discovered that Italian wages are many times those of their homelands. Providing other countries with employees who can be expected to return home has become a tradition in Yugoslavia, Spain, Portugal, Turkey, and Algeria. Meanwhile, thousands of Mexicans and other Latin Americans flock to jobs in the United States, remain a few years, and go home. They seek a better life, but among their own people.[47]

As with those coming back from Pittsburgh and Chicago in 1910 who showed off their savings and built "American houses," so the European guest-worker of today drives a German car back to his Spanish village and builds his new home in *el centro aleman* ("the German district"); in Portugal it is the *casa francesa* built by the worker returned from France. Ireland once had its "Yanks," who were sought out as a source of money and stories about life in a modern country, but today in the town of Alcudia de Guadix, Spain, the citizens turn for such things to the remigrants they jokingly call *los alemanes* ("the Germans"). And as occurred in southern Italy a century ago, land prices in Alcudia de Guadix have zoomed as remigrants carry back money and dreams of acquiring property.[48]

Studies of these modern remigrants focus on their desires for status and prestige while examining their interest in new equipment for farming and fruit raising. The debate over their impact on innovation in Third World homelands is as frequently heard today as it was when their European predecessors returned from America eighty or one hundred years ago.

From such evidence, it is apparent that the United States does not stand alone as a nation of either immigration or return migration. Rather, except for the variety of sources and the massive numbers involved, the American experience is largely within the mainstream of the world's historic migrations.

9. Finally, the story of the returned immigrant brings the historian face to face with the importance of human feelings, human emotions, in world events. Scholars often stress impersonal forces when discussing developments involving masses of people. But the fact that several million immigrants could turn around and leave a land with a higher standard of living and all the glitter of modernization, to cross the ocean again and return to a backward peasant village, with its distinctive culture and traditions, stands as supreme testimony to the pull of kin and home.

The Psalmist cried, "How shall we sing the Lord's song in a strange land?" And the longing to be within the family circle, in the familiar pathways and fields of home, has always been part of the human condition. The human heart must be given equal rank here with cold economic statistics and the pleadings of steamship agents. For the sense of being lost, away from moorings, left thousands of immigrants with the feeling that nothing seemed right in the New World—not holidays, not religious rites, not even the summer sunrise. They like the Psalmist felt lost in a strange land. The Swedish novelist of emigration, Vilhelm Moberg, reflected on these feelings in his autobiographical novel *A Time on Earth*:

> Man must have a root in the world; he must belong somewhere. He cannot abandon the land where he was born and adopt another country as his birthplace. Prattle about old and new mother countries is prattle only, and a lie. Either I have a country of my own, or I have not. Mother country is singular, never plural.
>
> The country you knew as child and young man was the country you left. That was your fate; you could never find another homeland.[49]

In the final analysis, the story of the returned immigrants is a record of the endurance of home and family ties. It provides further evidence that, for many, immigration demonstrated the strength and unity of the family—both in going to America and in returning—rather than the family's weakening or destruction. For it was to rejoin their people, to walk again on their own land, to sit in the parish church once more, that the temporary immigrants repacked their America trunks and booked passage again, this time for home. The journey to America had been round-trip. And as they had helped shape life in the United States, its world of work, its image of itself and of foreigners, now they would affect the lives of their own families, their villages, their homelands. It would be a different future on both continents because of the returned immigrants.[50]

Major Sources

Sources for the history of return migration in the years 1880–1930 are scattered across America and Europe, in government records, journalists' and travelers' accounts, and shipping, business, labor, religion, and folklore collections. Specific citations are provided in the endnotes; only important sources are mentioned here.

In Poland, major manuscript collections used for this study were the Wychodzstwo (Emigration) collections of the Archiwum Kurii Metropolitalnej w Krakowie (Archive of the Metropolitan Curia in Kraków). In Warsaw, the Archiwum akt Nowych (Archive of Modern Records) provided much material on post-1918 returns to Poland.

Irish manuscript collections used include the Irish Folklore Commission's Questionnaires Series, in the Department of Irish Folklore, University College Dublin; and the Archbishop Edward McCabe Papers, in the Dublin Diocesan Archives at Clonliffe College, Dublin.

The main American manuscript collections used include the Immigrants' Protective League Papers at the University of Illinois, Chicago Circle; the Terence V. Powderly Papers at Catholic University of America (on microfilm), and the Chicago Foreign Press Survey at the Chicago Historical Society.

Major U.S. government documents relied on include annual reports of both the Commissioner-General of Immigration and the Department of Labor; Reports from U.S. consuls; *Testimony . . . into the Alleged Violation of the Laws Prohibiting the Importation of Contract Laborers* (H. Misc. Doc. 572, 1888); U.S. Industrial Commission *Reports*

(1901); Dillingham Commission *Reports* (1911); and Thomas Kessner's "History of Repatriation," Appendix A in the staff report of the Select Commission on Immigration and Refugee Policy, *U.S. Immigration Policy and the National Interest* (1981).

Italian government documents used include the Commissariato dell' Emigrazione's main publications in the 1900–26 period, notably the periodical *Bollettino dell'Emigrazione*, the three-volume *Emigrazione e Colonie* (Rome, 1903–5), and the two-volume *L'Emigrazione Italiana dal 1910 al 1923* (Rome, 1926).

The twenty-volume report of the Emigrationsutredningen (the Royal Swedish Commission on Emigration), *Betänkande och bilagor*, issued 1908–13, was also valuable.

Notes

Chapter 1. A Two-Way Migration

1. *Gazeta Koscielna* (n.p., n.d.), quoted in *Dziennik Chicagoski*, 24 March 1894, translated by Chicago Foreign Press Survey, reel 58, Polish.

2. Frank Thistlethwaite, "Migration from Europe Overseas in the Nineteenth and Twentieth Centuries," XIe Congrès International des Sciences Historiques, *Rapports* (Stockholm, 1960), 5:40. J. D. Gould, "European Inter-Continental Emigration—The Road Home: Return Migration from the U.S.A.," *Journal of European Economic History* 9 (1980), 50. Marsha Penti, "The Role of Ethnic Folklore among Finnish-American Returnees" (Ph.D. diss., Indiana University, 1983), 1.

3. Miguel de Cervantes Saavedra, "The Jealous Estramaduran," in *The Exemplary Novels* (1613; rpt. New York, 1960), 105–37. William L. Sachse, "The Migration of New Englanders to England, 1640–1660," *American Historical Review* 53 (January 1948), 252–54, 260. Wilbur S. Shepperson, *Emigration and Disenchantment: Portraits of Englishmen Repatriated from the United States* (Norman, Okla., 1965), 3–4.

4. Charles Dickens, *American Notes for General Circulation* (London, 1842), 2:234–35, 237, quoted in Günter Moltmann, "American-German Return Migration in the Nineteenth and Early Twentieth Centuries," *Central European History* 13 (December 1980), 378.

5. Oscar Handlin estimates the total at "almost four million" for the years 1900–30; Handlin, "Immigrants Who Go Back," *Atlantic*, July 1956, 70.

6. Louis Adamic, *Laughing in the Jungle* (New York, 1932), 6.

7. U.S. Immigration Commission *Reports* (Washington, D.C., 1911), 4: 58. George R. Gilkey, "America: Myth and Reality," unpublished article in author's possession, 32, 37. Arnold Schrier, *Ireland and the American Emigration, 1850–1900* (Minneapolis, 1958), 138–39. Carlo Levi, *Christ Stopped at Eboli* (New York, 1947), 43, 127. Julianna Puskás, *From Hungary to the United States (1880–1914)* (Budapest, 1982), 80. Edward Steiner, *The Immigrant Tide: Its Ebb and Flow* (New York, 1909), 102–11.

8. The quotation is from Emily Green Balch, "Slav Emigration at Its Source," *Charities*, 7 April 1906, 78. See discussion of the remigrant prime ministers in Chapter 7.

9. Betty Boyd Caroli, *Italian Repatriation from the United States, 1900–1914* (New York, 1973), 41. Ingrid Semmingsen, *Norway to America: A History of the Migration* (Minneapolis, 1978), 120.

10. Halvdan Koht, *The American Spirit in Europe: A Survey of Transatlantic Influences* (Philadelphia, 1949), 185–86. Keijo Virtanen, *Settlement or Return: Finnish Emigrants (1860–1930) in the International Overseas Return Migration Movement* (Helsinki, 1979), 200–201. George R. Gilkey, "The United States and Italy: Migration and Repatriation," *Journal of Developing Areas* (October 1967), 26. Jonathan Sarna, "The Myth of No Return: Jewish Return Migration to Eastern Europe, 1881–1914," *American Jewish History* 71 (1981–82), 264–65. Puskás, *From Hungary*, 90n. Sten Carlsson, "Augustana Lutheran Pastors in the Church of Sweden," *Swedish-American Historical Quarterly* 35 (July 1984), 239–40. Alfred Vagts, *Deutsch-Amerikanische Rückwanderung* (Heidelberg, 1960), 96–98. Moltmann, "American-German Return Migration," 379. Roland Sarti, *Long Live the Strong: A History of Rural Society in the Apennine Mountains* (Amherst, Mass., 1985), 116–17. Carla Bianco, *The Two Rosetos* (Bloomington, Ind., 1974), 40–43.

11. Moltmann, "American-German Return Migration," 381–82. Reino Kero, "The Return of Emigrants from America to Finland," in University of Turku Institute of General History *Publications*, no. 4 (1972), 11–13. Virtanen, *Settlement or Return*, 43. Aulis Hautamäki, "Etelä-Pohjanmaan Järviseudun Amerikansiirtolaisuus, 1872–1917" (thesis, University of Jyväskylän, Finland, 1981), 103. Thomas J. Archdeacon, *Becoming American: An Ethnic History* (New York, 1983), 139. Imre Ferenczi and Walter F. Willcox, *International Migrations* (New York, 1929), 2: 196–200. Dino Cinel, *The National Integration of Italian Return Migration, 1870–1929* (Cambridge, 1991), 101–5. Donna Gabaccia discusses the problems in major Italian and U.S. sources in *Militants and Migrants: Rural Sicilians Become American Workers* (New Brunswick, N.J., 1988), 177–79.

12. Thistlethwaite, "Migration from Europe," 39–41.

13. Lars-Göran Tedebrand, *Västernorrland och Nordamerika, 1875–1913: Utvandring och Återinvandring* (Uppsala, 1972), 312. Daniel Kubat, ed., *The Politics of Return: International Return Migration in Europe* (Rome, 1984), 4. See analyses of the issue of statistical accuracy in Gould, "European Inter-Continental Emigration," 47–49, 85–87; Archdeacon, *Becoming American*, 139; Brinley Thomas, *Migration and Economic Growth: A Study of Great Britain and the Atlantic Economy* (Cambridge, 1973), 35–55; Thomas Kessner, "History of Repatriation," in U.S. Select Commission on Immigration and Refugee Policy, *U.S. Immigration Policy and the National Interest* (Washington, D.C., 1981), App. A, 296–309, 317–18. On the problems with pre-1880 German statistics, see Walter D. Kamphoefner, "The Volume and Composition of German-American Return Migration," in Rudolph J. Vecoli and Suzanne M. Sinke, eds., *A Century of European Migrations, 1830–1930* (Urbana, Ill., 1991), 296–99.

14. Wilhelm Schlag, "A Survey of Austrian Emigration to the United States," in Otto Hietsch, ed., *Österreich und die angelsächsische Welt* (Vienna, 1961), 141, quoted in Frances Kraljic, *Croatian Migration to and from the United States, 1900–1914* (Palo Alto, Calif., 1978), 40.

15. Kraljic, *Croatian Migration*, 95. Archdeacon, *Becoming American*, 139.

16. Kristian Hvidt, *Flight to America: The Social Background of 300,000 Danish Emigrants* (New York, 1984), 180–81. Virtanen, *Settlement or Return*, 69.

17. Rowland Tappan Berthoff, *British Immigrants in Industrial America* (Cambridge, Mass., 1953), 10. Dirk Hoerder, "Immigration and the Working Class: The Remigration Factor," *International Labor and Working Class History*, no. 21 (Spring 1982), 30. Archdeacon, *Becoming American*, 139.

18. Virtanen, *Settlement or Return*, 65–67, 221.

19. Archdeacon, *Becoming American*, 118–19.

20. Moltmann, "American-German Return Migration," 383–85. Also see Kamphoefner's critique, "Volume and Composition of German-American," 296–99.

21. Theodore Saloutos' study of Greek remigrants is not a statistical examination, but he emphasized the massive return flow; Saloutos, *They Remember America: The Story of the Repatriated Greek-Americans* (Berkeley, 1956).

22. Puskás, *From Hungary*, 26, based on official Hungarian statistics combined with Ferenczi and Willcox's statistics in *International Migrations*. Archdeacon, *Becoming American*, 139.

23. Kerby A. Miller, *Emigrants and Exiles: Ireland and the Irish Exodus to North America* (New York, 1985), 426. Marjolein 't Hart, "Heading for Paddy's Green Shamrock Shore: The Returned Emigrants in Nineteenth Century Ireland" (Master's thesis, University of Groningen, Holland, 1981), 21.

24. Francesco P. Cerase, "From Italy to the United States and Back: Returned Migrants, Conservative or Innovative?" (Ph.D. diss., Columbia University, 1971), 108. Dino Cinel, "Land Tenure Systems, Return Migration, and Militancy in Italy," *Journal of Ethnic Studies* 12 (Fall 1984), 56–57. Italy, Commissariato Generale dell'Emigrazione, *L'emigrazione italiana dal 1910 al 1923* (Rome, 1926), 1:208–9. Gould, "European Inter-Continental Emigration," 87. Virtanen, *Settlement or Return*, 68. Adam Walaszek, "Reemigranci ze Stanów Zjednoczonych i Kanady w Polsce. 1919–1923. 'Jak mozna bylo tak sobie to pieknie przedstawiac?'" *Przegląd Polonijny* 6, no. 1 (1980), 3–4.

25. Archdeacon, *Becoming American*, 139. Sarna, "Myth of No Return," 258–59.

26. Alfred Erich Senn and Alfonsas Eidintas, "Lithuanian Immigrants in America and the Lithuanian National Movement before 1914," *Journal of American Ethnic History* 6 (Spring 1987), 15.

27. Semmingsen, *Norway to America*, 120. J. E. Backer, "Norwegian Migration, 1856–1960," *International Migration* 4, nos. 3/4 (1966), 174. Knut Djupedal, "Tales of America," *Western Folklore* 49 (April 1990), 178.

28. Walaszek, "'How Was It Possible,'" 3–4.

29. Berthoff, *British Immigrants*, 10. Hoerder, "Immigration and the Working Class," 30.

30. Mark Stolarik, "From Field to Factory: The Historiography of Slovak Immigration to the United States," *Slovakia*, no. 28 (1978–79), 85, cited in Walaszek, "'How Was It Possible,'" 3. Archdeacon, *Becoming American*, 139.

31. Lars-Göran Tedebrand, "Remigration from America to Sweden," in Harald Runblom and Hans Norman, eds., *From Sweden to America: A History of the Migration* (Minneapolis, 1976), 201, 209. Tedebrand, "Strikes and Political Radicalism in Sweden and Emigration to the United States," in Dirk Hoerder, ed., *American Labor and Immigration History, 1877–1920s: Recent European Research* (Urbana, Ill., 1983), 222–23. John S. Lindberg, *The Background of Swedish Emigration to the United States: An Economic and Sociological Study in the Dynamics of Migration* (Minneapolis, 1930; rpt. 1971), 242.

32. Saloutos, *They Remember America*, 63, 67. Irish Folklore Commission Questionnaires, MS 1411, 236–37. Schrier, *Ireland and the American Emigration*, 136.

Louis Adamic, *The Native's Return: An American Immigrant Visits Yugoslavia and Discovers His Old Country* (New York, 1934), 25.

33. Thistlethwaite, "Migration from Europe Overseas," esp. 49–51, 57. Shepperson, *Emigration and Disenchantment*, vii–viii, 196. Cinel, *National Integration of Italian Return Migration*, 8. Theodore Saloutos, *Expatriates and Repatriates: A Neglected Chapter in United States History* (Rock Island, Ill., 1972), 19. In addition, a research agenda for the study of return migration has been proposed by Ewa Morawska in "Return Migrations: Theoretical and Research Agenda," in Vecoli and Sinke, *A Century of European Migrations*, 277–87.

34. Robert Foerster, *The Italian Emigration of Our Times* (New York, 1919; rpt. 1968), ii.

Chapter 2. Seasonal Migrations and the America Fever

1. "State of Labor in Europe, 1878: Italian Laborers in Germany," 46th Cong., 1st sess., H. Ex. Doc. 5, 192–93.

2. Antonio Mangano, "The Effect of Emigration upon Italy," *Charities*, 4 January 1908, 1329.

3. U.S. Commissioner-General of Immigration, *Annual Report*, 1931 (Washington, D.C., 1931), 218. An excellent recent compilation of immigration statistics is Stephan Thernstrom, ed., *Harvard Encyclopedia of American Ethnic Groups* (Cambridge, Mass., 1980), esp. 547, 1036–37, 1048. Harald Runblom, "A Brief History of a Research Project," in Runblom and Hans Norman, eds., *From Sweden to America: A History of the Migration* (Minneapolis, 1976), 11. Andrzej Brożek, *Polish Americans, 1854–1939* (Warsaw, 1985), 36–37. Jon Gjerde, *From Peasants to Farmers: The Migration from Balestrand, Norway, to the Upper Middle West* (Cambridge, 1985), 3, 12. Sigmund Skard, *The United States in Norwegian History* (Oslo, 1976), 82.

4. Emily Greene Balch, "Slav Emigration at Its Source," *Charities*, 2 June 1906, 326–27. Frances Kraljic, *Croatian Migration to and from the United States, 1900–1914* (Palo Alto, Calif., 1978), 14. Robert F. Foerster, *The Italian Emigration of Our Times* (New York, 1919, 1968), 63.

5. Alfred Schutz, *Collected Papers, I: The Problem of Social Reality* (The Hague, 1962), 1: 69–71, quoted in Ewa Morawska, *For Bread with Butter: The Life-Worlds of East Central Europeans in Johnstown, Pennsylvania, 1890–1940* (Cambridge, 1985), 63–64.

6. John J. Bukowczyk, *And My Children Did Not Know Me: A History of the Polish-Americans* (Bloomington, Ind., 1987), 12. Morawska, *For Bread with Butter*, 66–67. M. Mark Stolarik, *Immigration and Urbanization: The Slovak Experience, 1870–1918* (New York, 1989), 236–37. Roland Sarti, *Long Live the Strong: A History of Rural Society in the Apennine Mountains* (Amherst, N.J., 1985), 117–19. Timo Orta, "Finnish Emigration prior to 1893: Economic, Demographic, and Social Backgrounds," in Michael G. Karni et al., eds., *The Finnish Experience in the Western Great Lakes Region: New Perspectives* (Turku, Finland, 1975), 23.

7. Claudius Riegler, "Labor Migration of Skilled Workers, Artisans, and Technicians and Technology Transfer between Sweden and Germany before World War I," 164, and Dirk Hoerder, "An Introduction to Labor Migration in the Atlantic Economies," 23, in Hoerder, ed., *Labor Migration in the Atlantic Economies: The European and North American Working Classes during the Period of Industrialization* (Westport, Conn., 1985). John Bodnar, *The Transplanted: A History of Immigrants*

in Urban America (Bloomington, Ind., 1985), 45. Italy, Commissariato dell'Emigrazione, *Bollettino dell'Emigrazione*, 1912, no. 1, 6–7, 18–58.

8. Kazimiera Zawistowicz-Adamska, *Spolecznosc Wiejska* (Łódź, 1948), 154.

9. 1907 Survey, Wychodźstwo Collection, Archiwum Kurii Metropolitalnej w Krakowie, Poland (hereafter cited as Kraków Diocese Archives).

10. Oscar Handlin, *The Uprooted: The Epic Story of the Great Migrations That Made the American People* (New York, 1951), 7, 17.

11. Hans Norman and Harald Runblom, "Migration Patterns in the Nordic Countries," in Hoerder, *Labor Migration*, 34, 41. Robert C. Ostergren, *A Community Transplanted: The Trans-Atlantic Experience of a Swedish Immigrant Settlement in the Upper Middle West, 1835–1915* (Madison, Wis., 1988), 86. Gjerde, *From Peasants to Farmers*, 13, 15–16. Julianna Puskás, "Emigration from Hungary to the United States before 1914," *Studia Historica* (Budapest, 1975), 17. Abel Chatelain, *Les migrants temporaires en France de 1800 a 1915* (Lille, 1976), 2:1102. David Kertzer and Dennis Hogan, "On the Move: Migration in an Italian Community, 1865–1921," *Social Science History* 9 (Winter 1985), 8, and "Migration Patterns during Italian Urbanization, 1865–1921," *Demography* 22 (August 1985), 309. David DeChenne, "Labor and Immigration in a Southern Illinois Mill Town, 1890–1937" (D.A. diss., Illinois State University, 1989), 309. Cormac ó Gráda, "Seasonal Migration and Post-Famine Adjustment in the West of Ireland," *Studia Hibernica*, n. 13 (1973), 60.

12. Pamela L. R. Horn, "The National Agricultural Labourers' Union in Ireland, 1873–79," *Irish Historical Studies* 17 (March 1971), 71. *The American Review of Reviews* (September 1905), 362. Hoerder, *Labor Migration*, 22–23. Benjamin Murdzek, *Emigration in Polish Social-Political Thought, 1870–1914* (Boulder, Colo., 1977), 25–27. Lawrence Schofer, *The Formation of a Modern Labor Force: Upper Silesia, 1865–1914* (Berkeley, 1975), 24–25, 71–72. Caroline Golab, *Immigrant Destinations* (Philadelphia, 1977), 79–80, 86–87. Andrzej Jedrzejowski, "Danish Polonia between 1892–1921," *Przegląd Polonijny* 1, no. 2 (1975), 200. George Nellemann, *Polske landarbejdere i Danmark og deres efferkommere* (Copenhagen, 1981), 314, 316.

13. Gianfausto Rosoli, "Italian Migration to European Countries from Political Unification to World War I," in Hoerder, *Labor Migration*, 111. Foerster, *Italian Emigration*, 144, 148–49. Italy, Commissariato dell'Emigrazione, *Emigrazione e Colonie*, 1:1.225–26. Parish surveys, 1891, 1907, and 1913, Kraków Diocese Archives.

14. Kraków Priests' Convention, 1907, 24–27, Kraków Diocese Archives.

15. Gerard Moran, "'A Passage to Britain': Seasonal Migration and Social Change in the West of Ireland, 1870–1890," *Saothar* 13 (1988), 25. Chatelain, *Les migrants temporaires en France*, 2:1102–4. Morawska, *For Bread with Butter*, 41. Irena Lechowa, "Tradycje emigracyjne w Klonowej," *Prace i Materiały* (Łódź, 1960), 43–67.

16. Instytut Gospodarstwa Społecznego, *Szkoła Głowna Planowania Statystyki* (Warsaw, 1935–36), interviews 10 and 249.

17. Frank Thistlethwaite, "Migration from Europe Overseas in the Nineteenth and Twentieth Centuries," *XIᵉ Congrès International des Sciences Historiques Rapports* (Stockholm, 1960), 5:41–42. Franco Ramella, "Emigration from an Area of Intense Industrial Development: The Case of Northwestern Italy," in Rudolph J. Vecoli and Suzanne M. Sinke, eds., *A Century of European Migrations, 1830–1930* (Urbana, Ill., 1991), 271. Golab, *Immigrant Destinations*, 94, 97. Morawska, *For Bread with Butter*, 36–37. Klaus J. Bade, "German Emigration to the United States

and Continental Immigration to Germany in the Late Nineteenth and Early Twentieth Centuries," in Hoerder, *Labor Migration*, 132. Christoph Klessman, "Polish Miners in the Ruhr District: Their Social Situation and Trade Union Activity," in Hoerder, *Labor Migration*, 253–54, 256–57. Dirk Hoerder, "International Labor Markets and Community Building by Migrant Workers in the Atlantic Economies," in Vecoli and Sinke, *A Century of European Migrations*, 80–81.

18. Moran, "'A Passage to Britain,'"22, 24–26. William Thomas and Florian Znaniecki, *The Polish Peasant in Europe and America: Monograph of an Immigrant Group* (Boston, 1918), 1:398–99. John W. Briggs, *An Italian Passage: Immigrants to Three American Cities, 1890–1930* (New Haven, Conn., 1978), 65–68.

19. Andrzej Pilch, "The Economic Migration of the Galician Population in the 19th and 20th Centuries," *Przegląd Polonijny* 1, no. 2 (1975), 199. Golab, *Immigrant Destinations*, 99. Morawska, *For Bread with Butter*, 28–30. Gjerde, *From Peasants to Farmers*, 20–21. Hoerder, "International Labor Markets," discusses the question of surplus labor traveling about Europe.

20. John Malcolm Brinnin, *The Sway of the Grand Saloon: A Social History of the North Atlantic* (New York, 1971), 160–69, 241, 311. Philip Taylor, *The Distant Magnet: European Emigration to the U.S.A.* (New York, 1971), 116–17. Michael J. Piore, *Birds of Passage: Migrant Labor and Industrial Societies* (Cambridge, 1979), 149, 154. Terry Coleman, *Going to America* (New York, 1972), 242.

21. Marjolein 't Hart, "Heading for Paddy's Green Shamrock Shore: The Returned Emigrants in Nineteenth Century Ireland," (Master's thesis, University of Groningen, 1981), 33. Coleman, *Going to America*, 237. Basil Greenhill and Ann Giffard, *Traveling by Sea in the Nineteenth Century: Interior Design in Victorian Passenger Ships* (London, 1972), 25. Irish Folklore Commission Questionnaires, MS 1408, 97–98. Taylor, *Distant Magnet*, 116.

22. Greenhill and Giffard, *Traveling by Sea*, 9. Brinnin, *Sway of the Grand Saloon*, 6–8.

23. Brinnin, *Sway of the Grand Saloon*, 8. Taylor, *Distant Magnet*, 115–16, 119–20, covers U.S. laws of 1855, 1860, 1882, and 1908.

24. Taylor, *Distant Magnet*, 94. Dollar equivalents are given in *The World Almanac 1886* (New York, 1886), 29. E. L. Boas, passenger agent of the Hamburg-America Line, quoted in U.S. 50th Cong., 1st sess., H. Misc. Doc. 572, *Testimony Taken by the Select Committee . . . into the Alleged Violation of the Laws Prohibiting the Importation of Contract Laborers, Paupers, Convicts, and Other Classes* (Washington, D.C., 1888), 5. Kerby A. Miller, *Emigrants and Exiles: Ireland and the Irish Exodus to North America* (New York, 1985), 355. Witold Kula et al., comps., *Writing Home: Immigrants in Brazil and the United States, 1890–1891* (Boulder, Colo., 1986), 272–73, 375.

25. Piore, *Birds of Passage*, 154. U.S. 57th Cong., *Reports of the Industrial Commission on Immigration* (Washington, D.C., 1901), 15:xc, 115, 117. U.S. 50th Cong., H. Misc. Doc. 572, 39. *Bolletino dell'Emigrazione*, 1908, no. 4, 4–9, and 1912, no. 3, 468–73. Rudolph J. Vecoli, "Chicago's Italians prior to World War I: A Study of Their Social and Economic Adjustment" (Ph.D. diss., University of Wisconsin, 1962), 290. Roger David Simon, "The Birds of Passage in America, 1865–1914" (thesis, University of Wisconsin, 1966), 10. Isaac Hourwich, *Immigration and Labor: Economic Aspects of European Immigration to the United States* (New York, 1912), 97, 268. Also see Taylor, *Distant Magnet*, 94–95, and Kraljic, *Croatian Migration*, 53, 76.

26. Keijo Virtanen, *Settlement or Return: Finnish Emigrants (1860–1930) in the*

International Overseas Return Migration Movement (Helsinki, 1979), 184–85, n. 63.

27. U.S. 50th Cong., 1st sess., H. Misc. Doc. 572, pt. 2, *Reports of Diplomatic and Consular Officers Concerning Emigration from Europe to the United States* (Washington, D.C., 1889), 66. Dino Cinel, "Conservative Adventurers: Italian Migrants in Italy and San Francisco" (Ph.D. diss., Stanford University, 1979), 57.

28. U.S. Commissioner-General of Immigration, *Report, 1904*, 134. Report of Prefetto, Cosenza, 23 October 1891, cited in Cinel, "Conservative Adventurers," 65–66.

29. Robert Marzo, New York, quoted in 50th Congress, *Reports of Diplomatic and Consular Officers*, 81. See such varied sources on this as Mangano, "Effect of Emigration," *Charities*, 1 February 1908, 1478, 1480; Puskás, "Emigration from Hungary," 8; U.S. 50th Cong., *Contract Laborers*, 339; U.S. 50th Cong., *Reports of Diplomatic and Consular Officers*, 112.

30. U.S. 50th Cong., *Contract Laborers*, 100–101, 121. Grazia Dore, "Some Social and Historical Aspects of Italian Emigration to America," *Journal of Social History* 2 (Winter 1968), 118.

31. Gjerde, *Peasants to Farmers*, 130. Miller, *Emigrants and Exiles*, 353–54. U.S. 61st Cong., 3rd sess., S. Doc. 747, *Reports of the Immigration Commission* (Washington, D.C., 1911), 4:62–63 (hereafter cited as Dillingham Commission *Reports*). Marcus Braun, special immigrant inspector, in U.S. Commissioner-General of Immigration, *Report, 1903*, 88.

32. U.S. Commissioner-General of Immigration, *Report, 1903*, 87. Francesco P. Cerase, "From Italy to the United States and Back: Returned Migrants, Conservative or Innovative?" (Ph.D. diss., Columbia University, 1971), 26n. U.S. 50th Cong., *Contract Laborers*, 152–53. U.S. 50th Cong., *Reports of Diplomatic and Consular Officers*, 112. U.S. 57th Cong., *Reports of the Industrial Commission*, 15:xc, xci, 107. Kula et al., *Writing Home*, 317.

33. U.S. 50th Cong., *Contract Laborers*, 120–22, 335, 339.

34. U.S. 50th Cong., *Contract Laborers*, 116. Stoyan Christowe, *This Is My Country* (New York, 1938), 26–27.

35. George W. Hotwhick, U.S. Consulate, Trieste, to T. V. Powderly, 2 November 1907, in Terence Vincent Powderly Papers, 1864–1937, Catholic University of America, reel 80.

36. Broughton Brandenburg, *Imported Americans* (New York, 1904), 38–39. U.S. Commissioner-General of Immigration, *Report, 1903*, 95.

37. Josef Cybulski, from unidentified U.S. city, to wife and brother in Rumunki, Lipno district, Congress Poland, 16 February 1891, in Kula et al., *Writing Home*, no. 110, 222–23.

38. U.S. Commissioner-General of Immigration, *Report, 1903*, 87–89. Zoltan Kramar, ed., *From the Danube to the Hudson: U.S. Ministerial and Consular Dispatches on Immigration from the Habsburg Monarchy, 1850–1900* (Atlanta, Ga., 1978), 77. Trial information from Leopold Caro, *Emigracya: I Polityka Emigracyjna* (Poznań, 1914), 82–85; other sources are given in Murdzek, *Emigration in Polish Social-Political Thought*, 103. On other trials of agents, see Caro, *Emigracya*, 86, 92–93.

39. Caro, *Emigracya*, 92–93. Grace Abbott, "The Bulgarians of Chicago," *Charities*, 9 January 1909, 656–57. U.S. Commissioner-General of Immigration, *Report, 1909*, 112–13, quoted with approval in Dillingham Commission *Reports*, 2:385.

40. U.S. 50th Cong., *Contract Laborers*, 153. Braun report in U.S. Commissioner-General of Immigration, *Report, 1904*, 133. Caro, *Emigracya*, 94.

41. James Stuart Olson, *The Ethnic Dimension in American History* (New York, 1979), 203–10. Taylor, *Distant Magnet*, chap. 5, esp. 116–19. Robert DeC. Ward, "The Immigration Problem," *Charities*, 6 February 1904, 140. Powderly, Summary of Findings, 1907, in Powderly Papers, reel 76.

42. Hourwich, *Immigration and Labor*, 97–98.

43. Hon. Ferri, in *Bollettino dell'Emigrazione*, 1909, no. 12, 30, cited in Angelo Olivieri, "L'Italia ufficiale e la realtà dell'emigrazione in USA (1886–1914)," *Studi Emigrazione* 11 (March 1974), 41–42. Branko Mita Colakovic, *Yugoslav Migrations to America* (San Francisco, 1973), 62. On railroad and state propaganda, see Lars Ljungmark, *For Sale—Minnesota: Organized Promotion of Scandinavian Immigration, 1866–1873* (Stockholm, 1971), 17–22, and David Emmons, *Garden in the Grasslands: Boomer Literature of the Central Great Plains* (Lincoln, Neb. 1971), esp. 105–6. Marsha Penti, "The Role of Ethnic Folklore among Finnish-American Returnees" (Ph.D. diss., Indiana University, 1983), 283–85. Vilhelm Moberg, "Why I Wrote the Novel about Swedish Emigrants," *Swedish Pioneer Historical Society Journal* 17 (January 1966), 64.

44. Irish Folklore Commission Questionnaires, MS 1410, 98–100. Mangano, "Effect of Emigration" (1 February 1908), 1479. Brandenburg, *Imported Americans*, 39–41. Moberg, "Why I Wrote the Novel," 64. John Strusinski, College Point, N.Y., to Adam Strusinski, Rumunki, Lipno district, Congress Poland, 16 February 1891, in Kula et al., *Writing Home*, no. 262, 418.

45. George R. Gilkey, "The Effects of Emigration on Italy, 1900 to 1923" (Ph.D. diss., Northwestern University, 1950), 37, 141. Krystyna Duda-Dziewierz, *Wieś Malopolska A Emigracja Amerykańska* (Warsaw, 1938), 51–53. Brożek, *Polish Americans*, 24. Mangano, "Effect of Emigration" (1 February 1908), 1478.

46. Balch, "Slav Emigration," *Charities*, 3 February 1906, 598. David Doyle, "Unestablished Irishmen: New Immigrants and Industrial America, 1870–1910," 215, and Lars-Göran Tedebrand, "Strikes and Political Radicalism in Sweden and Emigration to the United States," 228–29, in Dirk Hoerder, ed., *American Labor and Immigration History, 1877–1920s: Recent European Research* (Urbana, Ill., 1983). Thomas and Znaniecki, *Polish Peasant*, 1:376–77.

47. Monika Glettler, *Pittsburg—Wien—Budapest: Programm und Praxis der Nationalitätenpolitik bei der Auswanderung der ungarischen Slowaken nach Amerika um 1900* (Vienna, 1980), 25. Irish Folklore Commission Questionnaires, MS 1411, 157. Dillingham Commission *Reports*, 4:154–55, 158–59, 270, 361–64, 386. J. D. Gould points out that England, not the United States, remained the destination for most short-term emigrants from Ireland. Ease of transport as well as wages were important in this choice. Most seeking permanent emigration abroad headed to America; Gould, "European Inter-Continental Emigration—the Road Home: Return Migration from the U.S.A.," *Journal of European Economic History* 9, no. 1 (1980), 73.

48. U.S. Department of Labor, *History of Wages in the United States from Colonial Times to 1928* (Washington, D.C., 1934), 256–60, 329–32. Paul H. Douglas, *Real Wages in the United States* (Boston, 1930), 143, 175. Complications in comparing U.S. and European workers' incomes are discussed in Walter D. Kamphoefner, Wolfgang Helbich, and Ulrike Sommer, eds., *News from the Land of Freedom: German Immigrants Write Home* (Munich, 1988; trans. Cornell University Press, 1991), 289–94. Kamphoefner et al. note that U.S. unskilled workers received wages that were often not much above those in Germany, but some aspects of living

conditions—such as an abundance of butter—were better in America. Unemployment, however, remained a more serious problem in the United States. Conditions in the Continental "periphery"—Poland, Italy, Bulgaria, Greece, Russia, Finland, Romania, Hungary—would have been far below those in Germany, however.

49. Gould, "European Inter-Continental Emigration," 67–69. Dillingham Commission *Reports*, 1:185. Dino Cinel, *The National Integration of Italian Return Migration, 1870–1929* (Cambridge, 1991), 126.

50. John Bodnar, Roger Simon, and Michael P. Weber, *Lives of Their Own: Blacks, Italians, and Poles in Pittsburgh, 1900–1960* (Urbana, Ill., 1982), 57, 59, 62–63. Dillingham Commission *Reports*, 9:49–50. DeChenne, "Labor and Immigration," 48–51.

51. J. W. White, Seaboard Railway, to W. H. Gates, Norfolk, Va., 5 July 1906; White to Terence Powderly, 2 June 1906; Powderly to White, 9 July 1906, in Powderly Papers, reel 76. Dillingham Commission *Reports*, 1:188. Bodnar develops this theme in *Transplanted*, 1–56, esp. 38 and 56.

52. Bade, "German Emigration," 126. Edward A. Steiner, *The Immigrant Tide: Its Ebb and Flow* (New York, 1909), 77. Harry Jerome, *Migration and Business Cycles* (New York, 1926), 202; see discussion of Jerome's theory in Cinel, "Conservative Adventurers," 58. Brinley Thomas, *Migration and Economic Growth: A Study of Great Britain and the Atlantic Economy* (Cambridge, 1973), chaps. 7, 10. Jeffrey G. Williamson, "Migration to the New World: Long Term Influences and Impact," *Explorations in Economic History*, Summer 1974, 372–73, 385.

53. Vecoli, "Chicago's Italians," 111. Grazia Dore, "Some Social and Historical Aspects," 110–11. Census figures given in George R. Gilkey, "The United States and Italy: Migration and Repatriation," *The Journal of Developing Areas* 2 (October 1967), 26–28.

54. Julianna Puskás, *From Hungary to the United States (1880–1914)* (Budapest, 1982), 48. Morawska, *For Bread with Butter*, 24–25. Josef J. Barton, *Peasants and Strangers: Italians, Rumanians, and Slovaks in an American City, 1890–1950* (Cambridge, Mass., 1975), 32. Kula et al., *Writing Home*, 13. Golab, *Immigrant Destinations*, 93, 98. Bodnar et al., *Lives of Their Own*, 40. Thomas and Znaniecki, *Polish Peasant*, 2:158.

55. Keijo Virtanen, comp., *Letters to Finland* (Ann Arbor, Mich., 1976), 1–2. Penti, "The Role of Ethnic Folklore," 113, 215. Gjerde, *From Peasants to Farmers*, 8, 122. Arne Hassing, "Norway's Organized Response to Emigration," *Norwegian-American Studies* 25 (1972), 58, 65. Sten Carlsson, "Chronology and Composition of Swedish Emigration to America," in Runblom and Norman, *From Sweden to America*, 132. Ljungmark, *For Sale—Minnesota*, 5. John S. Lindberg, *The Background of Swedish Emigration to the United States* (Minneapolis, 1930, 1971), 247–49.

56. Doyle, "Unestablished Irishmen," 204. Irish Folklore Commission Questionnaires, MS 1409, 61–62.

57. Barton, *Peasants and Strangers*, 32, 34, 36–39.

58. Bodnar, *Lives of Their Own*, 39. Emily Greene Balch, "The Peasant Background of Our Slavic Fellow-Citizens," *Survey* 24 (6 August 1910), 672–73.

59. Barton, *Peasants and Strangers*, 28–32. Cinel, "Conservative Adventurers," 66–69. Bodnar, *Lives of Their Own*, 45. Briggs, *An Italian Passage*, 1–14. Cinel, *National Integration of Italian Return Migration*, chap. 8 on regional differences.

60. A. William Hoglund, "No Land for Finns: Critics and Reformers View the Rural Exodus from Finland between the 1880's and World War I," 36–37, 43–45, and Timo Orta, "Finnish Emigration prior to 1893: Economic, Demographic, and

Social Backgrounds," 28–29, in Karni et al., *Finnish Experience.* Golab, *Immigrant Destinations,* 80–87, 93, 97. Balch, "Slav Emigration," *Charities,* 5 May 1906, 178–79. Stefan Kieniewicz, *The Emancipation of the Polish Peasantry* (Chicago, 1969), 182, 190–204, 212–13. Murdzek, *Emigration in Polish Social-Political Thought,* 141–42.

61. Maria Wierusyewska-Adamcyk, *Społeczność Wiejska Zaborowa w Procesie Przemian* (Warsaw, 1980), 81–82.

62. G. H. L. Zeegers quoted in Thistlethwaite, "Migration from Europe Overseas," 54. Glettler, *Pittsburg—Wien—Budapest,* 378. Morawska, *For Bread with Butter,* 66. Puskás, "Emigration from Hungary," 15. Williamson, "Migration to the New World," 376–77.

63. Kieniewicz, *Emancipation of the Polish Peasantry,* 182, 212, 216, 228–29. Murdzek, *Emigration in Polish Social-Political Thought,* 109. Golab, *Immigrant Destinations,* 52, 98–99. Balch, "Slav Emigration," *Charities,* 6 January 1906, 439–40; 2 June 1906, 325; 25 August 1906, 542–43. Hoglund, "No Land for Finns," 45. Dillingham Commission *Reports,* 4:265.

64. Thomas Kessner, *The Golden Door: Italian and Jewish Immigrant Mobility in New York City, 1880–1915* (New York, 1977), 35–37. Imre Ferenczi and Walter F. Willcox noted in their 1929 study, "In temporary emigration, the proportion of females is regularly very small"; Ferenczi and Willcox, *International Migrations* (New York, 1929), 1:210, see also 1:211, 1:444, 1:446. U.S. 13th Census (1910) *Abstract* (Washington, D. C., 1913), 190, quoted in Kraljic, *Croatian Migration,* 40, also see 19. Foerster, *Italian Emigration,* 342–43. Dillingham Commission *Report,* 4:138, 376, Table 21. Puskás, "Emigration from Hungary," 8. Gwendolyn Mink, *Old Labor and New Immigrants in American Political Development: Union, Party, and State, 1875–1920* (Ithaca, N.Y., 1986), 49. Thomas Archdeacon, *Becoming American: An Ethnic History* (New York, 1983), 135. Julianna Puskás, "Hungarian Overseas Migration: A Microanalysis," in Vecoli and Sinke, *A Century of European Migrations,* 225–26.

65. Isaac Hourwich, *Immigration and Labor: Economic Aspects of European Immigration to the United States* (New York, 1912), 198–99.

66. M. Mark Stolarik, "Immigration and Urbanization: The Slovak Experience, 1870–1918" (Ph.D. diss., University of Minnesota, 1974), 25. In addition to citations in note 64, for studies on male percentages from specific areas, see Ostergren, *A Community Transplanted,* 312–13; Hassing, "Norway's Organized Response," 58; J. E. Backer, "Norwegian Migration, 1856–1960," *International Migration* 4, nos. 3/4 (1966), 178, Table 4; Reino Kero, "The Return of Emigrants from America to Finland," University of Turku Institute of General History *Publications,* no. 4 (1972), 10–11; Virtanen, *Settlement or Return,* 126. Hourwich, *Immigration and Labor,* 198–99. Gould, "European Inter-Continental Emigration," 53. On exceptions to the heavily male emigration percentages, note the Irish: Thomas, *Migration and Economic Growth,* 73–74, 78; Miller, *Emigration and Exile,* 352; Arnold Schrier, *Ireland and the American Emigration, 1850–1900* (Minneapolis, 1958), 4; and Jews: Kessner, *The Golden Door,* 31–32. On age breakdown among emigrants, see Thomas, *Migration and Economic Growth,* 74, Table 16; Penti, "Role of Ethnic Folklore," 121–22; and Virtanen, *Settlement or Return,* 114–15.

67. Puskás, "Hungarian Overseas Migration," 225–27. Francis and Frances Tychewicz, Reynoldsville, Pa., to Matthew Fochnowski, Sadlowo, Rypin district, Congress Poland, 1 December 1890, reprinted in Kula et al., *Writing Home,* no. 275, 432.

68. Cinel, "Conservative Adventurers," 71–72. Cinel, *National Integration of*

Italian Return Migration, 101–5. Samuel L. Baily, "The Adjustment of Italian Immigrants in Buenos Aires and New York, 1870–1914," *American Historical Review* 88 (April 1983).

69. Balch, "Slav Emigration," *Charities*, 25 August 1906, 548. Abbott, "Bulgarians of Chicago," 651. See discussion in DeChenne, "Labor and Immigration," 51–52.

70. 1902 parish survey in Kraków Diocese Archives. Thomas and Znaniecki, *Polish Peasant*, 1:463. Virtanen, *Settlement or Return*, 79.

71. Kraków Priests' Convention, 28 November 1907, 24–25, Kraków Diocese Archives. *Harvard Encyclopedia of American Ethnic Groups*, 1048. Dr. Ernst Lundevall, Olands, in Swedish Royal Commission on Emigration, *Report* (Stockholm, 1908–13), 17:198. Quoted in Hassing, "Norway's Organized Response," 65.

72. An explanation of how varied backgrounds in Italy sent some away forever, others temporarily, is presented in Cinel, *National Integration of Italian Return Migration*, 112–15.

Chapter 3. Immigrants in an Industrializing Economy

1. All information on Frank Chmiel is taken from Chmiel *v.* Thorndike Co. (1902), 65 NE 47.

2. These changes are discussed in Brinley Thomas, *Migration and Economic Growth: A Study of Great Britain and the Atlantic Economy* (Cambridge, 1973), 152–53. Andrea Graziosi, "Common Laborers, Unskilled Workers: 1880–1915," *Labor History* 22 (Fall 1981), 512–14, 531–33, 538–39. David Brody, *Steelworkers in America: The Nonunion Era* (New York, 1960), 58–59.

3. U.S. 61st Cong., 3d sess., S. Doc. 747, *Reports of the Immigration Commission* (Washington, D.C., 1911), 1:495, 16:87 (hereafter cited as Dillingham Commission *Reports*). *Survey*, 1 April 1911, 49. Keijo Virtanen, comp., *Letters to Finland* (Ann Arbor, Mich., 1976), 3.

4. See discussion of this point in Crystal Eastman, *Work-Accidents and the Law* (New York, 1910), chap. 12.

5. Chmiel *v.* Thorndike Co., 65 NE 47, 48. In 1907 an immigrant child attempted to sue his employer after he was hurt on the job; he was turned down by the courts because he was not a citizen; see discussion in *United Mine Workers Journal*, 14 March 1907, 4. It should be noted here that the picker machine was one of the most notorious as a cause of work injuries in early twentieth-century textile mills. Tamara K. Hareven reports on an accident similar to Chmiel's involving an immigrant working in the Amoskeag mills in Manchester, New Hampshire. She observes that such cases were typical; Hareven, *Family Time and Industrial Time: The Relationship between the Family and Work in a New England Industrial Community* (Cambridge, 1982), 125–26. A similar machine was the cause of the pathetic case used by Jack London in the opening of *The Iron Heel*; London based his account on an accident reported in *Outlook*, 18 August 1906, 902–4.

6. Eric J. Hobsbawm, *Social Bandits and Primitive Rebels: Studies in Archaic Forms of Social Movement in the 19th and 20th Centuries* (Glencoe, Ill., 1959), 108, quoted in Herbert G. Gutman, *Work, Culture, and Society in Industrializing America* (New York, 1966, 1977), 86.

7. See discussion of these points in Jeffrey G. Williamson, "Migration to the New World: Long Term Influences and Impact," *Explorations in Economic History*, Summer 1974, 386–87. David Montgomery, *The Fall of the House of Labor: The*

Workplace, the State, and American Labor Activism, 1865–1925 (Cambridge, Mass., 1987), 47. Dillingham Commission *Reports*, 1:493. David M. Gordon, Richard Edwards, and Michael Reich, *Segmented Work, Divided Workers: The Historical Transformation of Labor in the United States* (Cambridge, Mass., 1982), 2–3. Michael J. Piore, *Birds of Passage: Migrant Labor and Industrial Societies* (Cambridge, 1979), 3.

8. U.S. Bureau of Labor, *Bulletin* (September 1907), 15:410–11. Caroline Golab, *Immigrant Destinations* (Philadelphia, 1977), 46, 48. Williamson, "Migration to the New World," 382, argues that in such conditions the lack of available land had very little to do with changing immigration levels in the late nineteenth century. For a discussion of how differing self-images were important in determining interest in remigration, see Herbert S. Klein, "AHR Forum: The Integration of Italian Immigrants into the United States and Argentina: A Comparative Analysis," *American Historical Review* 88 (April 1983), 306–29.

9. James F. Willis and Martin L. Primack, *An Economic History of the United States* (Englewood Cliffs, N.J., 1989), 241–42, 248–49. Brody, *Steelworkers in America*, 1. Dominic A. Pacyga, "Villages of Steel Mills and Packinghouses: the Polish Worker on Chicago's South Side, 1880–1921," in Frank Renkiewicz, ed., *The Polish Presence in Canada and America* (Toronto, 1982), 19–20.

10. Williamson, "Migration to the New World," 366.

11. Dillingham Commission *Reports*, 1: 139, tables 13 and 14; 145, table 19.

12. A. T. Lane, *Solidarity or Survival? American Labor and European Immigrants, 1830–1924* (Westport, Conn., 1987), 122–23. Graziosi, "Common Laborers," 512–14. Brody, *Steelworkers in America*, 96–98. Stephen Meyer, "Adapting the Immigrant to the Line: Americanization in the Ford Factory, 1914–1921," *Journal of Social History* 14 (Fall 1980), 69. John A. Fitch, *The Steel Workers* (New York, 1910), 68, 147. Dillingham Commission *Reports*, 16:85. Also see report by Peter Roberts, "The New Pittsburghers," *Charities*, 2 January 1909, 533.

13. Dillingham Commission *Reports*, 1:297–98. The commission also reported that the work force in copper mining had a background of 55.7 percent in farming or farm labor, although Finns—the major copper mining ethnic group—showed 74.8 percent with farm labor backgrounds. In farm implement manufacture, the record for 12,000 foreign-born workers showed these percentages coming from farming and farm labor backgrounds: Ruthenians, 89.9 percent; Serbians, 78.4 percent; Lithuanians, 74.4 percent; Slovenians, 74.3 percent. See *Reports*, 16:24, 14:425. *Survey*, 1 April 1911, 35.

14. Francesco Paolo Cerase, *From Italy to the United States and Back: Returned Migrants, Conservative or Innovative?* (Ph.D. diss., Columbia University, 1971), 58–59, 65.

15. Discussed in Rudolph J. Vecoli, "Chicago's Italians prior to World War I: A Study of Their Social and Economic Adjustment" (Ph.D. diss., University of Wisconsin, 1962), 227. Cerase, *From Italy to the United States*, 64. Dillingham Commission *Reports*. 1:561–64.

16. Julianna Puskás, *From Hungary to the United States (1880–1914)* (Budapest, 1982), 51–53. John Bodnar, Roger Simon, and Michael P. Weber, *Lives of Their Own: Blacks, Italians, and Poles in Pittsburgh, 1900–1960* (Urbana, Ill., 1982), 48. Branko Mita Colakovic, *Yugoslav Migrations to America* (San Francisco, 1973), 57. David M. Brownstone, Irene M. Franck, and Douglass L. Brownstone, *Island of Hope, Island of Tears* (New York, 1979, 1986), 60–62. Keijo Virtanen, "Finnish Migrants (1860–1930) in the Overseas Return Migration Movement," in Dirk Hoerder, ed., *Labor Migration in the Atlantic Economies* (Westport, Conn., 1985),

383. Theodore Saloutos, *They Remember America: The Story of the Repatriated Greek-Americans* (Berkeley, 1956), 136. Louis Adamic, *The Native's Return: An American Immigrant Visits Yugoslavia and Discovers His Old Country* (New York, 1934), chap. 7.

17. U.S. Commissioner-General of Immigration, *Annual Report, 1931*, 238.

18. Joseph Cybulski, in United States, to Sophie Cybulska, Rumunki, Lipno district, Congress Poland, 16 February 1891, in Witold Kula et al., *Writing Home: Immigrants in Brazil and the United States, 1890–1891* (Boulder, Colo., 1986), no. 110, 222–23.

19. Dillingham Commission *Reports*: on meatpacking, 13:147, and coal mining, 13:371–72, 410, 435. On the plate glass industry, 14:112–13; for copper mining and smelters, 16:62–63; for iron and steel, 8:148, 212, 308. Also see Anna-Leena Toivonen, "Etelä-Pohjanmaan Valtameren-takainen Siirtolaisuus, 1867–1930" (Ph.D. diss., Seinäjoen Kirjapaino, Finland, 1963), 208.

20. George Gilkey, "Italy and America: The Migrations of the Early Twentieth Century," unpublished paper, 3. Wolski letter, 2 November 1913, in William I. Thomas and Florian Znaniecki, comps., *The Polish Peasant in Europe and America: Monograph of an Immigrant Group* (Boston, 1918), 1:235. Lyddi and Petter, Stambaugh, Mich., to parents in Finland, 24 June 1900, in Virtanen, *Letters to Finland*, 10.

21. Krystyna Duda-Dziewierz, *Wieś Malopolska A Emigracja Amerykańska* (Warsaw, 1938), 51–64. Maria Wierusyewska-Adamcyk, *Społeczność Wiejska Zaborowa w Procesie Przemian* (Warsaw, 1980), 81–82, 113. Kazimiera Zawistowicz-Adamska, *Społeczność Wiejska: Doswiadczenia i Rozwazania z Badan Terenowych w Zaborowie* (Łódź, 1948), 19. Jerzy Fierich, *Przeszłość powiatu ropczyckiego w ustach mieszkańców* (Ropczyce, Poland, 1936), 58.

22. Massimo Livi Bacci, *L'immigrazione e l'assimilazione degli Italiani negli Stati Uniti secondo le statistiche demografiche americane* (Milan, 1961), 41. Ivan Lupis-Vukic, *O Iseljevanje i o Americi* (Zadar, 1910), 8, quoted in Frances Kraljic, *Croatian Migration to and from the United States, 1900–1914* (Palo Alto, Calif., 1978), 85.

23. Dillingham Commission *Reports*, 10:30, 13:25; also see 6:24–26, 14:47, 16:17, 85, 217. Robert C. Elliott testimony, U.S. 50th Cong., 1st sess., H. Misc. Doc. 572, "Testimony Taken by the Select Committee . . . to Inquire into the Alleged Violation of . . . Importation of Contract Laborers" (Washington, D.C., 1888), 599. Kenneth L. Roberts, "The Rising Irish Tide," *Saturday Evening Post* 192 (14 February 1920), 4.

24. Golab, *Immigrant Destinations*, 102–3. Stany Zjednoczone, *Pamiętniki Emigrantów* (Warsaw, 1977), 1:195–98. Adam Strucinski, Glassport, Pa., to wife in Poland, 12 February 1911, in Thomas and Znaniecki, *Polish Peasant*, 2:336–37.

25. Italy, Commissariato dell'Emigrazione, *Bollettino dell'Emigrazione*, 1912, no. 3, 49. Rudolph J. Vecoli, "Italian American Workers, 1880–1920: Padrone Slaves or Primitive Rebels?" in S. M. Tomasi, ed., *Perspectives in Italian Immigration and Ethnicity* (New York, 1977), 26. Maine Bureau of Labor quoted in Thomas Kessner, *The Golden Door: Italian and Jewish Immigrant Mobility in New York City, 1880–1915* (New York, 1977), 58. Vecoli, "Chicago's Italians," 279–80.

26. Emili Aalto, Kaleva, Mich., to his brother in Finland, 3 September 1902, in Virtanen, *Letters to Finland*, 11. Benjamin P. Murdzek, *Emigration in Polish Social-Political Thought, 1870–1914* (Boulder, Colo., 1977), 270, n. 28. Roberts, "New Pittsburghers," 537. A quarter of the steelworkers in Bethelehem, Pennsylvania, worked a seven-day week and a twelve-hour day, according to Frank Julian Warne,

The Immigrant Invasion (New York, 1913), 168–70. See also H. Arnold Barton, comp., *Letters from the Promised Land: Swedes in America, 1840–1914* (Minneapolis, 1975), 226–29. Irish Folklore Commission Questionnaires, MS 1409, 57.

27. Various examples of Poles commenting on hard work in America are given in Adam Walaszek, "'For in America Poles Work Like Cattle': Polish Peasant Immigrants and Work in America, 1890–1891," in Marianne Debouzy, ed., *In the Shadow of the Statue of Liberty: Immigrants, Workers, and Citizens in the American Republic, 1880–1920* (Paris, 1988), 98–99. Joseph Cybulski to Sophie Cybulska, Rumunki, Lipno district, Congress Poland, 16 February 1891, in Kula et al., *Writing Home*, no. 110, 222–23. Irish Folklore Commission Questionnaires, MS 1408, 194–95; also MS 1411, 236–37. Dr. Joh. Ajander, Värnamo district, 29 December 1907, in Royal Swedish Commission on Emigration, *Report* (Stockholm, 1908–13), 17:194–95. Reidar Grunde Simonsen, "Returned Emigrants: A Study of Repatriated Norwegians" (thesis, University of Oslo, 1982), 60.

28. Joseph John Parot, "The 'Serdeczna Matko' of the Sweatshops: Marital and Family Crises of Immigrant Working-Class Women in Late Nineteenth-Century Chicago," in Renkiewicz, *Polish Presence*, 156–57, 160–61.

29. Kula et al., *Writing Home*, no. 259, 413. Simonsen, "Returned Immigrants," 60. On the change from farm life to U.S. industry, including the change to living in industrial cities, see Matti E. Kaups, "The Finns in the Copper and Iron Ore Mines of the Western Great Lakes Region, 1864–1905: Some Preliminary Observations," in Michael G. Karni et al., eds., *The Finnish Experience in the Western Great Lakes Region: New Perspectives* (Turku, Finland, 1975), 55–57. Graziosi, "Common Laborers," 527–29, discusses the bosses' methods of driving their workers.

30. G. Beck, letter to *Survey* 24 (30 July 1910), 646–47. Charles Rumford Walker, *Steel: The Diary of a Furnace Worker* (Boston, 1922), 107.

31. John Reed, "Industrial Frightfulness in Bayonne," *Metropolitan Magazine*, January 1917, quoted in John J. Bukowczyk, "The Transformation of Working-Class Ethnicity: Corporate Control, Americanization, and the Polish Immigrant Middle Class in Bayonne, New Jersey, 1915–1925," *Labor History* 25 (Winter 1984), 56.

32. Rowland Tappan Berthoff, *British Immigrants in Industrial America* (Cambridge, Mass., 1953), 53. Also see Peter R. Shergold, "'Reefs of Roast Beef': The American Worker's Standard of Living in Comparative Perspective," in Dirk Hoerder, ed., *American Labor and Immigration History, 1877–1920s: Recent European Research* (Urbana, Ill., 1983), 83–84. *Bollettino dell'Emigrazione*, 1908, no. 8, 41. J. D. Gould, "European Inter-Continental Emigration—the Road Home: Return Migration from the U.S.A.," *Journal of European Economic History* 9 (1980), 67–68.

33. Vecoli, "Chicago's Italians," 311–17.

34. Frank Roney, *Frank Roney, Irish Rebel and California Labor Leader: An Autobiography* (Berkeley, 1931), 179–81. Letter from "a worker who was displaced by a child," in *Chicagoer Arbeiter-Zeitung*, 12 May 1895, reprinted in Hartmut Keil and John B. Jentz, eds., *German Workers in Chicago: A Documentary History of Working-Class Culture from 1850 to World War I* (Urbana, Ill., 1988), 74–76.

35. Ewa Morawska, *For Bread with Butter: The Life-Worlds of East Central Europeans in Johnstown, Pennsylvania, 1890–1940* (Cambridge, 1985), 114–15. Cajetan Kuczmarski, Pittsburgh, Pa., to Joseph Kuczmarski, Rakowo, Rypin district, Congress Poland, 7 December 1890, in Kula et al., *Writing Home*, no. 179, 318–19.

36. "Vampire" is the term used by Italian officials; see *Bollettino dell'Emigrazione*, 1908, no. 8, 4. Vecoli, "Chicago's Italians," 272. Dillingham Commission *Reports*, 18:339.

37. *La Parola dei Socialisti,* 12 and 20 March 1908, quoted in Vecoli, "Chicago's Italians," 249–50. Also see John R. Commons's description of padrone operations in his *Labor and Administration* (New York, 1964), 330–31. Edwin Fenton, "Immigrants and Unions, a Case Study: Italians and American Labor, 1870–1920" (Ph.D. diss., Harvard University, 1957), chaps. 3–4.

38. U.S. Bureau of Labor *Bulletin* (1907), 414–16, 420–21, 445–48, 482–84. Other discussions of the padrone problem include U.S. 50th Cong., *Contract Laborers,* 60–61; U.S. 51st Cong., 2d sess., H.R. 3472, *Report of the Select Committee on Immigration and Naturalization* (Washington, D.C., 1891), 504–5; U.S. Industrial Commission, *Reports . . . on Immigration* (Washington, D.C., 1901), 15:8; Vecoli, "Chicago's Italians," chap. 5; and Salvatore Mondello, *The Italian Immigrant in Urban America, 1880–1920, as Reported in the Contemporary Periodical Press* (New York, 1980), 80–83.

39. Morawska, *For Bread with Butter,* 104. Dillingham Commission *Reports,* 6:97; also see 14:449. Wictor Roos, Bessemer, Mich., to brother in Lappi, Tl., Finland, 29 November 1907, in Virtanen, *Letters to Finland,* no. 4, 14–15.

40. Golab, *Immigrant Destinations,* 113. Commons, *Labor and Administration,* 328. Graziosi, "Common Laborers," 537.

41. Golab, *Immigrant Destinations,* 49. Graziosi, "Common Laborers," 521. David Brody calls labor turnover in steel mills a stabilizing factor; employers could always count on new employees coming in the door as old employees left; Brody, *Steelworkers in America,* 109–11.

42. John R. Commons, *Industrial Goodwill* (New York, 1919, 1969), 1–5. Also see Graziosi, "Common Laborers," 517–18.

43. Commons, *Industrial Goodwill,* 3. Carleton Beals, "Those Who Have Gone Back," *Outlook,* 28 July 1926, 448.

44. Child labor was common in many parts of Europe. New York, *Thirteenth Annual Report of the Bureau of Factory Inspection—1898* (Albany, 1899), 789–90. Saloutos, *They Remember America,* 12. Angelo Olivieri, "L'Italia ufficiale e la realtà dell'emigrazione in USA (1886–1914)," *Studi Emigrazione* 11 (March 1974), 37, 40. Charlotte Erickson, *Invisible Immigrants: The Adaptation of English and Scottish Immigrants in Nineteenth-Century America* (Coral Gables, Fla., 1972), 237–38. Robert, "The New Pittsburghers," 547. Walaszek, "'For in America,'" 103–4.

45. Roberts, "The New Pittsburghers," 547. Morawska, *For Bread with Butter,* 124–25. U.S. Bureau of Labor *Bulletin* (1907), 478–80. Dillingham Commission *Reports,* 18:441. Walker, *Steel,* 28.

46. Dillingham Commission *Reports,* 18:441. *Charities,* 2 January 1909, 547. U.S. Bureau of Labor *Bulletin* (1907), 408–9. M. Mark Stolarik, "Immigration and Urbanization: The Slovak Experience, 1870–1918" (Ph.D. diss., University of Minnesota, 1974), 185–86. Barton, *Letters from the Promised Land,* 309. Also see discussion in Betty Boyd Caroli, *Italian Repatriation from the United States, 1900–1914* (New York, 1973), 57; Italy, Commissariato dell'Emigrazione, *Emigrazione e Colonie,* 2:141–44; Mondello, *Italian Immigrant,* 82–83; U.S. 50th Cong., *Contract Laborers,* 318; U.S. 51st Cong., *Report . . . on Immigration and Naturalization,* 587; Immigrants' Protective League, *4th Annual Report* (1913), 18–20; Robert F. Foerster, *The Italian Emigration of Our Times* (New York, 1919, 1968), 380.

47. *Survey,* 1 April 1911, 43, 47–48. Vecoli, "Chicago's Italians," 296–97. David DeChenne, "Labor and Immigration in a Southern Illinois Mill Town, 1890–1937" (D.A. diss., Illinois State University, 1989), 115–16. See descriptions in U.S. 50th Cong., *Contract Laborers,* 204–5.

48. F. Elisabeth Crowell, "The Housing Situation in Pittsburgh," *Charities,* 6 Feb-

ruary 1909, 871; also 9 November 1901, 398–400. Dominic T. Ciolli, "The 'Wop' in the Track Gang," *Immigrants in America Review* 2 (July 1916), 61–64, quoted in Vecoli, "Chicago's Italians," 312–15.

49. See U.S. Department of Labor report discussed in *Charities*, 6 February 1904, 142–43. Dillingham Commission *Reports*, 8:289, 1:729. Also Antonio Mangano, *Sons of Italy: A Social and Religious Study of the Italians in America* (New York, 1917, 1971), 11–14; Foerster, *Italian Emigration*, 385–86.

50. Joseph John Parot, "The 'Serdeczna Matko' of the Sweatshops: Marital and Family Crises of Immigrant Working-Class Women in Late Nineteenth-Century Chicago," in Renkiewicz, *Polish Presence*, 157. One Polonia city block had 457 persons per acre, one of the highest figures in Chicago. Stoyan Christowe, *This Is My Country* (New York, 1938), 51–53. Dillingham Commission *Reports*, 9:94. The best description of living conditions of the Bulgarians of Granite City is DeChenne, "Labor and Immigration," chap. 5. On Slovak boardinghouses, see M. Mark Stolarik, *Immigration and Urbanization: The Slovak Experience, 1870–1918* (New York, 1989), 112–15.

51. Robert C. Elliott testimony in U.S. 50th Cong., *Contract Laborers*, 600; John Webb testimony, ibid., 204–5. Adelbert M. Dewey testimony in U.S. 51st Cong., *Report . . . on Immigration and Naturalization*, 604–5. The anthracite region is covered in Peter Roberts, *Anthracite Coal Communities: A Study of the Demography, the Social, Educational, and Moral Life of the Anthracite Regions* (New York, 1904, 1970), chap. 5. Many immigrants would have been accustomed at home to having farm animals in their dwellings.

52. Dillingham Commission *Reports*, 17:174, 18:403–4. Vecoli, "Chicago's Italians," 311–12, 334. *Charities*, 2 January 1909, 540–43. Robert Elliott testimony in U.S. 50th Cong., *Contract Laborers*, 599–600. Better food was found in a visit to a labor camp not controlled by padroni; see U.S. Bureau of Labor *Bulletin* (1907), 461–67.

53. Cerase, "From Italy to the United States," 266–67. Sophie Nadrowska to Reynold Nadrowski, Ugoszcz, Rypin district, Congress Poland, 2 December 1890, in Kula et al., *Writing Home*, no. 220, 364. Ryszard Kantor, "The Position of Chicago in Modern Employment-Seeking Migrations of the Inhabitants of the Zaborów Parish (Province of Tarnów)," *Przegląd Polonijny* 10, no. 3 (1984), 152–53. Jon Gjerde, *From Peasants to Farmers: The Migration from Balestrand, Norway, to the Upper Middle West* (Cambridge, 1985), 140. George Prpic, quoted in Kraljic, *Croatian Migration*, 80. For similar comments about Finns, see Kaups, "Finns in the Copper and Iron Ore Mines," 86. Jane Addams, *Twenty Years at Hull-House* (New York, 1910, 1981), 89.

54. Cerase, "From Italy to the United States," 75. Simonsen, "Returned Emigrants," 20. Rudolph J. Vecoli, "Prelates and Peasants: Italian Immigrants and the Catholic Church," *Journal of Social History* 2 (Spring 1969), 230–31.

55. Walaszek, "'For in America,'" 100–101. Dillingham Commission *Reports*, 1:474. On separate industries' foreign-born workers, see *Reports*: iron and steel, 8:178; New England cotton manufacture, 10:209, 212, 213.

56. U.S. 50th Cong., *Contract Laborers*, 213, 323.

57. *Charities*, 2 January 1909, 544. Immigrants' Protective League Case Histories: I, "A Czeckoslovak Lost between Two Worlds, Chooses Repatriation," 1933, 3. Townsend dispatch of 4 October 1895, quoted in Zoltan Kramar, ed., *From the Danube to the Hudson: U.S. Ministerial and Consular Dispatches on Immigration from the Habsburg Monarchy, 1850–1900* (Atlanta, Ga., 1978), 85. Stephan Thern-

strom, ed., *Harvard Encyclopedia of American Ethnic Groups* (Cambridge, Mass., 1980), 740.

58. U.S. 50th Cong., *Contract Laborers*, 322–23. One Pole recalls in his memoir that he did not apply for U.S. citizenship because he wanted to go back to Poland; Zjednoczone, *Pamiętniki Emigrantów* 1, no. 2 (1912), 152.

59. U.S. Industrial Commission *Reports* (Washington, D.C., 1901), 15:44–45, 183. Dillingham Commission *Reports*, 1:150, 488–89; 6:185; 8:168, 320; 10:190; 13:168; 14:129, 131; 16:641.

60. Stolarik, "Immigration and Urbanization," 55–56.

61. Joel Perlmann, *Ethnic Differences: Schooling and Social Structure among the Irish, Italians, Jews, and Blacks in an American City, 1880–1935* (Cambridge, 1988), 102–9.

62. Lane, *Solidarity or Survival?*, 141.

63. Dillingham Commission *Reports*, 10:125. Foerster, *Italian Emigration*, 422. Also see Victor R. Greene, *The Slavic Community on Strike: Immigrant Labor in Pennsylvania Anthracite* (Notre Dame, Ind., 1968), 95–96.

64. Montgomery, *Fall of the House of Labor*, 174–75. Graziosi, "Common Laborers," 524–25. *Towarzystwo opieki nad wychodźcami 'OPATRZNOŚĆ' w Krakowie* (Kraków, 1908), 2. Dillingham Commission *Reports*, 6:104; also see 10:123.

65. Eccles Robinson, testimony in U.S. 50th Cong., *Contract Laborers*, 608. Colorado Bureau of Labor Statistics *Report, 1887–1888* (Denver, 1888), 255–70. Dillingham Commission *Reports*, 10:125. Brody, *Steelworkers in America*, 135–37. Gwendolyn Mink, *Old Labor and New Immigrants in American Political Development: Union, Party, and State, 1875–1920* (Ithaca, N.Y., 1986), 61–64.

66. Foerster, *Italian Emigration*, 402–3. Vecoli, "Chicago's Italians," 308–9, 429–30. Erickson, *Invisible Immigrants*, 49, 60, 118–21, 142. Monika Glettler, *Pittsburgh—Wien—Budapest: Programm und Praxis der Nationalitätenpolitik bei Auswanderung der ungarischen Slowaken nach Amerika um 1900* (Vienna, 1980), 26. Brody, *Steelworkers in America*, 261. Mink, *Old Labor and New Immigrants*, 61–64. Also see Lane, *Solidarity or Survival?* 57–73, and Greene, *Slavic Community*, chap. 4.

67. James A. Creelman, New York *Herald*, testimony in U.S. 50th Cong., *Contract Laborers*, 213. Victor Greene, however, argues that Slavs generally supported this strike; Greene, *Slavic Community*, 80, 96–97, and chap. 5.

68. *Chicagoer Arbeiter-Zeitung*, 29 April 1881, reprinted in Keil and Jentz, *German Workers in Chicago*, 47–49.

69. Robert Asher, "Union Nativism and the Immigrant Response," *Labor History* 23 (Summer 1982), 329–31, 338–39. Brody, *Steelworkers in America*, 142–44. *Survey*, 1 April 1911, 50–51. Also see Greene, *Slavic Community*, on pre-1880 examples, 60–63, and on union miscues, 86.

70. Lithuanian interview published in *The Independent*, 4 August 1904, quoted in Asher, "Union Nativism," 345–46. Pacyga, "Villages of Steel Mills," 23–24. Foerster, *Italian Emigration*, 402–3.

71. Vecoli, "Italian American Workers," 42. Asher, "Union Nativism," 332–33. Kessner, *Golden Door*, 69. Eugene Miller and Gioanna Panovsky, "Radical Italian Unionism: Its Development and Decline in Chicago's Mens Garment Industry, 1910–1930," paper presented to the 1981 conference "One Hundred Years of Organized Labor in Illinois, 1881–1981," Chicago. Graziosi, "Common Laborers," 536–37. Brody, *Steelworkers in America*, 59. Fenton, "Immigrants and Unions," 256–58.

72. Bukowczyk, "Transformation of Working-Class Ethnicity," 64–65. Edgar Syden Stricker, "The Settlement of Disputes under Agreements in the Anthracite Industry," in John R. Commons, ed., *Trade Unionism and Labor Problems* (New York, 1921, 1967), 508–10.

73. Greene, *Slavic Community*, 86, 109, 149, 211.

74. Dillingham Commission *Reports*, 16:620–21. Stolarik, "Immigration and Urbanization," 69–73, 116–19.

75. *Amalgamated Journal*, 16 January 1919, 14, 23; 5 September 1918, 18; 3 October 1918, 3, quoted in Brody, *Steelworkers in America*, 223–24.

76. Vecoli, "Chicago's Italians," 320. Graziosi, "Common Laborers," 526–28, 544. Dillingham Commission *Reports*, 18:404, 409. Julianna Puskás, "Hungarian Immigration and Socialism," in Debouzy, *In the Shadow of the Statue of Liberty*, 150.

77. Mondello, *The Italian Immigrant*, 98. New York Board of Health statistics, presumably 1910, quoted in Alberto Pecorini, "The Italians in the United States," *Forum*, January 1911, 17–18. *Charities*, 7 November 1908, 248; 26 October 1901, 341. Gerald Markowitz and David Rosner, "'The Street of Walking Death': Silicosis, Health, and Labor in the Tri-State Region, 1900–1950," *Journal of American History* 77 (September 1990), 545. David N. Doyle, "Unestablished Irishmen: New Immigrants and Industrial America, 1870–1910," in Hoerder, *American Labor and Immigration History*, 198.

78. Jan and Ewa Stelmach, Galicia, to children in Pittsburgh, 5 November 1909, 31 November 1910, 28 March 1911, in Thomas and Znaniecki, *The Polish Peasant*, 1:385–88. *Charities*, 2 January 1909, 543.

79. Eastman, *Work-Accidents*, 88.

80. Ibid., 86–87, 97.

81. Ibid., 14, 86, 121–22, 127, 128, 185. The relevant court cases are Deni *v.* Pennsylvania R. Co. (27 May 1897), 37 *At. Reporter* 558; Maiorano *v.* Baltimore & O. R. Co. (7 January 1907), 65 *Atlantic* 1077; and Liberato et al. *v.* Royer et al. (15 March 1926), 46 *S. Ct.* 373.

82. Robert C. Elliott testimony, U.S. 50th Cong., *Contract Laborers*, 600–601. Dillingham Commission *Reports*, 34:29, 40–41; also see 2:116–17.

83. Jan Nikodem memoir, in Instytut Gospodarstwa Społecznego, "Pamietniki wiejskich Dziataczy spotecznych" (Warsaw, 1935–36), no. 242. The Granite City situation is examined in DeChenne, "Labor and Immigration," 60. Italy, Commissariato Generale dell'Emigrazione, *L'emigrazione italiana dal 1910 al 1923* (Rome, 1926), 2:69.

84. Domicella and Francis Sawicki, Brooklyn, N.Y., to Catherine Sen, Dulsk, Golub-Dobrzyn, Congress Poland, 3 December 1890, no. 249, 400; Edward Bartz, Jersey City, N.J., to Johanna Retkin, Skepe, Lipno, Congress Poland, 3 January 1891, no. 79, 184–85; and Annie Berger, Chicago, Ill., to parents in Rypin, Congress Poland, 28 December 1890, no. 82, 188, in Kula et al., *Writing Home.*

85. Irish Folklore Commission Questionnaires, MS 1409, 303. See discussion in John B. Jentz and Hartmut Keil, "From Immigrants to Urban Workers: Chicago's German Poor in the Gilded Age and Progressive Era, 1883–1908," *Vierteljahrschrift für Sozial- und Wirtschaftsgeschichte*, no. 68 (1981), 97. On problems of Gaelic speakers, see Kerby A. Miller, *Emigrants and Exiles: Ireland and the Irish Exodus to North America* (New York, 1985), 518–19.

86. Reprinted in Isaac Metzker, ed., *A Bintel Brief: Sixty Years of Letters from the Lower East Side to the Jewish Daily Forward* (Garden City, N.Y., 1971), 76–77.

Chapter 4. Leaving the Land of Bosses and Clocks

1. Irish Folklore Commission Questionnaires, MS 1410, 124–25.
2. U.S. Secretary of Labor, *Eleventh Annual Report 1923* (Washington, D.C. 1923), 133, Table 4.
3. Kate Holladay Claghorn, "Immigration 1908–09," *Survey* 24 (9 April 1910), 91.
4. Italy, Parliament, *Inchiesta parlamentare sulle condizioni dei contadini nelle provincie meridionali e nella Sicilia* (Rome, 1909–11), 5:3.99, quoted in George R. Gilkey, "The Effects of Emigration on Italy, 1900 to 1923" (Ph.D. diss., Northwestern University, 1950), 151. *Forverts,* 24 November 1902, quoted in Zosa Szajkowski, "Deportation of Jewish Immigrants and Returnees before World War I," *American Jewish Historical Quarterly* 67 (June 1978), 305.
5. Edward A. Steiner, *On the Trail of the Immigrant* (New York, 1906), 334–35. See comments on this subject by the Dillingham Commission, in U.S. 61st Cong., 3d sess., S. Doc. 747, *Reports of the Immigration Commission* (Washington, D.C., 1911), 1:184 (hereafter cited as Dillingham Commission *Reports*). Also Marsha Penti, "The Role of Ethnic Folklore among Finnish-American Returnees" (Ph.D. diss., Indiana University, 1983), 134–35; Keijo Virtanen, *Settlement or Return: Finnish Emigrants (1860–1930) in the International Overseas Return Migration Movement* (Helsinki, 1979), 182; Charlotte Erickson, *Invisible Immigrants: The Adaptation of English and Scottish Immigrants in Nineteenth-Century America* (Coral Gables, Fla., 1972), 252; Alfred Vagts, *Deutsch-Amerikanische Rückwanderung* (Heidelberg, 1960), 6–7. For a summary of various scholars' findings, see Marjolein 't Hart, "Heading for Paddy's Green Shamrock Shore: The Returned Emigrants in Nineteenth Century Ireland" (Master's thesis, University of Groningen, 1981), 9–10.
6. Francesco Paolo Cerase, "From Italy to the United States and Back: Returned Migrants, Conservative or Innovative?" (Ph.D. diss., Columbia University, 1971), chap. 4. Dino Cinel, *The National Integration of Italian Return Migration, 1870–1929* (Cambridge, 1991), 115–21. Virtanen, *Settlement or Return,* 170. Theodore Saloutos, *Expatriates and Repatriates: A Neglected Chapter in United States History* (Rock Island, Ill., 1972), 13.
7. Reino Kero, "The Return of Emigrants from America to Finland," University of Turku Institute of General History *Publications,* no. 4 (1972), 17–18.
8. Keijo Virtanen, comp., *Letters to Finland* (Ann Arbor, Mich., 1976), 2, and *Settlement or Return,* 80–82. Julianna Puskás, "Hungarian Overseas Migration: A Microanalysis," in Rudolph J. Vecoli and Suzanne M. Sinke, eds., *A Century of European Migrations, 1830–1930* (Urbana, Ill., 1991), 227. Penti found three to four years typical among Finns; Penti, "Role of Ethnic Folklore," 223. Six to ten years was found to be typical for Italians; see Francesco Cerase, "Nostalgia or Disenchantment: Considerations on Return Migration," in Silvano M. Tomasi and Madeline H. Engel, eds., *The Italian Experience in the United States* (Staten Island, N.Y., 1970), 220–24. Dino Cinel, "Conservative Adventurers: Italian Migrants in Italy and San Francisco" (Ph.D. diss., Stanford University, 1979), 75, 77. Julianna Puskás, *From Hungary to the United States (1880–1914)* (Budapest, 1982), 80n. Lars-Göran Tedebrand, "Remigration from America to Sweden," in Harald Runblom and Hans Norman, eds., *From Sweden to America* (Minneapolis, 1976), 225. Thomas Kessner, "History of Repatriation," in U.S. Select Commission on Immigration and Refugee Policy, *U.S. Immigration Policy and the National Interest* (Washington, D.C., 1981), App. A, 309. M. Mark Stolarik, "Immigration and Urbaniza-

tion: The Slovak Experience, 1870–1918" (Ph.D. diss., University of Minnesota, 1974), 50. Charles Rumford Walker, *Steel: The Diary of a Furnace Worker* (Boston, 1922), 26. Stany Zjednoczone, *Pamiętniki Emigrantów* (Warsaw, 1977), 1:152–54, memoir 2.

9. The 1934 data were used by Reino Kero, "Return of Emigrants from America to Finland," 28. Virtanen, *Settlement or Return*, 182–83. The persons interviewed by Penti, "Role of Ethnic Folklore," were overwhelmingly positive about their American experiences.

10. Irish Folklore Commission Questionnaires, MS 1411, 95, 169; MS 1409, 55–56.

11. Jeremiah W. Jenks and W. Jett Lauck, *The Immigration Problem: A Study of American Immigration Conditions and Needs* (New York, 1922), 37. Dillingham Commission *Reports*, 1:181. Caroline Golab, *Immigrant Destinations* (Philadelphia, 1977), 164.

12. Tedebrand, "Remigration from America to Sweden," 206–7, 223. Robert C. Ostergren, *A Community Transplanted: The Trans-Atlantic Experience of a Swedish Immigrant Settlement in the Upper Middle West, 1835–1915* (Madison, Wis., 1988), 124–25. Walter D. Kamphoefner, "The Volume and Composition of German-American Return Migration," in Vecoli and Sinke, *A Century of European Migrations*, 301–3. Michael J. Piore, *Birds of Passage: Migrant Labor and Industrial Societies* (Cambridge, 1979), 153–54. Josef J. Barton, *Peasants and Strangers: Italians, Rumanians, and Slovaks in an American City, 1890–1950* (Cambridge, Mass., 1975), 55. High male percentages are shown in tables 95 and 96 in U.S. Commissioner-General of Immigration, *Annual Report, 1931* (Washington, D.C., 1931), 239–40. Virtanen, *Settlement or Return*, 126–29.

13. Adam Walaszek, *Reemigracja ze Stanów Zjednoczonych do Polski po i wojnie Światowej (1919–1924)* (Kraków, 1983), 176, and "Return Migration from the USA to Poland," 217, in Daniel Kubat, ed., *The Politics of Return: International Return Migration in Europe* (New York, 1984). Francesco Coletti, *Dell'emigrazione Italiana* (Milan, 1912), 78. Italy, Commissariato Generale dell'Emigrazione, *L'emigrazione italiana dal 1910 al 1923* (Rome, 1926), 1:59. Three-fourths of the Italians returning home in 1905–6 left singly, according to Betty Boyd Caroli, *Italian Repatriation from the United States, 1900–1914* (New York, 1973), 43. Frances Kraljic, *Croatian Migration to and from the United States, 1900–1914* (Palo Alto, Calif., 1978), 95. J. D. Gould, "European Inter-Continental Emigration—the Road Home: Return Migration from the U.S.A.," *Journal of European Economic History* 9, no. 1 (1980), 53, 64–66.

14. Tedebrand, "Remigration from America to Sweden," 223–24, 312, 314. Virtanen, *Settlement or Return*, 113, 118–23, 164. Lars Ljungmark, *Swedish Exodus* (Carbondale, Ill., 1979), 142.

15. Robert Park's "migrant industrials" phrase quoted in Rudolph J. Vecoli, "Chicago's Italians prior to World War I: A Study of Their Social and Economic Adjustment" (Ph.D. diss., University of Wisconsin, 1962), 287–88. Kraljic, *Croatian Migration*, 72–73. Caroli, *Italian Repatriation*, 43. Andrzej Brożek, *Polish Americans, 1854–1939* (Warsaw, 1985), 25. The Swedish study is in Tedebrand, "Remigration from America to Sweden," 203.

16. Harry Jerome, *Migration and Business Cycles* (New York, 1926), 100. Data on this subject from various sources are presented in Günter Moltmann, "American-German Return Migration in the Nineteenth and Early Twentieth Centuries," *Central European History* 13 (December 1980), 386. Wilbur S. Shepperson, *Emigration and Disenchantment: Portraits of Englishmen Repatriated from the United States*

(Norman, Okla., 1965), 5–6. Dillingham Commission *Reports*, 4:229. Month-by-month changes showing the impact of the 1907 Panic are charted in Italy, Commissariato dell'Emigrazione, *Bollettino dell'Emigrazione*, 1908, no. 6, 4, 6. Virtanen, *Settlement or Return*, 89–91, citing German studies also.

17. Ravenstein cited in Moltmann, "American-German Return Migration," 378, 387. Virtanen, *Settlement or Return*, 170.

18. Also, 22 were sick, and 41 were going to visit families, to marry, or for other "reasons of a social nature." Sherwood contended that some who said they were going home to visit were really unemployed; Herbert Francis Sherwood, "The Ebb and Flow of the Immigration Tide," *American Review of Reviews* 44 (December 1911), 700.

19. Leopold Caro, *Emigracya: I Polityka Emigracyjna* (Poznań, 1909, 1914), 95–96. Letter dated 21 July 1908, in William I. Thomas and Florian Znaniecki, *The Polish Peasant in Europe and America: Monograph of an Immigrant Group* (Boston, 1918), 2:113; also see 2:138–39.

20. Theodore Saloutos, *They Remember America: The Story of the Repatriated Greek-Americans* (Berkeley, 1956), 32, and "Exodus U.S.A.," in O. Fritiof Ander, ed., *In the Trek of the Emigrants: Essays Presented to Carl Wittke* (Rock Island, Ill., 1964), 199. Michael Just, *Ost- und südosteuropäische Amerikawanderung, 1881–1914* (Stuttgart, 1988), 64. Kraljic, *Croatian Migration*, 32.

21. Puskás, "Hungarian Overseas Migration," 227. David DeChenne, "Labor and Immigration in a Southern Illinois Mill Town, 1890–1937" (D.A. diss., Illinois State University, 1989), 59–62.

22. Jerome, *Migration and Business Cycles*, 48, 152, 204. Commissariato dell' Emigrazione, *L'emigrazione italiana*, 2:58. Branko Mita Colakovic, *Yugoslav Migrations to America* (San Francisco, 1973), 66.

23. Wolfgang Hell, "Amerikanisch-deutsche Rückwanderung," in Museum für Hamburgische Geschichte, ". . . *nach Amerika!*": *Auswanderung in die Vereinigten Staaten* (Hamburg, 1976), 56. Cinel, "Conservative Adventurers," 58, discusses the hypothesis based on high steerage rates. Rowland Tappan Berthoff, *British Immigrants in Industrial America* (Cambridge, Mass., 1953), 20. Samuel L. Baily, "The Adjustment of Italian Immigrants in Buenos Aires and New York, 1870–1924," *American Historical Review* 88 (April 1983), 296. Gould, "European Inter-Continental Emigration," 89–95. Robert F. Foerster, *The Italian Emigration of Our Times* (New York, 1919, 1968), 243–46.

24. Berthoff, *British Immigrants*, 17, 20, 42, 52, 76, 80, 82. The best single survey of British birds of passage is Roger David Simon, "The Birds of Passage in America, 1865–1914" (Thesis, University of Wisconsin, 1966).

25. Virtanen, *Settlement or Return*, 72–73. Ewa Morawska, *For Bread with Butter: The Life-Worlds of East Central Europeans in Johnstown, Pennsylvania, 1890–1940* (Cambridge, 1985), 39. Dillingham Commission *Reports*, 1:184, 6:165.

26. Arnold Schrier, *Ireland and the American Emigration, 1850–1900* (Minneapolis, 1958), 131–32. Giuseppe de Bartolo, "The Great Italian Emigration in the USA: The Case of Calabria," paper presented at the 20th Annual Conference of the American Italian Historical Association, 14 November 1987, 4. Virtanen, *Settlement or Return*, 71–72. Saloutos, *They Remember America*, 28. Kraljic, *Croatian Migration*, 38. John C. Cortis, testimony in U.S. 50th Cong., 1st sess., H. Misc. Doc. 572, *Testimony Taken by the Select Committee . . . to Inquire into the Alleged Violation of the Laws Prohibiting the Importation of Contract Laborers* (Washington, D.C., 1888), 52.

27. Dillingham Commission *Reports*, 41:333.

28. Avoiding shame by hanging on in America is a point made repeatedly by Germans quoted by Hell, "Amerikanisch-deutsche Rückwanderung," 56–58, and by Swedish Consul H. Lagercrantz in Swedish Royal Commission on Emigration, *Report* (Stockholm, 1908–13), 20:19–24. Steiner, *On the Trail of the Immigrant*, 250–51.

29. Irish Folklore Commission Questionnaires, MS 1409, 98, 144–46.

30. Ludwik Krzywicki, *Za Atlantykiem: Wrażenia z podróży po Ameryce* (Warsaw, 1895), 334. Irish Folklore Commission Questionnaires, MS 1141, 17–18, 66, 192. Emily Greene Balch, "Slav Emigration at Its Source," *Charities*, 25 August 1906, 549.

31. Sherwood, "The Ebb and Flow," 699. Edward A. Steiner, *The Immigrant Tide: Its Ebb and Flow* (New York, 1909), 24, 25–26, 341–42.

32. David N. Doyle, "Unestablished Irishmen: New Immigrants and Industrial America, 1870–1910," in Dirk Hoerder, ed., *American Labor and Immigration History, 1877–1920s: Recent European Research* (Urbana, Ill., 1983), 198. Foerster, *Italian Emigration of Our Times*, 462–64. Rudolph J. Vecoli, "Italian American Workers, 1880–1920: Padrone Slaves or Primitive Rebels?" in S. M. Tomasi, ed., *Perspectives in Italian Immigration and Ethnicity* (New York, 1977), 25. Cinel, "Conservative Adventurers," 115–16. Antonio Mangano, "The Effect of Emigration upon Italy," *Charities*, 1 February 1908, 1486; also see 7 November 1908, 248.

33. *Bolletino dell'Emigrazione*, 1908, no. 2, 80–88, 156; 1912, no. 2, 82–85, 797–98; and *L'emigrazione italiana*, 1:198–201.

34. Kero, "The Return of Emigrants," 16–17. Dr. Joh. Ajander and Dr. Ernst Lundevall, testimony before Swedish Royal Commission, *Report*, 17:194–95, 197–98.

35. Puskás, *From Hungary*, 138. Kraljic, *Croatian Migration*, 84.

36. *United Mine Workers Journal*, 9 January 1908, 4.

37. Carlo Levi tells of an Italian injured in a mining accident who held out until he obtained $3,000 compensation and then returned to Italy; Levi, *Christ Stopped at Eboli* (New York, 1947), 128–29. Stoyan Christowe reports the case of a Bulgarian who got $2,500 from a railroad company after a piece of chisel destroyed an eye; Christowe, *This Is My Country* (New York, 1938), 154–59. But most industrial accidents resulted in little or no compensation. Irish Folklore Commission Questionnaires, MS 1411, 52–53, 191–92. Crystal Eastman, *Work-Accidents and the Law* (New York, 1910), 128 and chap. 8. Eastman excludes from her determination eighty cases that meant no economic loss to survivors. Sherwood, "The Ebb and Flow," 699.

38. John R. Commons, *Industrial Goodwill* (New York, 1919, 1969), 130–31.

39. Walker, *Steel*, 90.

40. Irish Folklore Commission Questionnaires, MS 1408, 115. Amy Bernardy, *Italia randagia attraverso gli Stati Uniti* (Turin, 1913), 300–301. *Lietuva* (Chicago), 31 December 1909, in Chicago Foreign Press Survey, reel 44.

41. Irish Folklore Commission Questionnaires, MS 1407, 290; MS 1409, 56, 58. Letter of 1906 to *Jewish Daily Forward* reprinted in Isaac Metzker, ed., *A Bintel Brief: Sixty Years of Letters from the Lower East Side to the Jewish Daily Forward* (Garden City, N.Y., 1971), 59. The best example of Gutman's points on this topic are in his *Work, Culture, and Society in Industrializing America: Essays in American Working-Class and Social History* (New York, 1966–77), chap. 1, esp. 22–24.

42. Andrea Graziosi, "Common Laborers, Unskilled Workers: 1880–1915," *Labor History* 22 (Fall 1981), 520. Caro, *Emigracya*, 79–82, discusses the loss of work from Polish holidays.

43. Abraham Cahan, *Yekl and the Imported Bridegroom and Other Stories of the New York Ghetto* (New York, 1896, 1970), 154. Also see Cahan's *Rise of David Levinsky* on the theme of losses suffered in the process of achieving success in America. Jonathan D. Sarna, "The Myth of No Return: Jewish Return Migration to Eastern Europe, 1881–1914," *American Jewish History* 71 (December 1981), 263–67. Sarna stresses a multiplicity of reasons, including return to find a bride, as well as homesickness. After the Russian pogroms worsened, fewer Jews returned, Sarna concedes. Also see Polish Jews' letters in Witold Kula et al., comps., *Writing Home: Immigrants in Brazil and the United States, 1890–1891* (Boulder, Colo., 1986), such as no. 191, 331–32. Szajkowski, "Deportation of Jewish Immigrants," 304.

44. Francis Markowski, Troy, N.Y., to Antoinette Milewska, Wapielsk, Congress Poland, 9 December 1890, in Kula et al., *Writing Home*, no. 209, 351–52. Letter in Swedish Royal Commission, *Report*, 7:188–89, reprinted in H. Arnold Barton, comp., *Letters from the Promised Land: Swedes in America, 1840–1914* (Minneapolis, 1975), 283. Also see Emory Lindquist, "Appraisals of Sweden and America by Swedish Emigrants: The Testimony of Letters in Emigrationsutredningen (1907)," *Swedish Pioneer Historical Quarterly* 17 (April 1966), 92–93.

45. Irish Folklore Commission Questionnaires, MS 1409, 38. Carla Bianco, *The Two Rosetos* (Bloomington, Ind., 1974), 45. On the Irish immigrants' problems assimilating, see examples presented in Kerby A. Miller, with Bruce Boling and David N. Doyle, "Emigrants and Exiles: Irish Cultures and Irish Emigration to North America, 1790–1922," *Irish Historical Studies* 22 (September 1980), 97–125.

46. C. W. H., Canada, letter in Swedish Royal Commission, *Report*, 7: 188–89, reprinted in Barton, *Letters*, 283. See comments by Saloutos, *They Remember America*, 14–16, 33, 111. Steiner, *The Immigrant Tide*, 161.

47. Frank Paczkowski, St. Louis, Mo., to parents in Congress Poland, 20 January 1891, in Kula et al., *Writing Home*, no. 227, 372–73; also see no. 101, 211.

48. Hartmut Keil, "The German Immigrant Working Class of Chicago, 1875–90: Workers, Labor Leaders, and the Labor Movement," in Hoerder, *American Labor and Immigration History*, 160–61. The tenement tour is discussed in Vecoli, "Chicago's Italians," 132–33.

49. Irish Folklore Commission Questionnaires, MS 1407, 238; also MS 1410, 36.

50. Edit Fél and Tamás Hofer, *Proper Peasants: Traditional Life in a Hungarian Village* (Chicago, 1969), 375. Golab, *Immigrant Destinations*, 147–48. Virtanen, *Settlement or Return*, 176. Reidar Grunde Simonsen, "Returned Emigrants: A Study of Repatriated Norwegians" (thesis, University of Oslo, 1982), 96, 99.

51. John Muszenski, Bayonne, N.J., to Catherine Muszenska, Malszyce, Congress Poland, 27 February 1891, no. 218, 360; and Goldie Wolf, New York, to Frieda Rebecca Stop, Rypin, Congress Poland, 24 December 1890, no. 290, 452, in Kula et al., *Writing Home*. Irish Folklore Commission Questionnaires, MS 1411, 93.

52. Béla Gunda, "America in Hungarian Folklore," *New Hungarian Quarterly* 15 (Autumn 1974), 158–59. "Norway and America," by P. in Martin B. Ruud, trans. and ed., "Norwegian Emigrant Songs," in Norwegian American Historical Association, *Studies and Records* (1927), 14–15. Also see Metzker, *Bintel Brief*, 101–2, 115–16, 117–18.

53. Virtanen, *Settlement or Return*, 221–23. U.S. Industrial Commission, *Reports . . . on Immigration* (Washington, D.C., 1901), 15:53. One study of Irish in Butte, Montana, notes that Irishwomen held back the return movement; see Catherine Dowling, "Irish-American Nationalism in Butte, 1900–1916," *Montana*, Spring 1989, 59. Lars-Göran Tedebrand, *Västernorrland och Nordamerika 1875–1913: Utvandring och Återinvandring* (Uppsala, 1972), 314. This was found to be gener-

ally true in Sweden; Ljungmark, *Swedish Exodus*, 142. Irish women returning with dowries are noted frequently in Irish Folklore Commission Questionnaires, MS 1409, 18–19, 59–60, 259; MS 1411, 17–18. Schrier, *Ireland and the American Emigration*, 130–31. 't Hart, "Heading for Paddy's," 24.

54. Irish Folklore Commission Questionnaires, MS 1411, 193; also see 131–32; MS 1409, 40. 't Hart, "Heading for Paddy's," 24–25. Also see German examples in ". . . *nach Amerika!"* 56.

55. "Jak Jechałem Z Ameryki" [When I journeyed from America], in Harriet M. Pawlowska, ed., *Merrily We Sing: 105 Polish Folksongs* (Detroit, 1961), no. 77, 154–55.

56. Reprinted in Marcus Braun, *Immigration Abuses: Glimpses of Hungary and Hungarians* (New York, 1906, 1972), 103–4.

57. The national Italian debate is discussed in Cinel, *National Integration of Italian Return Migration*, chap. 4. *Bolletino dell'Emigrazione*, 1912, no. 3, 38–39. Other examples of Italian mistreatment are in Mrs. Harry Sternberger, "Are Our Foreign-Born Emigrating? An Analysis of the Experience of an Industrial City," *Survey*, 7 February 1920, 540. Angelo Olivieri, "L'Italia ufficiale e la realtá dell'emigrazione in USA (1886–1914)," *Studi Emigrazione* 11 (March 1974), 33–35. See debates on this subject in Italy, Camera dei Deputati, *Atti Parlamentari*, 23 November–3 December 1900, 398–964, esp. 601–9. The impact on the Italians' self-image of their labor on the bottom rungs of American industry is examined in Samuel L. Baily, "The Adjustment of Italian Immigrants in Buenos Aires and New York, 1870–1914," *American Historical Review* 88 (April 1983), 304–5.

58. For a description of Italian Catholic groups, see *Charities*, 7 May 1904, 476–82. Edwin Fenton, "Immigrants and Unions: A Case Study: Italians and American Labor, 1870–1920" (Ph.D. diss., Harvard University, 1957), 104–11, 118–19. *Bolletino dell'Emigrazione*, 1908, no. 5, 6–7, 51–52. Olivieri, "L'Italia ufficiale," 33–34. Gilkey, "The Effects of Emigration," 13.

59. Dr. Gustavo Tosti, "Italy's Attitude toward Her Emigrants," *North American Review* 180 (January–June 1905), 722–23. *Bolletino dell'Emigrazione*, 1908, no. 5, 20–21; 1912, no. 3, 39, 41.

60. Gilkey, "The Effects of Emigration," 135–36.

61. Caroli, *Italian Repatriation*, 70–71. *Bolletino dell'Emigrazione*, 1912, no. 4, 496–98.

62. Gilkey, "The Effects of Emigration," 136–38.

63. Stolarik, "Urbanization and Immigration," 137. See discussion in Puskás, *From Hungary*, 137, 193–95. John Bodnar, *The Transplanted: A History of Immigrants in Urban America* (Bloomington, Ind., 1985), 53–54. Zoltan Kramar, ed., *From the Danube to the Hudson: U.S. Ministerial and Consular Dispatches on Immigration from the Habsburg Monarchy, 1850–1900* (Atlanta, Ga., 1978), 43–45.

64. Robert E. Park, *The Immigrant Press and Its Control* (New York, 1922), 55, 432–33; it is unclear whether all of Park's figures are annual amounts. Monika Glettler, *Pittsburg—Wien—Budapest: Programm und Praxis der Nationalitätenpolitik bei Auswanderung der ungarischen Slowaken nach Amerika um 1900* (Vienna, 1980), 350, 358, 372–75. David M. Brownstone, Irene M. Franck, and Douglass L. Brownstone, *Island of Hope, Island of Tears* (New York, 1979, 1986), 48.

65. Glettler, *Pittsburg—Wien—Budapest*, 98–99, 124–27, 136, 147–49, 260, 273–75, 298.

66. Ibid., 319–21, 370 (note 20), chap. 3. Stolarik, "Immigration and Urbaniza-

tion," 137–40, 144. Braun, *Immigration Abuses*, 82–83, 119. "Are We Benefiting from Hungarian Immigration?" *American Review of Reviews*, March 1906, 356.

67. Glettler, *Pittsburg—Wien—Budapest*, 401–6.

68. Ivan Cizmic, "The Experience of South Slav Immigrants on Ellis Island and the Establishment of the Slavonic Immigrant Society in New York," in Marianne Debouzy, ed., *In the Shadow of the Statue of Liberty: Immigrants, Workers, and Citizens in the American Republic, 1880–1920* (Paris, 1988), 83. Bodnar, *Transplanted*, 50.

69. Brożek, *Polish-Americans*, 38–39. Zdzisław Dębicki, *Za atlantykiem* (Warsaw, 1921), 241. Bodnar, *Transplanted*, 50.

70. Saloutos, *They Remember America*, 30, 34. Ljungmark, *Swedish Exodus*, 133. Barton, *Letters from the Promised Land*, 210. Sture Lindmark, "Re-Immigration to Sweden from the United States, 1929–1932," *Swedish Pioneer Historical Quarterly* 17 (July 1966), 147. Virtanen, *Settlement or Return*, 189–90.

71. T. Jasieniecki, Michigan City, Ind., to Joseph Romecki, Ugoszcz, Congress Poland, 4 December 1890, in Kula et al., *Writing Home*, no. 146, 266. 1913 emigration survey, Miedzybrodzie report, in Archiwum Kurii Metropolitalnej w Krakowie, Kraków, Poland.

Chapter 5. Politics, Unions, and Postwar Americanism

1. Jeremiah W. Jenks and W. Jett Lauck, *The Immigration Problem: A Study of American Immigration Conditions and Needs* (New York, 1922), 36–40.

2. U.S. 51st Cong., 2d sess., H. R. 3472, *Report of the Select Committee on Immigration and Naturalization* (Washington, D.C., 1891), 549. *Chicago Evening Journal*, 11 April 1885, 14 January 1886, quoted in Rudolph J. Vecoli, "Chicago's Italians prior to World War I: A Study of Their Social and Economic Adjustment" (Ph.D. diss., University of Wisconsin, 1962), 408–9. Henry Sterne, U.S. Consul, Budapest, R. 76 (April 1887), in U.S. 50th Cong., 1st sess., H. Misc. Doc. 604, *Reports from Consuls of the United States* (Washington, 1887), 22:52. Also see Frank Julian Warne, *The Immigrant Invasion* (New York, 1913), 138–39.

3. Worthington C. Ford, report to Secretary of State (9 February 1887), in *Reports of Consuls* (1887), no. 76, 3. Timothy F. Lee, Immigration Inspector, U.S. Treasury Department, 1 May 1890, in U.S. 51st Cong., *Report . . . on Immigration and Naturalization*, 577.

4. Labor responses to the New Immigration are examined in Gwendolyn Mink, *Old Labor and New Immigrants in American Political Development: Union, Party, and State, 1875–1920* (Ithaca, N.Y., 1986), esp. 124–28, and by John Higham, *Strangers in the Land: Patterns of American Nativism, 1860–1925* (New York, 1975), chap. 6. Peter Roberts, "The New Pittsburghers," *Charities* 21 (2 January 1909), 543, and *Anthracite Coal Communities* (New York, 1904, 1970), 40, 52–54, 83, 284.

5. Warne, *Immigrant Invasion*, 7, 150–54, 162–65, 173, 178–79, 239–41, 315.

6. Sen. Henry Cabot Lodge, "The Restriction of Immigration," *North American Review* 152 (January 1891), 32.

7. Marcus Braun, *Immigration Abuses: Glimpses of Hungary and Hungarians* (New York, 1906, 1972), 102. Steiner testimony before Senate Subcommittee on Brewing and Liquor Interests and German Propaganda, U.S. 66th Cong., 1st sess.

(1919), 2:2823–24. See discussion in Robert E. Park, *The Immigrant Press and Its Control* (New York, 1992), 417–19.

8. Edwin Fenton, "Immigrants and Unions, a Case Study: Italians and American Labor, 1870–1920" (Ph.D. diss., Harvard University, 1957), 111. Park, *Immigrant Press*, 59–60. Warne, *Immigrant Invasion*, 243–44. Gustave Miller, New York, letter published in *Outlook*, 16 April 1919, 630–31.

9. U.S. Commissioner-General of Immigration, *Annual Report, 1904* (Washington, D.C., 1904), 43–45.

10. Mink, *Old Labor and New Immigrants*, 123. Vecoli, "Chicago's Italians," 418–19. In 1897 Idaho limited both public and private employment to citizens or those who had declared their intention to become citizens; Mark Wyman, *Hard-Rock Epic: Western Miners and the Industrial Revolution, 1860–1910* (Berkeley, 1979), 55–56. Higham, *Strangers in the Land*, 183.

11. Higham, *Strangers in the Land*, 103–5, 128–30, 189–93. Lodge, "Restriction of Immigration," 32, 36.

12. One version of the amendment banned public works employment by noncitizens or those who had not declared their intention to become citizens. Information on the Corliss amendment is drawn from *Congressional Record*, U.S. 54th Cong., 2d sess. (1896–97), 29: 1. 372; 2. 1217, 1288–29, 1925, 1930–31, 1937; 3. 17–19. A compendium of federal actions against return migration, with newspaper comment, is Neil Larry Shumsky, " 'Let No Man Stop to Plunder!' American Hostility to Return Migration, 1890–1924," *Journal of American Ethnic History* 11 (Winter 1992), 56–75.

13. A. T. Lane, *Solidarity or Survival? American Labor and European Immigrants, 1830–1924* (Westport, Conn., 1987), 47–49.

14. The best examination of the Chinese vis-à-vis American labor is Alexander Saxton, *The Indispensable Enemy: Labor and the Anti-Chinese Movement in California* (Berkeley, 1971). The quote is from Wyman, *Hard-Rock Epic*, 38–41.

15. *Congressional Record*, 48th Cong., 1st sess. (19 June 1884), 5349; see discussion in Mink, *Old Labor and New Immigrants*, 50–60, 108–9. Charlotte Erickson, *American Industry and the European Immigrant, 1860–1885* (New York, 1957), 172–73, 175.

16. Powderly and Adelbert M. Dewey testimony in U.S. 51st Cong., *Report . . . on Immigration and Naturalization*, 233, 604. Catherine Collomp, "Unions, Civics, and National Identity: Organized Labor's Reaction to Immigration, 1881–1897," *Labor History* 29 (Fall 1988), 460.

17. Dirk Hoerder, "German Immigrant Workers' Views of 'America' in the 1880s," in Marianne Debouzy, ed., *In the Shadow of the Statue of Liberty: Immigrants, Workers, and Citizens in the American Republic, 1880–1920* (Paris, 1988), 27–28. John R. Commons, *Labor and Administration* (New York, 1913, 1964), 317–18.

18. For example, an 1882 New York strike by a largely Irish union of freight handlers was broken up when the employer went to Castle Garden for New Immigrant strikebreakers; see Fenton, "Immigrants and Unions," 202–3. *United Mine Workers Journal*, 5 December 1907, 4; 12 December 1907, 6.

19. James T. Farrell, *The Young Manhood of Studs Loningan* (New York, 1934, 1948), 97.

20. Fenton, "Immigrants and Unions," 142–43. *Lietuva*, 28 January 1910, in Chicago Foreign Press Survey, reel 44, III.G.

21. Lane, *Solidarity or Survival?* 120, 173. But the United Mine Workers of America, particularly from 1900 on, was generally an exception to the AFL's anti–

New Immigrant policies—as it was an exception to the AFL's craft union approach to organization.

22. Mink argues that this set of circumstances also propelled the AFL into a Democratic party alliance; Mink, *Old Labor and New Immigrants*, 17, 38, 47–48, 150–51. Collomp, "Unions, Civics, and National Identity," 452, 460–61, 466, 474.

23. Lane, *Solidarity or Survival?* 95–110, 147. *United Mine Workers Journal*, 20 January 1910, 1–2; also see sympathetic reports on New Immigrants in issues of 25 April 1907, 6; 26 September 1907, 4; and 30 June 1910, 3.

24. It should be noted that according to Lane the New Immigrants' "apparent determination to return home when enough had been saved highlighted another immigrant characteristic condemned by labor critics: their ignorance of the United States except as the provider of economic opportunities." Lane adds that, because of their plans to leave, immigrants did not take part in American activities and did not become good American citizens; Lane, *Solidarity or Survival?* 63–64.

25. Commons, *Labor and Administration*, 151–53.

26. Charlotte Erickson, *Invisible Immigrants: The Adaptation of English and Scottish Immigrants in Nineteenth-Century America* (Coral Gables, Fla., 1972), 125–26. Herbert Gutman, *Work, Culture, and Society in Industrializing America: Essays in American Working-Class and Social History* (New York, 1966, 1977), 173. Dirk Hoerder, "An Introduction to Labor Migration in the Atlantic Economies, 1815–1914," in Hoerder, ed., *Labor Migration in the Atlantic Economies: The European and North American Working Classes during the Period of Industrialization* (Westport, Conn., 1985), 12. Higham summarizes the historical background of the antiimmigrant stance by organized labor in *Strangers in the Land*, 45–46.

27. U.S. 61st Cong., 3d sess., S. Doc. 747, *Reports of the Immigration Commission* (Washington, D.C., 1911), 1:46–47 (cited hereafter as Dillingham Commission *Reports*).

28. Wolfgang Hell, "Amerikanisch-deutsch Rückwanderung," in *". . . nach Amerika!" Auswanderung in die Vereinigten Staaten* (Hamburg, 1976), 56. Günter Moltmann, "American-German Return Migration in the Nineteenth and Early Twentieth Centuries," *Central European History* 13 (December 1980), 391.

29. Theodore Saloutos, *They Remember America: The Story of the Repatriated Greek-Americans* (Berkeley, 1956), 35–40. Granite City (Ill.) *Press-Record*, 4, 15, 22, and 25 October, and 1 November 1912. David DeChenne, "Labor and Immigration in a Southern Illinois Mill Town, 1890–1937" (D.A. diss., Illinois State University, 1989), 64–66.

30. *Survey*, 2 November 1912, 111–12.

31. *Survey*, 3 October 1914, 7–9. Letter to *Jewish Daily Forward* in 1914, reprinted in Isaac Metzker, ed., *A Bintel Brief* (Garden City, N.Y., 1971), 128–29.

32. See discussion of wartime immigration in Alan M. Kraut, *The Huddled Masses: The Immigrant in American Society, 1880–1921* (Arlington Heights, Ill., 1982), 18. Statistics from U.S. Department of Labor, *Annual Report of the Commissioner General of Immigration . . . 1931* (Washington D.C., 1931), 218–19, 229–30. Granite City *Press-Record*, 24 September 1914. *Survey*, 3 October 1914, 8. U.S. Department of Commerce, *Statistical Abstract of the United States, 1913*, 93, and *1916*, 103.

33. Monika Glettler, *Pittsburg—Wien—Budapest: Programm und Praxis der Nationalitätenpolitik bei der Auswanderung der ungarischen Slowaken nach Amerika um 1900* (Vienna, 1980), 352–53. Theodore Saloutos, "Exodus U.S.A.," in O. Fritiof Ander, ed., *In the Trek of the Immigrants* (Rock Island, Ill., 1964), 202–3. Miroslaw Frančić, *Komitet Obrony Narodowej W Ameryce, 1912–1918* (Wrocław,

1983), 220. Joseph T. Hapak, "The Polish Military Commission, 1917–1919," *Polish American Studies* 38 (Autumn 1981), 36–37, and "Selective Service and Polish Army Recruitment during World War I," *Journal of American Ethnic History* 10 (Summer 1991), esp. 51, 53. According to Andrzej Brożek, Haller's Army had 24,000–28,000 soldiers; he estimates that 190,000–300,000 Poles served in the U.S. Army; Brożek, *Polish Americans, 1854–1939* (Warsaw, 1985), 145–46.

34. Robert F. Foerster, *The Italian Emigration of Our Times* (New York, 1919, 1968), 33–34. Italy, Commissariato Generale dell'Emigrazione, *L'emigrazione italiana dal 1910 al 1923* (Rome, 1926), 1:936–37.

35. See discussion in David Brody, *Steelworkers in America: The Nonunion Era* (New York, 1960), 187–89, 195, chaps. 8–9.

36. Higham, *Strangers in the Land*, 103–5, 191–3, 200, 202–3. Philip Taylor, *The Distant Magnet: European Emigration to the U.S.A.* (New York, 1971), 243–50.

37. Higham, *Strangers in the Land*, 248. Theodore Saloutos, *Expatriates and Repatriates: A Neglected Chapter in United States History* (Rock Island, Ill., 1972), 16. Keijo Virtanen, *Settlement or Return: Finnish Emigrants (1860–1930) in the International Overseas Return Migration Movement* (Helsinki, 1979), 184.

38. Rollin Lynde Hartt, "Emigration from America," *Outlook*, 29 January 1919, 186–87. *Radnicka Straza* (Chicago), 7 November 1917, and *Magyar Tribune* (Chicago), 4 July 1919, in Chicago Foreign Press Survey.

39. U.S. Commissioner-General of Immigration, *Annual Report, 1931*, 229–30.

40. *Literary Digest*, 24 April 1920, 12–13. Harry Jerome, *Migration and Business Cycles* (New York, 1926), 24. "Emigrants and Immigrants," *Nation*, 18 September 1920, 316. Saloutos, "Exodus U.S.A.," 208–10. Hartt, "Emigration from America," 186–87.

41. *American Press Section of the Foreign Language Information Service*, June 27, 1921, no. 30.2. U.S. Commissioner-General of Immigration, *Annual Report, 1931*, 225. Reino Kero, "Emigration of Finns from North America to Soviet Karelia in the Early 1930s," in Michael G. Karni et al., *The Finnish Experience in the Western Great Lakes Region: New Perspectives* (Turku, Finland, 1975), 215–20.

42. Constantine M. Panunzio, "As 'They' See Us," *World Outlook*, May 1920, 4.

43. Frances Kraljic, *Croatian Migration to and from the United States, 1900–1914* (Palo Alto, Calif., 1978), 82–83, 99. On Hungary's plea, see reports in *Magyar Tribune* (Chicago), 26 March 1920, and 27 August 1920, in Chicago Foreign Press Survey, reel 29.

44. David N. Doyle, "Unestablished Irishmen: New Immigrants and Industrial America, 1870–1910," in Dirk Hoerder, ed., *American Labor and Immigration History, 1877–1920s: Recent European Research* (Urbana, Ill., 1983), 43. U.S. Statistical Abstract, 1921, 112. These totals, however, are higher than those reported ten years later in U.S. Commissioner-General of Immigration, *Annual Report, 1931*, 225. Arnold Schrier, *Ireland and the American Emigration, 1850–1900* (Minneapolis, 1958), 123. Catherine Dowling, "Irish-American Nationalism in Butte, 1900–1916," *Montana*, Spring 1989, 51–52.

45. Alan J. Ward, *The Easter Rising: Revolution and Irish Nationalism* (Arlington Heights, Ill., 1980), chap. 9.

46. William Galush, "Polish Americans and the New Poland: An Evidence of Changes in Ethnic Orientation," *Przegląd Polonijny* 6, no. 3 (1980), 140. Adam Walaszek, "Return Migration from the USA to Poland," in Daniel Kubat, ed., *The Politics of Return: International Return Migration in Europe* (Rome, 1981), 216. Stanisław Jan Zaleski, *Powrotna Fala* (Chicago, 1919), 45.

47. Adam Walaszek, *Reemigracja ze Stanów Zjednoczonych do Polski po i Wojnie Światowej (1919–1924)* (Kraków, 1983), chap. 3. Mieczysław Szawleski, *Mychodźtwo Polskie w Stanach Zjednoczonych Ameryki* (Kraków, 1924), 196–97. Polish Consulate-General in New York, Correspondence 1919–1929, in Polish Embassy files, Folder 2112, 87–92. M. Malinowski, *Jak Odbudowac Polske?* (Chicago, 1918?), 94. Zaleski, *Powrotna Fala*, 46.

48. Walaszek, *Reemigracja*, chap. 6. Brożek, *Polish Americans*, 53–54. Report, Military Minister, 24 November 1921; Association of Polish Veterans in America, letter of 24 February 1922; Polish Minister of Military Affairs, Warsaw, to Polish Embassy, Washington, in Polish Embassy (Washington) files, Folder 2278.

49. *Dziennik Chicagoski*, 6 January 1922, in Chicago Foreign Language Press Survey, reel 58, III. 6. Zaleski, *Powrotna Fala*, 54–60, 68. Stanisław Osada, *Jak sie ksztaltowala polska dusza Wychodztwa w Ameryce* (Pittsburgh, 1930), 175. Polish National Alliance Proceedings, Board of Directors, Jan A. Wedda report, January 1920, 40–44. Polish Consulate (London) report, 29 April 1922, Folder 59. U.S. Commissioner-General of Immigration, *Annual Report*, 1931, 224. *U.S. Statistical Abstract*, 1921, 112.

50. Walaszek, *Reemigracja*, 131–36.

51. Brożek, *Polish Americans*, 54. Osada, *Jak sie ksztaltowala polska*, 176–78, 184.

52. I take up the subject of Polish remigrants' activities in Poland further in succeeding chapters. Information in this paragraph on conditions in postwar Poland is taken from Walaszek, *Reemigracja*, 179, chap. 4; and from these files in Folder 9958 in the Polish Government's Archiwum akt Nowych, Warsaw: Polish Ministry of Foreign Affairs, "Reemigration," 17 May 1929; *Monitor* (Cleveland), 6 November 1931, 4 (copy in letter from Organizational Council of Poles from Abroad, 20 November 1931). Adam Walaszek, "Reemigranci ze Stanów Zjednoczonych i Kanady w Polsce, 1919–1923: 'Jak mozna bylo tak sobie to pieknie przedstawiac?'" *Przegląd Polonijny* 6, no. 1 (1980), 3. Polish Consulate (New York), 1923 Report, 103, Folder 2111.

53. Walaszek, "Return Migration from the USA to Poland," 216–17. Brożek, *Polish Americans*, 182–83. Szawleski, *Wychodźtwo Polskie*, 205.

54. "Prospective Emigration of Immigrants from the U.S.," 2 January 1919, in U.S. War Labor Policies Board Records. On the 1920 Hungarian land reform, see Edit Fél and Tamás Hofer, *Proper Peasants: Traditional Life in a Hungarian Village* (Chicago, 1969), 270. Postwar land reforms across Europe are discussed in Helen Douglas Irvine, *The Making of Rural Europe* (London, 1923), 204–6.

55. *Jewish Daily Forward*, 2 June 1919, reprinted in Park, *Immigrant Press*, 453–56. On Kellor's changing approach, see Higham, *Strangers in the Land*, 257–60.

56. Higham, *Strangers in the Land*, 256, 305. John Morton Bloom, *The Republican Roosevelt* (Cambridge, Mass., 1954, 1977), 157.

57. Lane, *Solidarity or Survival?* 194–95. Robert Asher, "Union Nativism and the Immigrant Response," *Labor History* 23 (Summer 1982), 334.

58. Brody, *Steelworkers in America*, chap. 12.

59. On Gompers' changing opinions, see Higham, *Strangers in the Land*, 305–6, and Asher, "Union Nativism," 335–36. Brody, *Steelworkers in America*, 276–77.

60. *Dawn*, 5 January 1924. Similar ideas were expressed in a Klan-controlled newspaper published in the 1920s in Pekin, Illinois; see Carl V. Hallberg, "'For God, Country, and Home': The Ku Klux Klan in Pekin, 1923–1925," *Journal of the Illinois State Historical Society* 77 (Summer 1984), 82–93.

61. Higham, *Strangers in the Land*, chaps. 9–11. A convenient compilation of the National Origins Act is in Leonard Dinnerstein and David M. Reimers, *Ethnic Americans* (New York, 1982), 61–62. Stephan Thernstrom, ed., *Harvard Encyclopedia of American Ethnic Groups* (Cambridge, Mass., 1980), 492–93

62. Iowa proclamation reprinted in Moses Rischin, ed., *Immigration and the American Tradition* (Indianapolis, Ind., 1976), 206–8.

63. *Survey*, 6 March 1920, 670–71. Polish Consulate (New York), report, 25 February 1924, 103, in Polish Consular Papers, Folder 2111. Stephen Meyer, "Adapting the Immigrant to the Line: Americanization in the Ford Factory, 1914–1921," *Journal of Social History* 14 (Fall 1980), 78–79.

64. George Seibel, "Going Back—and Why," *Nation*, 11 October 1919, 492–93. M. Mark Stolarik, *Immigration and Urbanization: The Slovak Experience, 1870–1918* (New York, 1989), 52–54. S. Miles Bouton, "What Is the Reason?" *Atlantic Monthly*, January 1921, 40–43.

65. Carleton Beals, "Those Who Have Gone Back," *Outlook*, 28 July 1926, 447.

66. Bouton, "What Is the Reason?" 41–42. Kero, "Emigration of Finns," 212. Swedish Royal Commission, *Report*, 20:19–24. Reidar Grunde Simonsen, "Returned Emigrants: A Study of Repatriated Norwegians" (thesis, University of Oslo, 1982), 64. Irish Folklore Commission Questionnaires, MS 1409, 33.

67. Samuel Baily and Franco Ramella, eds., *One Family, Two Worlds: An Italian Family's Correspondence across the Atlantic, 1901–1922* (New Brunswick, N.J., 1988), 2.

Chapter 6. Peasants Back on the Land

1. Nitti quoted in Francesco Paolo Cerase, "From Italy to the United States and Back: Returned Migrants, Conservative or Innovative?" (Ph.D. diss., Columbia University, 1971), 111–12. On the role of American houses, see also Adam Walaszek, *Reemigracja ze Stanów Zjednoczonych do Polski po i wojnie Światowej (1919–1924)* (Kraków, 1983), 141–48. Irish Folklore Commission Questionnaires, MS 1411, 67, 406. Julianna Puskás, *From Hungary to the United States (1880–1914)* (Budapest, 1982), 79–80. Robert F. Foerster, *The Italian Emigration of Our Times* (New York, 1919, 1968), 457. Dino Cinel, *The National Integration of Italian Return Migration, 1870–1929* (Cambridge, 1991), 163–64. U.S. 61st Cong., 3d sess., S. Doc. 747, *Reports of the Immigration Commission* (Washington, D.C., 1911), 4:232–33, 387 (hereafter cited as Dillingham Commission *Reports*). Maria Wierusyewska-Adamcyk, *Społeczność Wiejska Zaborowa w Procesie Przemian* (Warsaw, 1980), 85. Jerzy Fierich, *Przeszłość powiatu ropczyckiego w ustach mieszkańców* (Ropczyci, Poland, 1936), 57. George Gilkey, "The Effects of Emigration on Italy, 1900 to 1923" (Ph.D. diss., Northwestern University, 1950), 152. Anna-Leena Toivonen, "Etelä-Pohjanmaan Valtameren-takainen Siirtolaisuus, 1867–1930" (Ph.D. diss., Seinäjoen Kirjapaino, Finland, 1963), 209. Antonio Mangano, "The Effect of Emigration upon Italy," *Charities*, 2 May 1908, 171–72. Dino Cinel, "Conservative Adventurers: Italian Migrants in Italy and San Francisco" (Ph.D. diss., Stanford University 1979), 8, 105–6.

2. Carlo Levi, *Christ Stopped at Eboli* (New York, 1947), 43.

3. Adolfo Rossi, 1908, quoted in Dino Cinel, "Land Tenure Systems, Return Migration, and Militancy in Italy," *Journal of Ethnic Studies* 12 (Fall 1984), 59. Ewa Morawska, *For Bread with Butter: The Life-Worlds of East Central Europeans in Johnstown, Pennsylvania, 1890–1940* (Cambridge, 1985), 68–69. Betty Boyd

Caroli, *Italian Repatriation from the United States, 1900–1914* (New York, 1973), 85.

4. Stefan Kieniewicz, *The Emancipation of the Polish Peasantry* (Chicago, 1969), 223. Rudolph J. Vecoli, "Chicago Italians prior to World War I: A Study of Their Social and Economic Adjustment" (Ph.D. diss., University of Wisconsin, 1962), 118–19. Keijo Virtanen, *Settlement or Return: Finnish Emigrants (1860–1930) in the International Overseas Return Migration Movement* (Helsinki, 1979), 195–96. Cinel, "Land Tenure," 63. Italy, Commissariato Generale dell'Emigrazione, *L'emigrazione italiana dal 1910 al 1923* (Rome, 1926), 1:182–86. Caroline Golab, *Immigrant Destinations* (Philadelphia, 1977), 87. Puskás, *From Hungary*, 80–81. Virginia Yans-McLaughlin, *Family and Community: Italian Immigrants in Buffalo, 1880–1930* (Ithaca, N.Y., 1971, 1977), 29. Emily Greene Balch, "The Peasant Background of our Slavic Fellow Citizens," *Survey* 24 (6 August 1910), 670.

5. Irish Folklore Commission Questionnaires, MS 1407, 36–37. Benjamin P. Murdzek, *Emigration in Polish Social-Political Thought, 1870–1914* (Boulder, Colo., 1977), 99–100. Cinel, "Conservative Adventurers," 108–9. B. J. Hovde, "Notes on the Effects of Emigration upon Scandinavia," *Journal of Modern History* 6 (September 1934), 278. Dollar totals of funds sent home from the United States are reported in Dillingham Commission *Reports*, 37:69.

6. Morawska, *For Bread with Butter*, 69–70. Krzysztof Groniowski, "The Socio-Economic Base of Polish Emigration to North America, 1854–1939," in Frank Renkiewicz, ed., *The Polish Presence in Canada and America* (Toronto, 1982), 5–6. Murdzek, *Emigration in Polish Social-Political Thought*, 151–52, estimates the Galician total as slightly lower. Cinel, "Conservative Adventurers," 106–8, and *National Integration of Italian Return Migration*, 209–11. Foerster, *Italian Emigration*, 446–49. Levi, *Christ Stopped at Eboli*, 122.

7. Virtanen, *Settlement or Return*, 199. Edward A. Steiner, *The Immigrant Tide: Its Ebb and Flow* (New York, 1909), 67. Frances Kraljic, *Croatian Migration to and from the United States, 1900–1914* (Palo Alto, Calif., 1978), 70. Mangano, "Effect of Emigration," *Charities*, 4 April 1908, 14–15. Murdzek, *Emigration in Polish Social-Political Thought*, 153.

8. Adolfo Rossi, "Vantaggi e danni dell'emigrazione nel Mezzogiorno d'Italia," *Bollettino dell'Emigrazione* 13 (1908), 36–37, quoted in Cinel, *National Integration of Italian Return Migration*, 120.

9. Kazimiera Zawistowicz-Adamska, *Społeczność wiejska* (Łódź, 1948), 19–20. Mangano, "Effect of Emigration," *Charities*, 4 April 1908, 18.

10. Cinel, "Conservative Adventurers," 5. Inspector John J. Quinlan, testimony on 25 July 1899, U.S. 57th Cong., Industrial Commission, *Reports* (Washington, D.C., 1901), 15:22. Julianna Puskás, "Hungarian Overseas Migration: A Microanalysis," in Rudolph J. Vecoli and Suzanne M. Sinke, eds., *A Century of European Migrations, 1830–1930* (Urbana, Ill., 1991), 227.

11. Cinel, "Conservative Adventurers," iv, 84–85. Cinel cites the *Inchiesta Parlamentare*'s 1910 finding: districts without land for sale in southern Italy produced few emigrants. The relation between the availability of land for sale, emigration, and militancy is a major theme of J. S. MacDonald, "Agricultural Organization, Migration, and Labour Militancy in Rural Italy," *Economic History Review* (2d ser.) 16 (August 1963), 61–75.

12. Joseph Kurowski, Detroit, to brother in Poland, 10 January 1891, in Witold Kula et al., comps., *Writing Home: Immigrants in Brazil and the United States, 1890–1891* (Boulder, Colo., 1896), 320; Kula defines a *parobek* as "a farmhand, day laborer, country servant, one engaged in husbandry." Morawska, *For Bread with Butter*, 75–76.

13. Cinel, "Land Tenure," 67–68. Reino Kero, "The Return of Emigrants from America to Finland," University of Turku Institute of General History *Publications*, no. 4 (1972), 21. Virtanen, *Settlement or Return*, 75, 77. Lars-Göran Tedebrand, "Remigration from America to Sweden," in Harald Runblom and Hans Norman, eds., *From Sweden to America: A History of the Migration* (Minneapolis, 1976), 213, 217.

14. Hans Norman and Harald Runblom, eds., *Amerika-emigrationen* (Cikada, Uddevalls, Sweden, 1980), 186, Table 20:4.

15. Arnold Schrier, *Ireland and the American Emigration, 1850–1900* (Minneapolis, 1958), 139. Cinel, "Conservative Adventurers," 83–85.

16. Golab, *Immigrant Destinations*, 87. Emily Greene Balch, "Slav Emigration at Its Source," *Charities*, 5 May 1906, 181–82. Murdzek, *Emigration in Polish Social-Political Thought*, 153–54.

17. Puskás, *From Hungary*, 81. Leopold Caro, *Emigracya: I Polityka Emigracyjna* (Poznań, 1914), 79–82. Foerster, *Italian Emigration*, 451–52.

18. This change is discussed in Cinel, "Conservative Adventurers," 112–13.

19. *En Smålandssocken Emigerar* (Långasjö, Sweden, 1967), 815. Cinel, *National Integration of Italian Return Migration*, 185–86. Steiner, *Immigrant Tide*, 66–67. Mieczysław Szawleski, *Wychodźtwo Polskie w Stanach Zjednoczonych Ameryki* (Lwów, 1924), 352.

20. George R. Gilkey, "The United States and Italy: Migration and Repatriation," *Journal of Developing Areas* 2 (October 1967), 34–35, and "America—Myth and Reality," unpublished article, 28–29. Foerster, *Italian Emigration*, 452. Cinel, "Conservative Adventurers," 113–14. Pasquale Villari and Investigator Jarach, quoted in Gilkey, "Effects of Emigration," 71–72.

21. Virtanen, *Settlement or Return*, 189. Gilkey, "Effects of Emigration," 160–61. Cinel, "Conservative Adventurers," 118–19. Gilkey, "United States and Italy," 33–34. Theodore Saloutos, *They Remember America: The Story of the Repatriated Greek-Americans* (Berkeley, 1956), 104.

22. Murdzek, *Emigration in Polish Social-Political Thought*, 93, 122–26. Szawleski, *Wychodźtwo Polskie*, 351. Swedish Royal Commission on Emigration, *Report* (Stockholm, 1908–13), 20:37–40.

23. Lt.-Gen. von Mueller and Prof. Hans Delbrueck, in *Preussische Jahrbücher* (Berlin), quoted in *American Monthly Review of Reviews*, April 1906, 486. Also see Murdzek, *Emigration in Polish Social-Political Thought*, 23–24.

24. Caroli, *Italian Repatriation*, 60. Mangano, "Effect of Immigration," *Charities*, 4 April 1908, 18–19. Cinel, "Conservative Adventurers," 110–11. Cinel, *National Integration of Italian Return Migration*, 164–68, 172–76, 197. Murdzek, *Emigration in Polish Social-Political Thought*, 154–55. Puskás, *From Hungary*, 82–83. Balch, "Slav Emigration," *Charities*, 2 June 1906, 327–28. Gilkey, "Effects of Emigration," 65–66. Also see Groniowski, "Socio-Economic Base," 5–6, and William I. Thomas and Florian Znaniecki, eds., *The Polish Peasant in Europe and America: Monograph of an Immigrant Group* (Boston, 1918), 2:301n.

25. Murdzek, *Emigration in Polish Social-Political Thought*, 154–59. Puskás, *From Hungary*, 84n. Mangano, "Effect of Emigration," *Charities*, 4 April 1908, 13.

26. Mangano, "Effect of Emigration," *Charities*, 4 April 1908, 170–71. Adam Walaszek, "Polish Mechanics' Association in America, 1919–1945," *Przegląd Polonijny* 12, no. 2 (1986), 138–39. Commissariato dell'Emigrazione, *L'emigrazione italiana*, 1:186–87. Cinel discusses "returnees of retirement," who did not buy land but used their savings as retirement funds; Cinel, *National Integration of Italian Return Migration*, 117, 223.

27. Schrier, *Ireland and the American Emigration*, 138–39. Irish Folklore Commission Questionnaires, MS 1410, 107–8. Mangano, "Effect of Emigration," *Charities*, 4 April 1908, 170–71. Gilkey, "America—Myth and Reality," 32, 37. Levi, *Christ Stopped at Eboli*, 127. Josef J. Barton, *Peasants and Strangers: Italians, Rumanians, and Slovaks in an American City, 1890–1950* (Cambridge, Mass., 1975), 1–2. Saloutos, *They Remember America*, 78–79. Berit Brattne, in cooperation with Sune Åkerman, "The Importance of the Transport Sector for Mass Emigration," in Harald Runblom and Hans Norman, eds., *From Sweden to America: A History of the Migration* (Minneapolis, 1976), 182–86.

28. Jonathan D. Sarna, "The Myth of No Return: Jewish Return Migration to Eastern Europe, 1881–1914," *American Jewish History* 71 (December 1981), 264. Reino Kero, "The Industrial Enterprise of Returning Finnish Emigrants," *Turun Historiallinen Arkisto* 38 (Turku, Finland, 1982), 347–49.

29. The description of Polish postwar enterprises is taken from two works by Adam Walaszek: *Reemigracja*, chap. 4, 141–48, and "Polish Mechanics' Association," 138–39. Feliks Gross, *The Polish Worker: A Study of a Social Stratum* (New York, 1945), 158.

30. Cerase, *From Italy to the United States*, 290–91. *Inchiesta Parlamentare* (Rome, 1910), 5:3.112–13, quoted in Cinel, "Land Tenure Systems," 59. Earlier studies are noted in Cerase, *From Italy to the United States*, 290–91. Also see studies by numerous modern scholars collected in Daniel Kubat, ed., *The Politics of Return* (New York, 1984). On Cerase's categories, see *From Italy to the United States*, 192, 222.

31. Yans-McLaughlin, *Family and Community*, 21, 262. Kraljic, *Croatian Migration*, 66.

32. See discussion in Theodore C. Blegan, *Norwegian Migration to America* (Northfield, Minn., 1940), 469–70, and Grazia Dore, "Some Social and Historical Aspects of Italian Emigration to America," *Journal of Social History* 2 (Winter 1968), 97–98.

33. Utrandringskomiteen, 1912–13, *Indstilling* III, quoted in Hovde, "Notes on the Effects of Emigration," 278. Jonathan Bell, Ulster Folk and Transport Museum, Hollywood, Northern Ireland, letter to author, 16 January 1989 (hereafter cited as Bell Letter).

34. Szawleski, *Wychodźtwo Polskie*, 352. Ingrid Semmingsen, *Veien Mot Vest: Annen del utvandringen fra Norge, 1865–1915* (Oslo, 1950), 464. Marsha Penti, "The Role of Ethnic Folklore among Finnish-American Returnees" (Ph.D. diss., Indiana University, 1983), 359. Irish Folklore Commission Questionnaires, MS 1409, 41. Gilkey, "Effects of Emigration," 77.

35. Bell Letter. Aulia Hautamäki, "Etelä-Pohjanmaan Järviseudun Amerikansiirtolaisuus, 1872–1917" (thesis, University of Jyväskylän, Finland, 1981), 102. Virtanen, *Settlement or Return*, 204–5. Gilkey states that "how much their contribution counted" in the southern Italian livestock-raising change is "undeterminable"; Gilkey, "Effects of Emigration," 78.

36. Fierich, *Przeszłość powiatu*, 57. Gilkey, "Effects of Emigration," 80–81. Mangano, "Effect of Emigration," *Charities*, 4 April 1908, 14–15. The 1912 report cited in Kraljic, *Croatian Migration*, 69–70. Puskás, *From Hungary*, 75–76. Germany's agricultural transformation was more extensive than these and, as a consequence, the role of immigrants there is difficult to assess, according to one study. Many Germans worked on American farms, and their letters home were filled with reports on the advantages of farm mechanization. But U.S. salespeople and advertising were active in Europe as well, and by 1900 Germany was challenging France for

first place as the destination of exports of farm equipment from America. See Walter D. Kamphoefner, Wolfgang Helbich, and Ulrike Sommer, eds., *News from the Land of Freedom: German Immigrants Write Home* (Munich, 1988; trans. Cornell University Press, 1991), 54–61.

37. Reino Kero, "American Technology in Finland before World War I," in *Studia Historica in Honorem Vilho Niitemaa* (Turku, Finland, 1987), 160–61. Penti, "Role of Ethnic Folklore," 132–33. Semmingsen, *Veien Mot Vest*, 464.

38. Irish Folklore Commission Questionnaires, MS 1409, 21. Bell Letter. 1907 survey of diocese, in Archiwum Kurii Metropolitalnej w Krakowie, Kraków, Poland. Semmingsen, *Veien Mot Vest*, 462.

39. Hautamäki, "Etelä-Pohjanmaan," 102. Penti, "Role of Ethnic Folklore," 327. Semmingsen, *Veien Mot Vest*, 464.

40. Juris Silenieks, "Kārlis Ulmanis," in Longins Apkalns and Vito V. Simanis, eds., *Latvia* (St. Charles, Ill., 1984), 148–49.

41. Gilkey relies heavily on the *Inchiesta Parlamentare* in his discussion; Gilkey, "Effect of Emigration," 78–79, 81–82. Mangano, "Effect of Emigration," *Charities*, 6 June 1908, 332–33.

42. Semmingsen, *Veien Mot Vest*, 464–65. Norwegian commission report of 1912–13, quoted in Blegen, *Norwegian Migration*, 474. Dr. Ernst Lundevall, letter of 19 January 1908, Swedish Royal Commission, *Report*, 17:198.

43. Irish Folklore Commission Questionnaires, MS 1411, 259, 364; MS 1407, 49–53, 54–56, 57. Schrier, *Ireland and the American Emigration*, 134–35.

44. Villari quoted in Cerase, *From Italy to the United States*, 119. Gilkey, "Effects of Emigration," 150.

45. Krystyna Duda-Dziewierz, *Wieś Malopolska A Emigracja Amerykańska* (Warsaw, 1938), 129. Barbara Golda, "Konsekwencje emigracji w życiu wiejskiej spoleczności polskiej," *Przegląd Polonijny* 2, no. 1 (1976), 117. Bell Letter.

46. Cerase, *From Italy to the United States*, 64–66. Irish Folklore Commission Questionnaires, MS 1407, 54–56; MS 1409, 82. Also see Ernst Lundevall letter of 19 January 1908, Swedish Royal Commission, *Report*, 17:198. J. D. Gould, "European Inter-Continental Emigration—the Road Home: Return Migration from the U.S.A.," *Journal of European Economic History* 9 (1980), 67.

47. Gilkey, "Effects of Emigration," 161. Mangano, "Effect of Emigration," *Charities*, 4 April 1908, 18–19. *Inchiesta Parlamentare* quoted in Cinel, "Conservative Adventures," 116–18, 120–39. Cinel, *National Integration of Italian Return Migration*, 203, 217. Foerster, *Italian Emigration*, 456–57.

48. Ingrid Semmingsen, "Emigration and the Image of America in Europe," in Henry Steele Commager, ed., *Immigration and American History: Essays in Honor of Theodore C. Blegen* (Minneapolis, 1961), 45. Kero, "American Technology," 161. Knut Djupedal, "Tales of America," *Western Folklore* 49 (April 1990), 179.

49. Semmingsen, *Veien Mot Vest*, 462. G. Gerhard Magnusson, in Swedish Royal Commission, *Reports*, 8:2.82–84, quoted in H. Arnold Barton, comp., *Letters from the Promised Land: Swedes in America, 1840–1914* (Minneapolis, 1975), 293.

50. Cinel, "Conservative Adventurers," 358. Cinel, *National Integration of Italian Return Migration*, 226–27. Cerase, "From Italy to the United States," 122–23.

51. Cinel, "Conservative Adventurers," 102–4, 120–39.

52. John M. Synge, *The Aran Islands* (Marlboro, Vt., 1907; rpt., n.d.), 9–10.

53. Foerster, *Italian Emigration*, 453–54. Walaszek, *Reemigracja*, 179. Doreen Warriner, *Economics of Peasant Farming* (London, 1939), 107–8. Virtanen, *Settlement or Return*, 191. Duda-Dziewierz, *Wieś Malopolska*, 86–88.

54. Schrier, *Ireland and the American Emigration*, 140–42.

55. The "Americanization" of Europe through inventions is discussed in Halvdan Koht, *The American Spirit in Europe: A Survey of Transatlantic Influences* (Philadelphia, 1949), esp. chaps. 6 and 10. Virtanen, *Settlement or Return*, 210. Kraljic, *Croatian Migration*, 70, 73. Penti, "Role of Ethnic Folklore," 34–35. Lars Ljungmark, *For Sale—Minnesota: Organized Promotion of Scandinavian Immigration, 1866–1873* (Stockholm, 1971), 135. Sarti, *Long Live the Strong: A History of Rural Society in the Apennine Mountains* (Amherst, Mass., 1985), 131–32.

56. Kero, "American Technology," 162–63, 167.

57. Marjolein 't Hart, "Heading for Paddy's Green Shamrock Shore: The Returned Emigrants in Nineteenth Century Ireland" (Master's thesis, University of Groningen, 1981), 23. Saloutos, *They Remember America*, 88–89, 123. Steiner, *Immigrant Tide*, 102–11.

58. Levi, *Christ Stopped at Eboli*, 131–32.

59. Stany Zjednoczone, *Pamiętniki Emigrantów* (Warsaw, 1977), 169–73. Saloutos, *They Remember America*, 123–24.

60. Alfred Vagts, *Deutsch-Amerikanische Rückwanderung* (Heidelberg, 1960), 70–85.

61. Wolfgang Hell, "Amerikanisch-deutsche Rückwanderung," in *". . . nach Amerika!" Auswanderung in die Vereinigten Staaten* (Hamburg, 1976), 58.

62. Saloutos, *They Remember America*, 105.

63. Toivonen, "Etelä-Pohjanmaan," 209. Szawleski, *Wychodźtwo Polskie*, 352. Irish Folklore Commission Questionnaires, MS 1409, 70.

64. Cerase, "From Italy to the United States," 303–7. Men returning to Sambuca in western Sicily after five to eight years' work as padroni in Louisiana did not rise into the village elite; they "did not substantially improve their economic status or the occupational aspirations of their children." Not everyone who emigrated found that the road to riches ran through the United States. Donna Gabaccia, *Militants and Migrants: Rural Sicilians Become American Workers* (New Brunswick, N.J., 1988), 86. Walaszek, *Reemigracja*, 178–79. Monika Glettler, *Pittsburgh—Wien—Budapest: Programm und Praxis der Nationalitätenpolitik bei der Auswanderung der ungarischen Slowaken nach Amerika um 1900* (Vienna, 1980), 401. Keijo Virtanen, "Finnish Migrants (1860–1930) in the Overseas Return Migration Movement," in Dirk Hoerder, ed., *Labor Migration in the Atlantic Economies: The European and North American Working Classes during the Period of Industrialization* (Westport, Conn., 1985), 395.

65. Puskás, *From Hungary*, 83. Gabaccia, *Militants and Migrants*, 158–59.

Chapter 7. Workers' Ideas Carried Back

1. Sten Carlsson, "Augustana Lutheran Pastors in the Church of Sweden," *Swedish-American Historical Quarterly* 35 (July 1984), 246.

2. Ella Lonn, *Foreigners in the Union Army and Navy* (Baton Rouge, La., 1951), 74–75.

3. Halvdan Koht, *The American Spirit in Europe: A Survey of Transatlantic Influences* (Philadelphia, 1949), 202–4. Sune Åkerman and Hans Norman, "Political Mobilization of the Workers: The Case of the Worcester Swedes," in Dirk Hoerder, ed., *American Labor and Immigration History, 1877–1920s: Recent European Research* (Urbana, Ill., 1983), 235.

4. Robert F. Foerster, *The Italian Emigration of Our Times* (New York, 1919;

rpt. 1968), 323. Alberto Pecorini, "The Italians in the United States," *Forum*, January 1911, 16. Louis Adamic, *Laughing in the Jungle* (New York, 1932), 6.

5. M. Malinowski, *Jak Odbudowac Polske?* (Chicago, 1918?), 29–33.

6. Julianna Puskás, *From Hungary to the United States (1880–1914)* (Budapest, 1982), 85–86, 113.

7. Humbert L. Gualtieri, *The Labor Movement in Italy* (New York, 1946), 166. Dirk Hoerder, "Immigration and the Working Class: The Remigration Factor," *International Labor and Working Class History*, no. 21 (Spring 1982), 34. Joseph G. Rayback, *A History of American Labor* (New York, 1966), 149, 154. Feliks Gross, *The Polish Worker: A Study of a Social Stratum* (New York, 1945), 157–58.

8. Theodore Saloutos notes further that many Greek remigrants had been small shopkeepers and had an antilabor bias; Saloutos, *They Remember America: The Story of the Repatriated Greek-Americans* (Berkeley, 1956), 126.

9. The miners' ethnicity is examined in Mark Wyman, *Hard-Rock Epic: Western Miners and the Industrial Revolution, 1860–1910* (Berkeley, 1979), 41–42, 51.

10. Joyce L. Kornbluh, ed., *Rebel Voices: An I.W.W. Anthology* (Ann Arbor, Mich., 1965), esp. 1–2.

11. Eugene V. Debs, Crystal Falls, Mich., to Phil Wagner, 24 June 1916, in J. Robert Constantine, ed., *Letters of Eugene V. Debs* (Urbana, Ill., 1990), 2:240–43.

12. Odd Lovoll, "*Gaa Paa*: A Scandinavian Voice of Dissent," *Minnesota History* 52 (Fall 1990), 89–90. B. J. Hovde, "Notes on the Effects of Emigration upon Scandinavia," *Journal of Modern History* 6 (September 1934), 273. T. K. Derry, *A History of Modern Norway, 1814–1972* (Oxford, 1973), 315.

13. Lovoll, "*Gaa Paa*," 89–90. Letter of Synnøve Standal, Arbeiderbevegelsens Arkiv og Bibliotek, Oslo, Norway, to author, 30 November 1990.

14. Keijo Virtanen, *Settlement or Return: Finnish Emigrants (1860–1930) in the International Overseas Return Migration Movement* (Helsinki, 1979), 214–15. Douglas Ollila, Jr., "From Socialism to Industrial Unionism (IWW): Social Factors in the Emergence of Left-Labor Radicalism among Finnish Workers on the Mesabi, 1911–19," in Michael G. Karni et al., eds., *The Finnish Experience in the Western Great Lakes Region: New Perspectives* (Turku, Finland, 1975), 161–62. John H. Hodgson, *Communism in Finland: A History and Interpretation* (Princeton, N.J., 1967), 16–19.

15. Virtanen, *Settlement or Return*, 214, 216. L. A. Puntila, *The Political History of Finland, 1809–1966* (London, 1975), 95.

16. Michael Brook, "Joe Hill Was Not the Only Swedish-American Wobbly," paper delivered at "Voices of Dissent" conference, St. Paul, Minn., 20 May 1989. Sigfrid Stenberg, Borlänge, Sweden, to Ralph Chaplin, n.p., 23 January 1925, copy in Ralph Chaplin Papers, Washington State Historical Society, Tacoma, Wash.

17. Bruno Cartosio, "Sicilian Radicals in Two Worlds," in Marianne Debouzy, ed., *In the Shadow of the Statue of Liberty: Immigrants, Workers, and Citizens in the American Republic, 1880–1920* (Paris, 1988), 132–35. Virtanen, *Settlement or Return*, 214.

18. Puskás, *From Hungary*, 87. Gualtieri, *Labor Movement in Italy*, 15–16. Donna Gabaccia, *Militants and Migrants: Rural Sicilians Become American Workers* (New Brunswick, N.J., 1988), 156.

19. Terje I. Leiren, *Marcus Thrane: A Norwegian Radical in America* (Northfield, Minn., 1987), 135–37.

20. Dino Cinel, "Conservative Adventurers: Italian Migrants in Italy and San Francisco" (Ph.D. diss., Stanford University, 1979), 127–28. Francesco Saverio Nitti quoted in Francesco Paolo Cerase, "From Italy to the United States and Back: Re-

turned Migrants, Conservative or Innovative?" (Ph.D. diss., Columbia University, 1971), 117. Theodore C. Blegen, *Norwegian Migration to America* (Northfield, Minn., 1940), 475–76.

21. John W. Briggs, *An Italian Passage: Immigrants to Three American Cities, 1890–1930* (New Haven, Conn., 1978), 56–57. Foerster, *Italian Emigration*, 460–61, 518–20. Krystyna Duda-Dziewierz, *Wieś Malopolska A Emigracja Amerykańska* (Warsaw, 1938), 121–22. George R. Gilkey, "The Effects of Emigration on Italy, 1900 to 1923" (Ph.D. diss., Northwestern University, 1950), 147, 156. Puskás, *From Hungary*, 89. Thomas Kessner, "History of Repatriation," in U.S. Select Commission on Immigration and Refugee Policy, *U.S. Immigration Policy and the National Interest* (Washington, D.C., 1981), App. A, 371, no. 92. Giuseppe de Bartolo, "The Great Italian Emigration in the USA: The Case of Calabria," paper presented 14 November 1987 at the 20th Annual Conference of the American Italian Historical Association, Chicago, Ill. Bertrand M. Tipple, "The Emigration Crisis in Italy," *Methodist Review* 106 (May 1923), 452. Dino Cinel, *The National Integration of Italian Return Migration, 1870–1929* (Cambridge, 1991), 93.

22. Duda-Dziewierz, *Wieś Malopolska*, 137. Barbara Golda, "Konsekwencje emigracji w życiu wiejskiej spolecznści polskiej," *Prezeglqd Polonijny* 2, no. 1 (1976), 122. Betty Boyd Caroli, *Italian Repatriation from the United States, 1900–1914* (New York, 1973), 65. Instytut Gospodarstwa Społecznego, Szkoła Głowna Planowania Statystyki, "Pamietniki wiejskich Dziataczy spotecznych" (Warsaw, 1935–36), no. 242. Pamela L. R. Horn, "The National Agricultural Labourers' Union in Ireland, 1873–9," *Irish Historical Studies* 17 (March, 1971), 342. Irish Folklore Commission Questionnaires, MS 1410, 134–35. K. R. M. Short, *The Dynamite War: Irish-American Bombers in Victorian Britain* (Dublin, 1979), 20. In Sweden, democracy was preached among workers' groups by a remigrant named Isidor Kjellberg, publisher of *Östgolen*, according to Franklin D. Scott, "American Influences in Norway and Sweden," *Journal of Modern History* 18 (March 1946), 43.

23. Virtanen, *Settlement or Return*, 208–9. Saloutos, *They Remember America*, 127. Cinel, *National Integration of Italian Return Migration*, 93–94.

24. Instytut Gospodarstwa Społecznego, "Pamietniki," no. 91. Gross, *Polish Worker*, 157–58. Czesław Lechicki, "Hammerling Ludwik," *Polski Słownik Biograficzny* 9 (1960–61), 263–64. Norbert Barlicki, *Aleksander Dębski, Zycie i działalność* (Warsaw, 1937), chap. 1. Adam Walaszek, *Polscy Robotnicy, Praca I Związki Zawodowe w Stanach Zjednoczonych Ameryki, 1880–1922* (Wrocław, 1988), 103. Irish Folklore Commission Questionnaires, MS 1410, 304–5. Saloutos, *They Remember America*, 127.

25. Virtanen, *Settlement or Return*, 209. Keijo Virtanen, "Finnish Migrants (1860–1930) in the Overseas Return Migration Movement," in Dirk Hoerder, ed., *Labor Migration in the Atlantic Economies: The European and North American Working Classes during the Period of Industrialization* (Westport, Conn., 1985), 394. Anna-Leena Toivonen, "Etelä-Pohjanmaan Valtameren-takainen Siirtolaisuus, 1867–1930" (Ph.D. diss., Seinäjoen Kirjapaino, Finland, 1963), 205. Frances Kraljic, *Croatian Migration to and from the United States, 1900–1914* (Palo Alto, Calif., 1978), 83.

26. Tokoi technically was vice-chairman of the Finnish Senate's financial section, a post that became prime minister in the situation prevailing during 1917. Scott, "American Influences," 44. Virtanen, *Settlement or Return*, 215. Anthony F. Upton, *The Finnish Revolution, 1917–1918* (Minneapolis, 1980), 29, 104. Puntila, *Political History of Finland*, 95. Dr. Alfred Bilmanis, *Latvia as an Independent State* (Washington, D.C., 1947), 357. R. O. G. Urch, *Latvia: Country and People* (London,

1938), 103–4. *Latvia: Past and Present, 1918–1968* (Waverly, Iowa, 1968, 1969), 33. Edgars Kunsdorfs, *The Life of Kārlis Ulmanis* (Tumba, Sweden, 1978), 599–614. Juris Silenieks, "Kārlis Ulmanis," in Longins Apkalns and Vito V. Simanis, eds., *Latvia* (St. Charles, Ill., 1984).

27. Virtanen, *Settlement or Return*, 215. Peter Kivisto, "Finnish Americans and the Homeland, 1918–1958," *Journal of American Ethnic History* 7 (Fall 1987), 10. John O. Crane and Sylvia Crane, *Czechoslovakia: Anvil of the Cold War* (New York, 1991), xviii, xxi, 7, 235–36, 320. New York *Times*, 11 March 1948, 4.

28. *Atlantis* (New York), 20 March 1909, quoted in Saloutos, *They Remember America*, 127.

29. The Bresci story is told in Richard Suskind, *By Bullet, Bomb, and Dagger* (New York, 1971), 119–22.

30. Alan J. Ward, *The Easter Rising: Revolution and Irish Nationalism* (Arlington Heights, Ill., 1980), 48–49. Ward, *Easter Rising*, 50–52, 64, 71–72. Short, *Dynamite War*, 239. Thomas C. Garvin, "Troubles," *Wilson Quarterly*, Spring 1985, 59.

31. Dublin *Review*, July 1882, quoted in Thomas N. Brown, *Irish-American Nationalism, 1870–1890* (Philadelphia, 1966), 116. Sylvester Malone, "Some Modern Theories of Land Tenure," *Irish Ecclesiastical Record* (3d ser.) 16 (1895), 429–41. J. F. Hogan, "Agrarian Socialism," *Irish Ecclesiastical Record* (4th ser.) 27 (1910), 577–605. Speech by Mr. J. Forbes Maguire at Unionist Convention for Provinces of Leinster, Munster, and Connaught, 23 June 1892, *Report of Proceedings* (Dublin, 1892), 167.

32. Desmond Bowen, *Paul Cardinal Cullen and the Shaping of Modern Irish Catholicism* (Dublin, 1983), 267. Short, *Dynamite War*, 7–8, 11–12. Ward, *Easter Rising*, 52–54, 72–73. Lonn, *Foreigners in the Union Army*, 74–75. Arnold Schrier, *Ireland and the American Emigration, 1850–1900* (Minneapolis, 1958), 125–26. C. J. Woods, "Ireland and Anglo-Papal Relations, 1880–85," *Irish Historical Studies* 18 (March 1972), 29.

33. Bowen, *Paul Cardinal Cullen*, 271, 280, 292. Kerby Miller, *Emigrants and Exiles: Ireland and the Irish Exodus to North America* (New York, 1985), 426. E. D. Steele, "Cardinal Cullen and Irish Nationality," *Irish Historical Studies* 19 (March 1975), 240–44.

34. William O'Connor Morris, *Ireland, 1798–1898* (London, 1898), 259–61. "Resolutions of the Irish Bishops on the Land Bill of 1881, Education, and Other Subjects," 26 April and 18 September 1881, in *Irish Ecclesiastical Record* (3d ser.) 2 (1881), 627–31.

35. Eric Foner, "Class, Ethnicity, and Radicalism in the Gilded Age: The Land League and Irish-America," *Marxist Perspectives*, Summer 1978, 9–11. Ward, *Easter Rising*, 41–44. Brown, *Irish-American*, 117–19. Miller, *Emigrants and Exiles*, 426.

36. Bowen, *Paul Cardinal Cullen*, 259, 271–72. Letter from unknown to Archbishop Edward McCabe, 10 September 1882; also see letters of 1 February and 9 June 1882, and undated marked "360/1" in 1883; also unknown to Fr. Walsh, Templetown, Co. Wexford, 1884, in "Letters from Religious (Nuns)," 360/7, in Archbishop Edward McCabe Papers, Dublin Diocesan Archives, Clonliffe College, Dublin.

37. Woods, "Ireland and Anglo-Papal Relations," 56–57.

38. Michael F. Funchion, *Chicago's Irish Nationalists, 1881–1890* (New York, 1976), 38–41, 82–87. Foner, "Class, Ethnicity," 9. Ward, *Easter Rising*, 64, 66. Brown, *Irish-American*, 162–63, 174–75.

39. Joseph Lee, *The Modernisation of Irish Society, 1848–1918* (Dublin, 1973), 150–56. Ward, *Easter Rising*, 8, 123–24.

40. Miller, *Emigrants and Exiles*, 426, 544–45. On the vast political changes in western Ireland, see K. Theodore Hoppen, "National Politics and Local Realities in Mid-Nineteenth Century Ireland," in Art Cosgrove and Donal McCartney, eds., *Studies in Irish History: Presented to R. Dudley Edwards* (Dublin, 1979), 225–26. Irish historian David N. Doyle argues that "the Irish War of Independence was more closely linked to the great emigration than Irish historians, focusing upon the activities of professional revolutionaries, have cared to concede"; Doyle, "Unestablished Irishmen: New Immigrants and Industrial America, 1870–1910," in Dirk Hoerder, ed., *American Labor and Immigration History, 1877–1920s: Recent European Research* (Urbana, Ill., 1983), 218.

41. The German and Russian fears are discussed in Benjamin P. Murdzek, *Emigration in Polish Social-Political Thought, 1870–1914* (Boulder, Colo., 1977), 169.

42. Adam Walaszek, "Reemigranci ze Stanów Zjednoczonych i Kanady w Polsce, 1919–1923: 'Jak mozna bylo tak sobie to pieknie przedstawiac?'" *Przegląd Polonijny* 6, no. 1 (1980), 13–15.

43. Duda-Dziewierz, *Wieś Malopolska*, 133–34. Walaszek, "Reemigranci ze Stanów," 27, note 69.

44. U.S. Minister Jackson, dispatch of 18 November 1854, quoted in Zoltan Kramar, ed., *From the Danube to the Hudson: U.S. Ministerial and Consular Dispatches on Immigration from the Habsburg Monarchy, 1850–1900* (Atlanta, Ga., 1978), 24–25. *Znanje* (Chicago), 11 September 1920, in Chicago Foreign Press Survey, reel 9.

45. See report by 1904 visitor to Croatian emigrants in the United States, in Kraljic, *Croatian Migration*, 58–59; also see 67–68, 80–81. Emily Greene Balch, "Slav Emigration at Its Source," *Charities*, 7 April 1906, 78. Edward A. Steiner, *The Immigrant Tide: Its Ebb and Flow* (New York, 1909), 147.

46. Balch, "Slav Emigration," *Charities*, 7 April 1906, 78. Monika Glettler, *Pittsburg—Wien—Budapest: Programm und Praxis der Nationalitätenpolitik bei der Auswanderung der ungarischen Slowaken nach Amerika um 1900* (Vienna, 1980), 273–76, 319–22.

47. M. Mark Stolarik, *Immigration and Urbanization: The Slovak Experience, 1870–1918* (New York, 1989), 187–91.

48. Puskás, *From Hungary*, 84, 87. The Heves County statement was made in 1904.

Chapter 8. Churches, Traditions, and the Remigrant

1. Lawrence B. Davis, *Immigrants, Baptists, and the Protestant Mind in America* (Urbana, Ill., 1973), chap. 4. On the rush to "plant" in the American frontier, see Mark Wyman, *Immigrants in the Valley: Irish, Germans, and Americans in the Upper Mississippi Country, 1830–1860* (Chicago, 1984), chap. 5. Halvdan Koht, *The American Spirit in Europe: A Survey of Transatlantic Influences* (Philadelphia, 1949), 188–89.

2. Monika Glettler, *Pittsburg—Wien—Budapest: Programm und Praxis der Nationalalitätenpolitik bei der Auswanderung der ungarischen Slowaken nach Amerika um 1900* (Vienna, 1980), 124–26, 136–40.

3. Instytut Gospodarstwa Społecznego, *Szkoła Głowna Planowania Statystyki* (Warsaw, 1935–36), no. 91.

4. Diocese of Kraków, 1913 survey of parishes, in Archiwum Kurii Metropolitalnej w Krakowie.

5. Pastor I. Strandh, letter, 16 July 1908, in Swedish Royal Commission on Emigration, *Report* (Stockholm, 1908–13), 17:169–70. Liam Kennedy, "The Early Response of the Irish Catholic Clergy to the Co-operative Movement," *Irish Historical Studies* 21 (March 1978), 57n. E. D. Steele, "Cardinal Cullen and Irish Nationality," *Irish Historical Studies* 19 (March 1975), 243–44. M. F. Shinnors, "Ireland and America: Some Notes of a Mission Tour in the United States," *Irish Ecclesiastical Record* (4th ser.) 11 (1902), 114–26, 385–99. But also see rebuttal to Shinnors: John Talbot Smith, "The Irish in the United States," ibid., 532–44. Schrier, *Ireland and the American Emigration*, 62.

6. Wyman, *Immigrants in the Valley*, 184–85.

7. Lars Ljungmark, *Swedish Exodus* (Carbondale, Ill., 1979), 140. Robert C. Ostergren, *A Community Transplanted: The Trans-Atlantic Experience of a Swedish Immigrant Settlement in the Upper Middle West, 1835–1915* (Madison, Wis., 1988), 309. Franklin D. Scott, "American Influences in Norway and Sweden," *Journal of Modern History* 18 (March 1946), 38–39. Elizabeth Malcolm, '*Ireland Sober, Ireland Free': Drink and Temperance in Nineteenth-Century Ireland* (Syracuse, N.Y., 1986), 56, 61–66. *The Temperance Cyclopedia* (Glasgow, Scotland, n.d., ca. 1850s). Emily Greene Balch, "Slav Emigration at Its Source," *Charities*, 7 April 1906, 76. Peter A. Ming, "The Churches of Europe against Alcoholism: The Catholic Church," *Proceedings of the Fifteenth International Congress against Alcoholism* (Washington, D.C., 1920) 86, 89.

8. Antonio Mangano, "The Effect of Emigration upon Italy," *Charities*, 4 April 1908, 16. Edward A. Steiner, *On the Trail of the Immigrant* (New York, 1906), 337–38. Dino Cinel, "Conservative Adventurers: Italian Migrants in Italy and San Francisco" (Ph.D. diss., Stanford University, 1979), 104, 120–39. Julianna Puskás, *From Hungary to the United States (1880–1914)* (Budapest, 1982), 87.

9. Barbara Golda, "Konsekwencje emigracji w życiu wiejskiej społeczności polskiej," *Przegląd Polonijny* 2, no. 1 (1976), 120–22. Mieczysław Szawleski, *Wychodźtwo Polskie w Stanach Zjednoczonych Ameryki* (Lwów, 1924), 353. Roland Sarti, *Long Live the Strong: A History of Rural Society in the Apennine Mountains* (Amherst, Mass., 1985), 30, 40, 42–43, 250 (notes 25 and 28).

10. Dino Cinel, *The National Integration of Italian Return Migration, 1870–1929* (Cambridge, 1991), 93. Unnamed peasant in Podlasie, Poland, to newspaper *Zaranie*, ca. 1906–7, reprinted in William I. Thomas and Florian Znaniecki, *The Polish Peasant in Europe and America: Monograph of an Immigrant Group* (Boston, 1918), 4:169.

11. George M. Stephenson, *The Religious Aspects of Swedish Immigration: A Study of Immigrant Churches* (Minneapolis, 1932), 5–8.

12. Antonio Mangano, *Sons of Italy: A Social and Religious Study of the Italians in America* (New York, 1917; rpt. 1971), 92–93. Report of convention of priests of the Kraków diocese, 28 November 1907, Pt. 4: Emigration, 25–27, in Archiwum Kurii Metropolitalnej w Krakowie.

13. Golda, "Konsekwencje emigracji," 122. Krystyna Duda-Dziewierz, *Wieś Małopolska A Emigracja Amerykańska* (Warsaw, 1938), 134–36. Antonio Mangano, "Effect of Emigration," *Charities*, 2 May 1908, 176–77.

14. Chiesa Metodista Episcopale Italiana, *XXXVII sessione della conferenza annuale tenuta a Venezia dal 5 al 10 ottobre 1920* (Rome, 1920), 56. Mangano, *Sons of Italy*, 153. Francesco Paolo Cerase, "From Italy to the United States and Back:

Returned Migrants, Conservative or Innovative?" (Ph.D. diss., Columbia University, 1971), 309.

15. Mangano, *Sons of Italy*, 91–94. *Ann. Stat. Ital.* 4 (2d ser., 1914), 29, cited in George Gilkey, "The Effects of Emigration on Italy, 1900 to 1923" (Ph.D. diss., Northwestern University, 1950), 114. The Roman Catholic total reported in the 1911 Italian religious census exceeded 30 million.

16. Cerase, "From Italy to the United States," 313–14, 321–22.

17. Ibid., 315, 318.

18. Chiesa Metodista Episcopale Italiana, *XXXVIII sessione della conferenza annuale tenuta a Napoli dal 25 al 29 Maggio 1921* (Rome, 1921), 42. Mangano, *Sons of Italy*, 93–94, 164–65, 168–69, 175, 191. Cerase, "From Italy to the United States," 325–26.

19. Paul Fox, *The Polish National Catholic Church* (Scranton, Pa., n.d., ca. 1955), chap. 1, 30, 32–40, 63, 65–70, 115–18.

20. Ibid., 40–42.

21. Adam Walaszek, *Reemigracja ze Stanów Zjednoczonych do Polski po i Wojnie Światowej (1919–1924)* (Kraków, 1983), 37–38. Fox, *Polish National Catholic Church*, 63.

22. Fr. Romuald Moskala, "Niebezpieczeństwo idące z Ameryki," *Przegląd Powszechny* 145–46 (January 1920), 75–80.

23. *Ameryka Echo* quoted in Adam Walaszek, "Reemigranci ze Stanów Zjednoczonych i Kanady w Polsce. 1919–1923. 'Jak mozna bylo tak sobie to pieknie przedstawiac?'" *Przegląd Polonijny* 6, no. 1 (1980), 13–16, 28 (note 73). The PNCC had to cut all ties with its American branches in 1950, under orders of Poland's Communist regime; Fox, *Polish National Catholic Church*, 63.

24. Fox, *Polish National Catholic Church*, 42–51, 54, 60–65. Bronisław Krupski, "Dawn of the National Church in Poland," *PNCC Studies* 11 (1990), 72–113. Prof. Joseph W. Wieczerzak, PNCC Commission on History and Archives, letter to author, 19 December 1990.

25. Puskás, *From Hungary*, 88. Edward A. Steiner, *Immigrant Tide: Its Ebb and Flow* (New York, 1909), 129, 135–36. Alfred Vagts, *Deutsch-Amerikanische Rückwanderung* (Heidelberg, 1960), 65–70. *Baptist Missionary Magazine* 88 (March 1908), 108–10.

26. Adolf Olson, *A Centenary History: As Related to the Baptist General Conference of America* (Chicago, 1952), 16, 460, 577. *Baptist Missionary Magazine*, 88 (March 1908), 108–10. Stephenson, *Religious Aspects*, 97, 127, 135.

27. Davis, *Immigrants, Baptists*, 105. Stephenson, *Religious Aspects*, chap. 5, 83, 87–88. Olson, *Centenary History*, 5–8, 36, 40–42. Scott, "American Influences," 40–41.

28. Davis, *Immigrants, Baptists*, 105. Stephenson, *Religious Aspects*, 74–75.

29. Information in following paragraphs on different denominations operating in Sweden is from Stephenson, *Religious Aspects*, 93–105, 116–25.

30. Marvin R. O'Connell, *John Ireland and the American Catholic Church* (St. Paul, Minn., 1988), 265.

31. Sten Carlsson, "Augustana Lutheran Pastors in the Church of Sweden," *Swedish-American Historical Quarterly* 35 (July 1984), 244, 246–47. Stephenson, *Religious Aspects*, 18–20, 99, 193–95.

32. Stephenson, *Religious Aspects*, 3, 8–10, 143–45. Swedish Royal Commission, *Report*, 20:47.

33. Keijo Virtanen, *Settlement or Return: Finnish Emigrants (1860–1930) in the*

International Overseas Return Migration Movement (Helsinki, 1979), 210–11; Virtanen, "Finnish Migrants (1860–1930) in the Overseas Return Migration Movement," in Dirk Hoerder, ed., *Labor Migration in the Atlantic Economies: The European and North American Working Classes during The Period of Industrialization* (Westport, Conn., 1985), 394.

34. Andrew Jenson, ed., *Encyclopedic History of the Church of Jesus Christ of Latter-Day Saints* (Salt Lake City, Utah, 1941), 92–94, 237–38, 280, 596.

35. Scott, "American Influences," 42.

36. Béla Gunda, "America in Hungarian Folklore," *The New Hungarian Quarterly* 15 (Autumn 1974), 157. Gunda also notes the contention by another folklorist that remigrants introduced the Christmas tree to Norway.

37. Dr. Ernst Lundevall, letter of 19 January 1908 to Swedish Royal Commission, in its *Report*, 17:198. Gino Arias, *La questione meridionale* (Bologna, 1921), 1: 458, quoted in George Gilkey, "Italy and America: The Migrations of the Early Twentieth Century," unpublished paper in possession of the author. Italy, Commissariato Generale dell'Emigrazione, *L'emigrazione italiana dal 1910 al 1923* (Rome, 1926), 1:197–98. Jerzy Fierich, *Przeszłość powiatu ropczyckiego w ustach mieszkańców* (Ropczyce, Poland, 1936), 67.

38. Theodore Saloutos, *They Remember America: The Story of the Repatriated Greek-Americans* (Berkeley, 1956), 63–64. Kazimiera Zawistowicz-Adamska, *Społeczność Wiejska* (Łódź, 1948), 71–83. Frances Kraljic, *Croatian Migration to and from the United States, 1900–1914* (Palo Alto, Calif., 1978), 68. Puskás, *From Hungary*, 88n. Walaszek, *Reemigracja*, 135–36. Irish Folklore Commission Questionnaires, MS 1407, 45. Arnold Schrier, *Ireland and the American Emigration, 1850–1900* (Minneapolis, 1958), 133–34.

39. Marsha Penti, "The Role of Ethnic Folklore among Finnish-American Returnees" (Ph.D. diss., Indiana University, 1983), 302–3.

40. Gunda, "America in Hungarian Folklore," 161. Fierich, *Przeszłość*, 57. Joseph Lopreato, *Peasants No More: Social Class and Social Change in an Underdeveloped Society* (San Francisco, 1967), 177. Penti, "Role of Ethnic Folklore," 328. Anna-Leena Toivonen, "Etelä-Pohjanmaan Valtameren-takainen Siirtolaisuus, 1867–1930" (Ph.D. diss., Seinäjoen Kirjapaino, Finland, 1963), 210. Maisa Martin, "American Finnish: A Degenerate or Creative Language?" paper read at the conference "The Making of Finnish America: An Ethnic Culture in Transition," University of Minnesota, 7 November 1991. Compilation of remigrant Finnish words by Pertti Virtaranta, provided by Martin. Irish Folklore Commission Questionnaires, MS 1409, 81; MS 1410, 124–25. Schrier, *Ireland and the American Emigration*, 136.

41. Gunda, "America in Hungarian Folklore," 157, 158, 160. The grinder song originated in Norwalk, Virginia.

42. Sarti, *Long Live the Strong*, 135–36.

43. Saloutos, *They Remember America*, 125. Toivonen, "Etelä-Pohjanmaan," 210. Penti, "Role of Ethnic Folklore," 321–22.

44. Golda, "Konsekwencje emigracji," 117–18. Saloutos, *They Remember America*, 91, 123. Betty Boyd Caroli, *Italian Repatriation from the United States 1900–1914* (New York, 1973), 64–65. Ingrid Semmingsen, *Veien Mot Vest* (Oslo, 1950), 465–58. Irish Folklore Commission Questionnaires, MS 1408, 14. Salvatore Mondello, *The Italian Immigrant in Urban America, 1880–1920, as Reported in the Contemporary Periodical Press* (New York, 1980), 56.

45. Virtanen, *Settlement or Return*, 201. *Inchiesta Parlamentare* quoted in U.S. 61st Cong., 3d sess., S. Doc. 747, *Reports of the Immigration Commission* (Wash-

ington, D.C., 1911), 4:224. Irish Folklore Commission Questionnaires, MS 1407, 321. Duda-Dziewierz, *Wieś Malopolska*, 79–85.

Chapter 9. The America Trunk Comes Home

1. See descriptions of the America trunk in Marsha Penti, "The Role of Ethnic Folklore among Finnish-American Returnees" (Ph.D. diss., Indiana University, 1983), 322–26, 659. Penti found remigrants who still prized their items from America sixty years later.

2. Charles Dickens, *American Notes for General Circulation* (London, 1842), 2: 234–35.

3. See Chapter 1, note 5.

4. The Italian estimate, however, makes no allowance for multiple voyages by the same person—the birds of passage. Betty Boyd Caroli, *Italian Repatriation from the United States, 1900–1914* (New York, 1973), 41. Ingrid Semmingsen, *Norway to America: A History of the Migration* (Minneapolis, 1987), 120.

5. John Lardner, "The Mayor of Futani," *New Yorker*, 27 May 1944, 28–29, 35. George Gilkey, interview, 5 June 1986.

6. Norma Ashbrook, interview, 5 April 1990.

7. C. B. Iannace, *La scoperta dell'america* (Padova, 1971), 16, quoted in Rudolph J. Vecoli, "Italian American Workers, 1880–1920: Padrone Slaves or Primitive Rebels?" in S. M. Tomasi, ed., *Perspectives in Italian Immigration and Ethnicity* (New York, 1977), 25–26. See also Caroline Golab, *Immigrant Destinations* (Philadelphia, 1977), 163.

8. See discussion in Franco Ramella, "Emigration from an Area of Intense Industrial Development: The Case of Northwestern Italy," in Rudolph J. Vecoli and Suzanne M. Sinke, eds., *A Century of European Migrations, 1830–1930* (Urbana, Ill., 1991), 270–71.

9. Mary Jo Brown, interview, 16 May 1986.

10. Broughton Brandenburg, *Imported Americans* (New York, 1904), 32.

11. *United Mine Workers' Journal*, 2 February 1907, 1; 25 April 1907, 6; 26 September 1907, 4, 7; 12 December 1907, 6. As an industrial union, the Mine Workers were a rarity within the craft-dominated AFL.

12. Stoyan Christowe, *This Is My Country* (New York, 1938), 22–23. Adam Walaszek, *Reemigracja ze Stanów Zjednoczonych do Polski po i Wojnie Światowej (1919–1924)* (Kraków, 1983), 141–48. Joseph Lopreato, *Peasants No More: Social Class and Social Change in an Underdeveloped Society* (San Francisco, 1967), 156–57, 175–77, 188, 222–23.

13. Knut Djupedal, "Tales of America," *Western Folklore* 49 (April 1990), 178–81, 184.

14. Roland Sarti, *Long Live the Strong: A History of Rural Society in the Apennine Mountains* (Amherst, Mass., 1985), 39, 131–34. Lars Ljungmark, *Swedish Exodus* (Carbondale, Ill., 1979), 135. George Gilkey, interview, 5 June 1986.

15. Ingrid Semmingsen, *Veien Mot Vest* (Oslo, 1950), 467. On retention of backward farming practices, see Cormac ó Gráda, "Seasonal Migration and Post-Famine Adjustment in the West of Ireland," *Studia Hibernica*, no. 13 (1973), 72, and Dino Cinel, "Conservative Adventurers: Italian Migrants in Italy and San Francisco" (Ph.D. diss., Stanford University, 1979), 83–85.

16. Philip S. Bagwell and G. E. Mingay, *Britain and America, 1850–1939: A Study of Economic Change* (London, 1970), 73–80.

17. Semmingsen, *Veien Mot Vest*, 467. Robert F. Foerster, *The Italian Emigration of Our Times* (New York, 1919; 1968), 455–56. Frances Kraljic, *Croatian Migration to and from the United States, 1900–1914* (Palo Alto, Calif., 1978), 68. Arnold Schrier, *Ireland and the American Emigration, 1850–1900* (Minneapolis, 1958), 140. Edward A. Steiner, *The Immigrant Tide: Its Ebb and Flow* (New York, 1909), 71–73.

18. On the spread of English, see Penti, "Role of Ethnic Folklore," 622–24; Irish Folklore Commission Questionnaires, MS 1407, 279; Sten Carlsson, "Augustana Lutheran Pastors in the Church of Sweden," in *Swedish-American Historical Quarterly* 35 (July 1984), 246.

19. Julianna Puskás referred to the remigrants' "developing consciousness of their national or ethnic identity" as the greatest change in their thinking; Puskás, *From Hungary to the United States (1880–1914)* (Budapest, 1982), 89–90.

20. Stainsław Osada, *Jak sie ksztaltowala polska dusza Wychodztwa w Ameryce* (Pittsburgh, 1930), 176–78. Andrzej Brozek, *Polish Americans, 1854–1939* (Warsaw, 1985), 183. Penti, "Role of Ethnic Folklore," 622–24, 628–29.

21. Kristian Hvidt, *Flight to America: The Social Background of 300,000 Danish Emigrants* (New York, 1975), 180. Keijo Virtanen, "Attitudes to the Return Migration in Early 20th Century Finland" (Rostock, East Germany, 1987), 4. Theodore Saloutos, *They Remember America: The Story of the Repatriated Greek-Americans* (Berkeley, 1956), 113. Louis Adamic, *The Native's Return* (New York, 1934), 161–62, 166–67, 280. Osada, *Jak sie ksztaltowala polska*, 176–78, 191.

22. Handlin, "Immigrants Who Go Back," 70. Faith H. Eikaas, "You Can't Go Home Again? Culture Shock and Patterns of Adaptation, Norwegian Returnees," in Robert E. Rhoades, ed., *The Anthropology of Return Migration* 20 (Spring 1979), 112–13. Penti, "Role of Ethnic Folklore," 148–64, 391–93. Caroli, *Italian Repatriation*, 86, 88. Francesco Paolo Cerase estimated that 400 World War I veterans attended the American Legion's 1966 Italian convention; Cerase, "From Italy to the United States and Back: Returned Migrants, Conservative or Innovative?" (Ph.D. diss., Columbia University, 1971), 172n.

23. Ingrid Semmingsen, "Emigration and the Image of America in Europe," in Henry Steele Commager, ed., *Immigration and American History: Essays in Honor of Theodore C. Blegen* (Minneapolis, 1961), 45. Anna-Leena Toivonen, "Etelä-Pohjanmaan Valtameren-takainen Siirtolaisuus, 1867–1930" (Ph.D. diss., Seinäjoen Kirjapaino, Finland, 1963), 204–5.

24. Cerase, "From Italy to the United States," chap. 4. Cinel, "Conservative Adventurers," 128–29. William I. Thomas and Florian Znaniecki, *The Polish Peasant in Europe and America: Monograph of an Immigrant Group* (Boston, 1918), 4:73–74. Saloutos, *They Remember America*, 70–71, 128–29. See also Lopreato, *Peasants No More*, chap. 8, and George R. Gilkey, "The United States and Italy: Migration and Repatriation," *Journal of Developing Areas* 2 (October 1967), 30–33. On remigrants having little or no impact, see the following: 1924 Finnish report, quoted in Virtanen, "Attitudes to the Return Migration," 3; Keijo Virtanen, *Settlement or Return: Finnish Emigrants (1860–1930) in the International Overseas Return Migration Movement* (Helsinki, 1979), 217; Ljungmark, *Swedish Exodus*, 135; George R. Gilkey, "The Effects of Emigration on Italy, 1900 to 1923" (Ph.D. diss., Northwestern University, 1950), 156; Puskás, *From Hungary*, 87–88; Carlo Levi, *Christ Stopped at Eboli* (New York, 1947), 123–24.

25. Benjamin P. Murdzek, *Emigration in Polish Social-Political Thought, 1870–1914* (Boulder, Colo., 1977), 74–75. Virtanen, "Attitudes to the Return Migration," 1–2. Ann-Sofie Kälvemark, "Swedish Emigration Policy in an International Perspec-

tive, 1840–1925," in Harald Runblom and Hans Norman, eds., *From Sweden to America: A History of the Migration* (Minneapolis, 1976), 112–13, and Kalvemark, *Reaktionen mot utvandringen: Emigrationsfrågan i svensk debatt och politik, 1901–1904* (Uppsala, 1972), 225–26. Monika Glettler, *Pittsburg—Wien—Budapest: Programm und Praxis der Nationalitätenpolitik bei der Auswanderung. der ungarischen Slowaken nach Amerika um 1900* (Vienna, 1980), 319–22. James Davenport Whelpley, "Control of Emigration in Europe," *North American Review* 180 (January–June 1905), 866–87. For a summary of U.S. and British government investigations, see Philip Taylor, *The Distant Magnet: European Emigration to the U.S.A.* (New York, 1971), 297.

26. Günter Moltmann, "American-German Return Migration in the Nineteenth and Early Twentieth Centuries," *Central European History* 13 (December 1980), 392. *Literary Digest*, 24 April 1920, 12–13. U.S. 50th Cong., 1st sess., H. Misc. Doc. 604, "Reports from Consuls of the United States" (Washington, D.C., 1887), no. 76 (April 1887). Whelpley, "Control of Emigration," 865. The 1891 U.S. law required ships to carry home all immigrants rejected by U.S. Customs officials; William S. Bernard, "Immigration: History of U.S. Policy," in Stephan Thernstrom, ed., *Harvard Encyclopedia of American Ethnic Groups* (Cambridge, Mass., 1980), 491. The best survey of Italian laws is Gilkey, "Effects of Emigration," 123–33. U.S. Department of Commerce and Labor, *Bulletin of the Bureau of Labor*, 15:72.485 (September 1907).

27. Italy, Commissariato dell'emigrazione, *Bolletino dell'Emigrazione*, 1910, no. 11, 226, quoted in Thomas Kessner, "History of Repatriation," App. A to U.S. Select Commission on Immigration and Refugee Policy, *U.S. Immigration Policy and the National Interest* (Washington, D.C., 1981), 323. Gilkey, "Effects of Emigration," 135–36. Leopold Caro, *Emigracya: I Polityka Emigracyjna* (Poznań, 1914), 353. Foerster, *Italian Emigration*, 486–91.

28. The first Italian law on emigration, enacted in 1889, sought to restrict the operations of ticket agents; Dino Cinel, *The National Integration of Italian Return Migration, 1870–1929* (Cambridge, 1991), 86–87. Gilkey, "Effects of Emigration," 136–38. Grazia Dore, "Some Social and Historical Aspects of Italian Emigration to America," *Journal of Social History* 2 (Winter 1968), 121–22. Monte S. Finkelstein, "The Johnson Act, Mussolini and Fascist Emigration Policy, 1921–1930," *Journal of American Ethnic History* 8 (Fall 1988), 38–55. Nazi Germany created a foundation to encourage and assist remigration, providing free return tickets and a promise of no taxes for a year for qualified workers and engineers; Alfred Vagts, *Deutsch-Amerikanische Rückwanderung* (Heidelberg, 1960), 29–31.

29. Kälvemark, *Reaktionen*, 226, 232–33. Hans Norman and Harald Runblom, "Migration Patterns in the Nordic Countries," Dirk Hoerder, ed., *Labor Migration in the Atlantic Economies: The European and North American Working Classes during the Period of Industrialization* (Westport, Conn., 1985), 55. George M. Stephenson, *The Religious Aspects of Swedish Immigration: A Study of Immigrant Churches* (Minneapolis, 1932), 443–45. Nils Runeby, "Americanism, Taylorism, and Social Integration," *Scandinavian Journal of History* 3 (1978), 21–22. B. J. Hovde, "Notes on the Effects of Emigration upon Scandinavia," *Journal of Modern History* 6 (September, 1934), 257–58.

30. Sture Lindmark, "Re-Immigration to Sweden from the United States, 1929–1932," *Swedish Pioneer Historical Quarterly* 17 (July 1966), 147. Stephenson, *Religious Aspects*, 441, 443–45. The recommendations are in Swedish Royal Commission on Emigration, *Report* (Stockholm, 1908–13), 20:41–50.

31. Ljungmark, *Swedish Exodus*, 133–34. As late as 1911 only 19.3 percent of

the Swedish adult population was eligible to vote; John S. Lindberg, *The Background of Swedish Emigration to the United States* (Minneapolis, 1930; 1971), 30–31. H. Arnold Barton, comp., *Letters from the Promised Land: Swedes in America, 1840–1914* (Minneapolis, 1975), 306–310. Lars-Göran Tedebrand, "Strikes and Political Radicalism in Sweden and Emigration to the United States," in Dirk Hoerder, ed., *American Labor and Immigration History, 1877–1920s: Recent European Research* (Urbana, Ill., 1983), 224–27.

32. Gilkey, "Effects of Emigration," 165. Ewa Morawska, *For Bread with Butter: The Life-Worlds of East Central Europeans in Johnstown, Pennsylvania, 1890–1940* (Cambridge, 1985), 329.

33. Steiner, *Immirant Tide*, 31.

34. Carla Bianco found these mixed attitudes in most of her interviews in Italian villages; Bianco, *The Two Rosetos* (Bloomington, Ind., 1974), 44–45. Halvdan Koht discusses European criticisms in Koht, *The American Spirit in Europe: A Survey of Transatlantic Influences* (Philadelphia, 1949), chap. 11. Angelo Olivieri, "L'Italia ufficiale e la realtá dell'emigrazione in USA (1886–1914)," *Studi Emigrazione* 11 (March 1974), 43–44.

35. Levi, *Christ Stopped at Eboli*, 123. *Inchiesta Parlamentare*, 6:1.614, quoted in Gilkey, "Effects of Emigration," 156.

36. Cerase, "From Italy to the United States," 292–93. Caroli, *Italian Repatriation*, 85–90. Irish Folklore Commission Questionnaires, MS 1408, 322. Penti, "Role of Ethnic Folklore," 329, 599–600. On Norwegians, see Reidar Grunde Simonsen, "Returned Emigrants: A Study of Repatriated Norwegians" (thesis, University of Oslo, 1982), 63–65.

37. Saloutos, *They Remember America*, 110–11, 113, 127–29. Handlin, "Immigrants Who Go Back," 74.

38. Djupedal, "Tales of America," 183. Semmingsen, *Veien Mot Vest*, 469. Moltmann, "American-German Return Migration," 392. A 1960s study of Zaborów, Poland, found that 32 percent of the village population still had family members outside the country, and more than two-thirds of that total was in the United States; Maria Wierusyewska-Adamcyk, *Spoleczność Wiejska Zaborowa w Procesie Przemian* (Warsaw, 1980), 86. See also Penti, "Role of Ethnic Folklore," 329.

39. Theodore Saloutos, *Expatriates and Repatriates: A Neglected Chapter in United States History* (Rock Island, Ill., 1972), 18–19. Frank Thistlethwaite, "Migration from Europe Overseas in the Nineteenth and Twentieth Centuries," in Comite International des Sciences Historiques, XIe Congrès International des Sciences Historiques, *Rapports* (Stockholm, 1960), 5:37, 40.

40. This point has been made by the late Herbert G. Gutman, most forcefully in his *Work, Culture, and Society in Industrializing America: Essays in American Working-Class and Social History* (New York, 1977), 40. Even the continued ambivalence of Italians toward their life in the United States has been linked by one scholar to the prevalence of return migration within the group; Cinel, *National Integration of Italian Return Migration*, 5–6.

41. Murdzek, *Emigration in Polish Social-Political Thought*, 270, note 28. Marcus Lee Hansen, *The Immigrant in American History* (Cambridge, Mass., 1940), 82. Dirk Hoerder, "Immigration and the Working Class: The Remigration Factor," *International Labor and Working Class History*, no. 21 (Spring 1982), 37. Robert C. Ostergren, *A Community Transplanted* (Madison, Wis., 1988). 147. Jon Gjerde, *From Peasants to Farmers* (Cambridge, 1985), chap. 6.

42. Julainna Puskás, "Emigration from Hungary to the United States before 1914," *Studia Historica*, no. 113 (1975), 16. Penti, "Role of Ethnic Folklore," 30,

211. Sarti, *Long Live the Strong*, 16–17. Murdzek, *Emigration in Polish Social-Political Thought*, 139–40.

43. Statistics are based on Stephan Thernstrom, ed., *Harvard Encyclopedia of American Ethnic Groups* (Cambridge, Mass., 1980), 1049. *Gazeta Koscielna*, n.p., n.d., quoted in *Dziennik Chicagoski*, 24 March 1894, translated by Chicago Foreign Press Survey, reel 58.

44. Maisa Martin (University of Jyväskylä, Finland), interview, and presentation entitled "American Finnish: A Degenerate or Creative Language?" at the conference "The Making of Finnish America: An Ethnic Culture in Transition," University of Minnesota, 7 November 1991. Pertti Virtaranta, compilation of immigrant contributions to Finnish language, provided to the author by Maisa Martin.

45. See discussion on this point in Dore, "Some Social and Historical Aspects," 122.

46. John J. Kulczycki, "'Scapegoating' the Foreign Worker: Job Turnover, Accidents, and Diseases among Polish Coal Miners in the German Ruhr," *Polish American Studies* 46 (1989), 43, 45, 49–55. Gianfausto Rosoli, "Italian Migration to European Countries from Political Unification to World War I," in Dirk Hoerder, ed., *Labor Migration in the Atlantic Economies*, 112–13. Foerster, *Italian Emigration*, 141.

47. See discussion on European temporary workers in Ivo Baučić, *The Effects of Emigration from Yugoslavia and the Problems of Returning Emigrant Workers* (The Hague, 1972), 1–2. Hoerder, "Immigration and the Working Class," 34–37. Russell King, "Italian Migration: the Clotting of the Haemorrhage," *Geography* 70 (April 1985), 173.

48. Robert E. Rhoades, "From Caves to Main Street: Return Migration and the Transformation of a Spanish Village," 57, 60, 68, and Caroline B. Brettell, "Emigrar para Voltar: A Portuguese Ideology of Return Migration," 4, 6, in Rhoades, ed., *The Anthropology of Return Migration* 20 (Spring 1979). Robert L. Vivolo, "Emigration and Agriculture in a Sicilian Village," 73, and Daniel Kubat, "Introduction," 1–8, in Kubat, ed., *The Politics of Return: International Return Migration in Europe* (Rome, 1984). Baučić, *Effects of Emigration from Yugoslavia*, 15, 24–25, 27, 32–34. See discussion of the study of modern remigration in two other chapters in Kubat's *Politics of Return*: Emilio Reyneri and Clara Mughini, "Return Migration and Sending Areas: From the Myth of Development to the Reality of Stagnation," 34, and Russell King, Jill Mortimer, and Alan Strachan, "Return Migration and the Development of the Italian Mezzogiorno," 84.

49. Psalm 137:4. Cinel, *National Integration of Italian Return Migration*, 5–6. Vilhelm Moberg, *A Time on Earth* (New York, 1965), 219–20.

50. The persistent strength of the family during immigration and beyond is emphasized by Virginia Yans-McLaughlin in *Family and Community: Italian Immigrants in Buffalo, 1880–1930* (Ithaca, N.Y., 1971; 1977), 20–21.

Index

CPSIA information can be obtained
at www.ICGtesting.com
Printed in the USA
LVHW101810210223
740054LV00002B/18

9 780801 428753